AF650414

ENERGY COOPERATION
BETWEEN
INDIA AND THE CASPIAN REGION

ENERGY COOPERATION
BETWEEN
INDIA AND THE CASPIAN REGION

NGANGOM DHRUBA TARA SINGH

FOREWORD BY
AIR VICE MARSHAL **ANIL GOLANI** (RETD)

Centre for Air Power Studies
New Delhi

in association with

KW Publishers Pvt Ltd
New Delhi

Copyright © 2025 Centre for Air Power Studies, New Delhi

The Centre for Air Power Studies is an independent, non-profit, academic research institution established in 2002 under a registered Trust to undertake and promote policy-related research, study and discussion on the trends and developments in defence and military issues, especially air power and the aerospace arena, for civil and military purposes. Its publications seek to expand and deepen the understanding of defence, military power, air power and aerospace issues without necessarily reflecting the views of any institution or individuals except those of the authors.

Centre for Air Power Studies
P-284, Arjan Path
Subroto Park
New Delhi 110010

Tele: (91-11) 25699131

E-mail: capsnetdroff@gmail.com
website: www.capsindia.org

All rights reserved. No part of this book may be reproduced or transmitted in any form or by any means, electronic or mechanical, including photocopying, recording or by any information storage and retrieval system, without permission in writing.

ISBN 978-81-984037-4-2 Hardback

Published in India by Kalpana Shukla

KW Publishers Pvt Ltd
4676/21, First Floor, Ansari Road
Daryaganj, New Delhi 110002
Phone: +91 11 43528107
Marketing: kw@kwpub.in
Editorial: production@kwpub.in
Website: www.kwpub.in

Printed and bound in India

CENTRE FOR AIR POWER STUDIES

VISION

To be an independent centre of excellence on national security contributing informed and considered research and analyses on relevant issues.

MISSION

To encourage independent and informed research and analyses on issues of relevance to national security and to create a pool of domain experts to provide considered inputs to decision-makers. Also, to foster informed public debate and opinion on relevant issues and to engage with other think-tanks and stakeholders within India and abroad to provide an Indian perspective.

Contents

Contents

Foreword

Rising temperatures and the challenges of climate change have forced many countries to look at alternative and renewable sources of energy. The implementation of this, however, has been voluntary to a large extent with consensus eluding the deliberations at the COP summits every year, ignoring the concerns of developing countries. While India has taken the lead to build a global alliance on solar energy, and has invested significantly in nuclear, wind power or eolic energy, it cannot do away with hydrocarbons that fuel its growth to becoming a developed nation. The demand for oil and gas is likely to continue unabated across both developing and developed nations across the world. Energy security is a vital and important constituent of national security. Nations that produce and export oil and gas rely upon its revenues for their economy and are concerned about its demand, while nations that import oil and gas depend upon the availability, accessibility and affordability of energy for their economic growth and are concerned about its supply. Securing supplies through protection of the trade routes and diversification of supplies becomes important for countries like India that are largely dependent upon the import of oil and gas for its requirement.

The littoral countries of the Caspian Sea, Russia, Kazakhstan, Turkmenistan, Iran and Azerbaijan are rich in hydrocarbon reserves. Each nation of the region has its own oil and gas industry which is governed by its own national policies as well as the geopolitics of the region. The Russia-Ukraine war that continues unabated has disrupted the supply and availability of oil and gas with sanctions being imposed on Russia and the European Union and other nations looking at alternate sources of energy to meet their domestic requirements. The Caspian Sea region witnessed the evolution of Azerbaijan, Kazakhstan and Turkmenistan, three new players post the disintegration of the Soviet Union. In the last three and a half decades since then, this region has witnessed the increasing presence of non regional actors like the United States, European Union and China, all of them for vested interests in the energy sector, while Russia tries to maintain its control over these states that were a part of the erstwhile Soviet Union. The development of the oil and gas industry in the Caspian Sea region has been influenced by the national politics of the newly formed states, the influence of Russia and the political upheaval in Iran apart from the presence of extra regional actors in the nation. The Caspian Sea Agreement of 2018 has to a large extent resolved the sovereignty of the littoral states in the Caspian Sea, however the division and exploitation of seabed resources remains unaddressed. The connectivity and pipelines for securing energy have emerged as a new battleground with extra regional powers exercising their influence over the littoral states.

Oil and gas play an important role in India's energy mix, and its import is going to more than double in the coming years to fulfil its escalating energy requirements even as the share of clean and renewable energy increases. India's Integrated Energy Policy looks at exploration of oil and gas within the country, its relations with Russia, Iran and other nations rich in hydrocarbon reserves and the easy availability and accessibility of energy to meet its burgeoning demand in the years to come. Despite the promise of renewables, certain sectors like aviation and shipping are likely to continue with their reliance on fossil fuels in the foreseeable future. The Caspian Sea littoral states are a significant source of energy with their abundant reserves and could serve India's interests with its proximity to the region. There are however challenges in the region due to unresolved territorial disputes, high transportation costs, regulatory uncertainties and the geopolitical landscape that is privy to contestation between global powers. This requires a nuanced approach by India which considers connectivity and India's cultural and historical connections with the countries of the Caspian Sea region as important factors. The International North South Trade Corridor (INSTC) and the Turkmenistan- Afghanistan- Pakistan-India (TAPI) projects are efforts to tap the energy resources of the Caspian Sea region.

With the Russia-Ukraine conflict and the sanctions on import of natural gas from Russia, the intra-regional cooperation between the Caspian Sea countries has only increased. Iran has become an important player with its admission to the BRICS and the SCO groupings in the last two years. This is going to result in increasing contestation in the region between regional and non regional actors posing significant challenges for India. This book provides an overview of India's energy requirements and how it could capitalize on fulfilling the same from the countries of the Caspian Sea region. With a detailed analysis of the energy sector of each of the littoral states of the Caspian Sea, the book calls for a dedicated and nuanced approach to forging long term energy partnerships and leveraging its historical and cultural linkages with deft diplomacy to overcome the existing challenges and meet its requirements. I am sanguine that Dr. Ngangom Dhruba Tara Singh's dedicated efforts to explore this subject would serve as an important document for policy makers, academicians and strategists.

Air Vice Marshal **Anil Golani** (Retd)

Preface

Energy has been central to the Caspian Sea countries of Azerbaijan, Russia, Kazakhstan, Turkmenistan, and Iran. It has shaped their political, economic, and geopolitical interactions. The region's vast oil and gas reserves have drawn significant attention from both regional and global actors, making the Caspian region an important player in the global energy coliseum. The Caspian region has a long history of energy production. Since the mid-19th century, Baku, Azerbaijan, has become the world's focal point for energy resources, and its impressive energy production pinned Baku and the surrounding region on the global energy map in both world wars. After the break-up of the Union of Soviet Socialist Republics (USSR), the emergence of energy-rich Caspian Sea littoral states and their transit capability drove the attention of many actors. In the mid-1990s, many major energy-consuming countries became aware of the energy potential of the Caspian region states, and simultaneously, the newly emerged countries opened to foreign investments and became important actors in the energy market.

In recent times, since the beginning of Russia's special military operation in 2022, the importance of the Caspian region spiked, and there has been a change in the global energy security concerns. While the demand for energy resources has been consistent, one can witness a shift in countries' varying approaches or policies to ensure their energy security. The conflict has introduced geopolitical risks and changes in the energy supply chain, and its repercussions can be witnessed in the decisions made by the countries of

Europe and Asia. For instance, the decision of European countries to halt energy imports from Russia has pushed the latter to look at Asian markets for exports and the former to look at the Caspian region for imports. As the conflict has prompted a global reassessment of energy policies, a renewed focus on diversification is clearly visible.

With renewed global interest in the Caspian region fuelled by the ongoing conflict, India needs to look at the region and reassess its approach. While India's energy partnership with Russia, a Caspian littoral country, has increased because of affordable imports, it is important to acknowledge that the future of affordable oil and gas for India remains uncertain. Therefore, India must look at ways to strengthen energy cooperation with Caspian littoral states endowed with abundant energy resources.

India's demand for hydrocarbons is projected to grow in the forthcoming years. India's oil demand is anticipated to double by 2040, hitting 9.1 million barrels per day (Figure 1); and its natural gas consumption is projected to triple by 2050, mostly attributable to industrial demand (Figure 2). From these predicted estimates, it can be established that both oil and gas will continue to remain significant for India's economic growth.

Figure 1: Oil demand in India from 2013 to 2040
(in million barrels per day)*

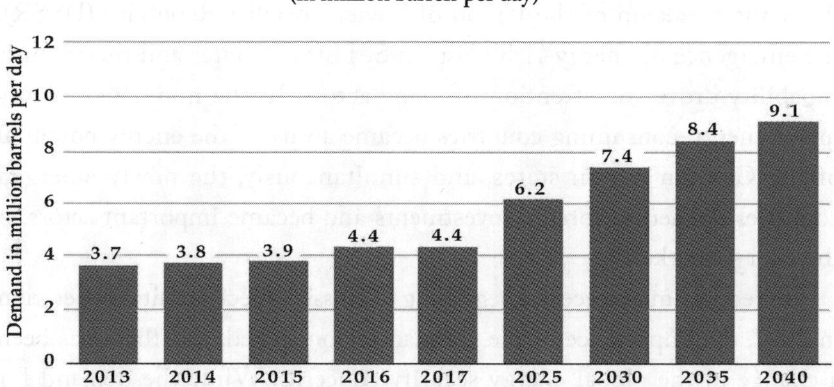

Source: Statista Data, 2024. https://www.statista.com/statistics/543336/projected-oil-demand-in-india/.

* This paper employs both the U.S. Measuring System (e.g., barrels, million cubic feet) and the Indian Measuring System (e.g., metric tonnes, cubic metres) for oil and gas measurements. A conversion table between these units is provided in Appendix I.

Figure 2: Natural Gas Consumption in India from 2022 to 2050 (in billion cubic feet per day)*

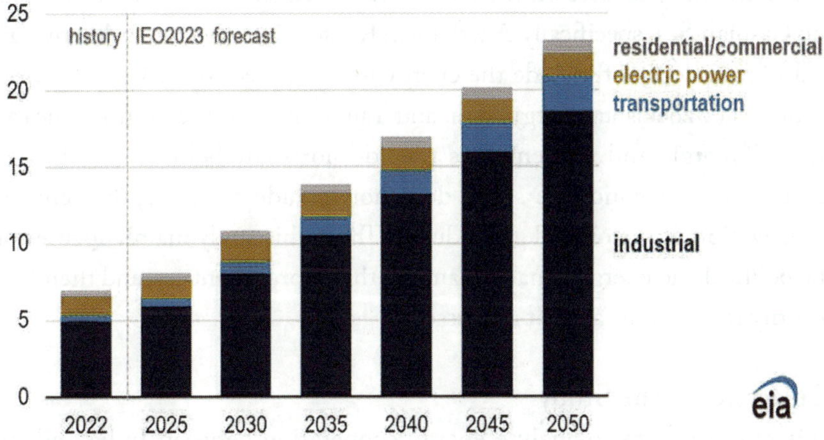

Source: US EIA Data, 2024. https://www.eia.gov/todayinenergy/detail.php?id=61423
* This paper employs both the U.S. Measuring System (e.g., barrels, million cubic feet) and the Indian Measuring System (e.g., metric tonnes, cubic metres) for oil and gas measurements. A conversion table between these units is provided in Appendix I.

Motivated by their energy requirements and geopolitical milieu, both India and the countries of the Caspian region find themselves with converging objectives for potential cooperation. The changing geopolitical landscape of the Caspian region since Russia's military operation in Ukraine has propelled the littoral states to seek more reliable partners for their energy exports, while India is on the lookout for nearby and secure sources of hydrocarbon imports to fuel its economic expansion. This convergence of interests offers a promising ground for energy cooperation.

When it comes to examining India's relations with the Caspian littoral states, earlier studies have often encompassed a broad range of topics, which include energy, cultural exchange, political cooperation, diplomatic ties, and military-to-military relations. While this comprehensive approach offers a valuable overview, it can sometimes result in a lack of in-depth analysis of specific aspects of the relationship. This tendency towards breadth can obscure the nuances and complexities that characterise individual areas of cooperation. In this regard, this book is an endeavour to explore avenues for stronger energy cooperation between India and the Caspian region.

Before beginning this study, the following caveats are in order: Firstly, this study solely focuses on the energy issues related to the littoral states of the Caspian Sea, specifically Azerbaijan, Russia, Kazakhstan, Turkmenistan, and Iran. It does not include the energy issues related to the Central Asian countries (Uzbekistan, Kyrgyzstan, and Tajikistan) and the South Caucasus states (Georgia and Armenia), as they do not share boundaries with the Caspian Sea. Second, the study does not include an in-depth technical investigation of the oil and gas industry. Third, this study mainly focuses on the political and energy dynamics among the littoral countries, and therefore, security interactions are not addressed.

Objectives of the Study

This research aims to analyse energy cooperation between India and the Caspian region. It primarily focuses on how to foster energy cooperation between India and the Caspian littoral countries. Specifically, the study will explore the following areas:

(a) Understand the notion of energy security in the Indian context.
(b) Examine the development of the oil and gas industry in the Caspian Sea region and the interplay of energy with the region's geopolitics.
(c) Understand the significance of oil and gas in India's present energy mix.
(d) Analyse the present status of India's energy cooperation with Caspian region countries and in what manner regional energy cooperation initiatives can facilitate India's energy security.
(e) Explore ways for future energy cooperation.

Plan of Study

The plan of this book has been developed to answer the research objectives. This study includes five main chapters, followed by a sixth chapter, the conclusion.

Chapter 1 seeks to understand energy security in the Indian context. This chapter delves into the dynamic concept of energy security in modern literature, highlighting its crucial significance in the current global scenario. It also explores the complex correlation between energy and geopolitics in the Caspian Sea region, uncovering how political and strategic factors influence energy policies.

Chapter 2 is devoted to explaining the development and hydrocarbon profile of Caspian littoral countries. It seeks to examine how the oil and gas industry in the Caspian Sea states has evolved over time. Additionally, it explores the status of hydrocarbon reserves in the Caspian Sea littoral states and how these reserves vary across the region.

Chapter 3 deals with the energy politics in the region. It discusses the ownership and control of the oil and gas resources in the region, the current legal status of the Caspian Sea, the objectives of major countries—Russia, China, the United States, and the European Union—in the region, connectivity approaches and initiatives, such as transport corridors and pipelines' influence on the region's energy politics, and the ongoing conflict in Ukraine and how this conflict has shaped regional energy dynamics.

Chapter 4 delves into the significance of oil and gas in India's energy profile. In the context of India's growing energy demands, this chapter seeks to elucidate the significance of oil and gas within the country's energy basket. Employing a descriptive approach, the chapter focuses on oil and gas in the present energy landscape and their significance in India's context. Further, it provides insight into the upstream, midstream, and downstream sectors and endeavours to understand government policies concerning oil and gas.

Chapter 5 deals with India's energy cooperation with the Caspian Sea littoral states. The objective is to examine the present status of India's energy cooperation with the Caspian Sea states along with how regional energy cooperation, both bilateral and multilateral, can facilitate India's energy security. It analyses India's strategy on connectivity and the potential of the Caspian connectivity initiatives, mainly the International North-South Transport Corridor (INSTC) and the Turkmenistan-Afghanistan-Pakistan-India (TAPI) gas pipeline.

Finally, Chapter 6, the conclusion, focuses on exploring prospects for future energy cooperation in the Caspian region.

This book, which endeavours to explore India's energy security through regional energy cooperation in the Caspian region, will be of interest to a wide range of individuals. It will be valuable for policymakers and officials involved in energy policy, particularly in India. It will also prove beneficial for academicians and researchers in the fields of international relations and energy studies. Additionally, think tanks and strategic analysts working on geopolitics, energy security, and cooperation will find this book relevant. Finally, general readers who are interested in understanding the impact of energy resources on international relations and regional dynamics will find this book informative.

Acknowledgements

After working for the Centre for Air Power Studies (CAPS) for the last three years, I am grateful to everyone who helped and supported me in completing my book project. I am deeply grateful to my friends and colleagues, whose insights have enriched this book immeasurably.

This book would not have been possible without the constant support and encouragement of several key individuals throughout this journey. First and foremost, I want to express my sincere gratitude to my guide, Dr Manpreet Sethi, for her invaluable mentorship, constant encouragement, and unwavering support. Her insightful feedback and guidance were instrumental in shaping this project and ensuring its successful completion. I am indebted to Dr Manpreet Sethi for helping to mould me as a researcher and scholar.

I would like to thank Air Vice Marshal Anil Golani, Director General, CAPS, for his continuous support and encouragement throughout this research. His belief in my abilities and his willingness to provide me the necessary resources were crucial to the successful completion of this project.

My sincere thanks to Air Vice Marshal Ashish Vohra, Additional Director General, CAPS, for his motivational words.

I am deeply indebted to the external experts—Prof. Rajan Kumar, Prof. Abuzar Khairi, Dr Akanksha Singh, and Dr Athar Zafar—for their valuable feedback on my research. Their expertise and perspectives provided crucial insights that greatly enhanced the quality of this work.

I am also grateful to those with whom I have had the pleasure of working during my project tenure. My interactions with Gp Capt (Dr) Rajneesh Kumar, Dr Joshy Paul, Javed Alam, Radhey Tambi, and Prahlad Kumar Singh were extremely helpful, and I benefitted immensely from them.

I extend my sincere thanks to Sushma Zutshi, Surbhi Sareen Sharma, and Rohit Singh Rajput for their unwavering support. Their commitment and expertise in assisting with literature searches and providing relevant resources were invaluable in my research endeavours.

I would like to express my sincere gratitude to my teachers at my alma mater, St. Joseph's College, Bangalore, and Jawaharlal Nehru University, for their unwavering support and guidance throughout my academic journey. Their dedication and mentorship were invaluable, and I am deeply indebted to them for their contributions to my academic and personal development.

Last, but not least, I want to thank my family for their unconditional love, support, and encouragement. Words cannot fully express my gratitude. I am truly indebted to my parents, and sister, Dr Ngangom Pravina Devi, for always being there and encouraging me to give my best.

I would like to express my sincere appreciation to CAPS for providing me with the platform to pursue this research in such a conducive and rewarding environment. The officers, fellow researchers, and the entire staff have been extremely helpful and supportive throughout my journey.

Thank you all once again.

With regards,

Ngangom Dhruba Tara Singh

Tables, Figures and Maps

Tables

Figures

Maps

Abbreviations

APERC	Asia Pacific Energy Research Centre
APOC	Anglo-Persian Oil Company
ASEAN	Association of Southeast Asian Nations
AIOC	Azerbaijan International Operating Company
ACG	Azeri–Chirag–Gunashli
ACSC	Azerbaijan Caspian Shipping Closed Joint-Stock Company
BRI	Belt and Road Initiative
BTC	Baku–Tbilisi–Ceyhan Pipeline
BTE	Baku–Tbilisi–Erzurum Pipeline (also known as South Caucasus Pipeline)
BRICS	Brazil, Russia, India, China, South Africa
M3	Cubic Metres
BCM	Billion Cubic Metres
TCM	Trillion Cubic Metres
Ft3	Cubic Feet
BCF	Billion Cubic Feet
TCF	Trillion Cubic Feet
MT	Metric Tonne or Ton
MMT	Million Metric Tonne
BBL	Barrel
MBPD	Million Barrels Per Day
CAC	Central Asia-Center gas pipeline system

CIS	Commonwealth of Independent States
CEFTA	Central European Free Trade Agreement
CPC	Caspian Pipeline Consortium
CNPC	China National Petroleum Corporation
CSTO	Collective Security Treaty Organization
EC	European Commission
EU	European Union
EIA	U.S. Energy Information Administration
EurAsEC	Eurasian Economic Community
IEA	International Energy Agency
INSTC	International North–South Transport Corridor
JCPOA	Joint Comprehensive Plan of Action
NATO	North Atlantic Treaty Organization
NCOC	North Caspian Operating Company
NEP	New Economic Policy
NIOC	National Iranian Oil Company
NIGC	National Iranian Gas Company
NIORDC	National Iranian Oil Refining and Distribution Company
NIGC	National Iranian Gas Company
ONGC	Oil and Natural Gas Corporation Limited
SAARC	South Asian Association for Regional Cooperation
SGC	Southern Gas Corridor
SCO	Shanghai Cooperation Organisation
SOCAR	State Oil Company of the Republic of Azerbaijan
TAPI	Turkmenistan–Afghanistan–Pakistan–India Gas Pipeline
TAP	Trans Adriatic Pipeline
TANAP	Trans-Anatolian Natural Gas Pipeline
TITR	Trans-Caspian International Transport Route
USSR	Union of Soviet Socialist Republics
UGSS	Unified Gas Supply System
UNGA	United Nations General Assembly
WEF	World Economic Forum

The Caspian Region

Source: BBC News.

1

Introduction: India's Energy Security

The Caspian Sea is the largest water body located inland and surrounded by five littoral countries: Russia, Kazakhstan, Turkmenistan, Iran, and Azerbaijan. This unique geographical position fosters a complex web of interactions, driven by the sea's rich resources, complex legal status, and strategic importance. The sea is a valuable reservoir of natural resources, as its depths contain extensive oil and natural gas deposits, fuelling the economies of all five littoral states. There has been disagreement about dividing the seabed resources among the states. The disagreement is because of historical claims and different interpretations of international law.

The Caspian Sea serves as a dynamic centre for geopolitical affairs. The exploration and discovery of fresh oil and gas deposits continue to influence the economic interests of the riparian states. Over the last three decades, the Caspian Sea region has experienced significant developments. For instance, when it comes to energy transit, multiple transnational energy pipelines, such as the Baku-Tbilisi-Ceyhan (BTC) pipeline and the Baku-Tbilisi-Erzurum (BTE) gas pipeline (also known as the South Caucasus Gas Pipeline), have been built. Since 1991, the involvement of external actors has exacerbated the complexity of the geopolitical landscape, as every transit development or energy project has been characterised as a component of competition among major global powers.

The protracted conflict between Russia and Ukraine has profoundly influenced the geopolitics of the Caspian region, owing to its proximity to the theatre of battle. Studies have noted that the ongoing crisis extends beyond military engagement between Russia and Ukraine to encompass a multifaceted tussle and power play, including Russia, the United States (U.S.), and Europe. More precisely, the response from Washington and its European allies is intended to weaken Russia's economic, military, and diplomatic capabilities, as well as Moscow's capacity to exert influence in its 'near abroad'.[1]

Many countries have demonstrated diverse responses to the ongoing crisis between Russia and Ukraine. For example, the reluctance of the U.S. allies in West Asia, the South Caucasus, and Central and South Asia to align with either the U.S. or Russia signifies a notable increase in autonomy in world politics. Further, the ongoing crisis has had a substantial influence on the restructuring of regional alliances in the Caspian region. The West and Russia are competing to draw Caspian countries into their own areas of influence, using new energy and connectivity programmes as key drivers.

Concept of Energy Security in Existing Writings

Energy has consistently played a crucial role in driving economic progress, serving as the cornerstone for military might and facilitating human development throughout world history. Today, it is crucial to guarantee the adequate reliability, inexpensiveness, accessibility, and security of energy sources. The notion of energy security, at a fundamental level, is commonly understood as "having access to the requisite volumes of energy at affordable prices…access to the required energy should be impervious to disruptions: that alternative supplies should be readily available at affordable prices and sufficient with respect to both available volume and time required for distribution."[2] The concept of energy security is not new, and there is a plethora of literature, as it has consistently been a subject of debate and varying interpretations concerning its exact definition.

From an institutional perspective, various agencies have come forward with their definition of the concept. The International Energy Agency (IEA) sees ensuring the security of oil supplies as one of the agency's main activities. It defines energy security as the "uninterrupted availability of energy sources at an affordable price."[3] Energy security encompasses two distinct aspects:

the long-term and the short-term. In the former, energy security primarily deals with timely investments to supply energy in agreement with economic developments and requirements for a sustainable environment. In the latter, energy security concentrates on the ability of the energy system to react responsively to any sudden developments in demand and supply. In the past, energy security was mainly associated with the supply of oil, which continues to remain the primary issue.[4] The Asia Pacific Energy Research Centre (APERC) sees energy security as the "ability of an economy to guarantee the availability of energy resource supply in a sustainable and timely manner with the energy price being at a level that will not adversely affect the economic performance of the economy. Factors that can influence energy security are the 4As: availability, accessibility, acceptability, and affordability" (Cherp and Jewell quoted APERC).[5] The European Commission (EC) defines energy security as "uninterrupted physical availability of energy products on the markets at an affordable price for all consumers."[6] According to the World Economic Forum (WEF), it is "*autonomy*, energy supply that is within the control of a country and free from disruption by external agents; *reliability*, or distribution that is safe and meets demand without interruption; *affordability*, or prices commensurable with the buying power of consumers; and *sustainability*, or sufficient supply of energy to support a high quality of life without damaging the environment."[7]

In light of the definitions presented above, it is possible to deduce that energy security is a multifaceted concept that takes into account both long-term and short-term factors. It focuses on ensuring a reliable and affordable supply of energy to meet a country's economic and social needs. While historically tied mainly to the availability of oil, the notion has broadened to encompass sustainability and environmental dimension.

There appears to be a shared understanding among these definitions: affordability and uninterrupted availability are the key. The IEA and the European Commission emphasise cost, while the WEF expands the definition to include control over energy sources (autonomy) and environmental responsibility (sustainability). The APERC introduces the 4As framework, highlighting the importance of social and environmental factors alongside price and physical availability.

Energy security is a concept that varies across countries. For countries that rely heavily on oil and gas imports, energy security is primarily about ensuring a stable supply. In contrast, countries that are dependent on exporting oil and gas consider energy security in terms of maintaining consistent demand for their resources. For example, the U.S. considers the availability of sufficient supplies at affordable rates, maintaining strategic oil reserves, securing Middle Eastern supplies, securing shipping routes against piracy, and mitigating threats to energy infrastructure as essential components of energy security. For Russia, energy security means maintaining state control over the resources it supplies to global markets. One main aspect of this is close monitoring of foreign investments in its oil and gas sector. China views energy security as the ability to adjust to its new dependency on global markets, engage in energy diplomacy, purchase stakes in foreign oil and gas fields, and protect vulnerable seaways. Japan considers energy security as balancing its domestic resource scarcity through trade and investments, diversification, and engagement with Asian countries to mutually develop energy resources. Saudi Arabia prioritises ensuring the security of demand for its oil and gas exports, while Colombia and Venezuela focus on minimising attacks on their energy facilities to ensure energy security.[8]

Geopolitics, embodying the state-centric realism viewpoint on international relations and national security, was intricately linked to the notion of energy security in the 20th century. At first, the geopolitical strategy mostly concentrated on the potential interruptions in the flow of oil from the Middle East to industrialised countries. Subsequently, it broadened its scope to encompass additional regions like Europe and Asia, while also incorporating alternative energy sources like natural gas. Presently, there is a growing trend or inclination to include non-state actors in the analysis of energy security and to emphasise the significance of institutions and systems of global governance. This includes addressing concerns such as environmental protection and global climate change.[9]

As previous studies have extensively dealt with the concept, this study does not intend to present a new cosmetic notion for energy security. Despite concerted efforts to establish a clear definition, there is a lack of agreement over the precise parameters that characterise energy security. Luft et al.

summarise this ambiguity by stating that where countries stand on energy security is determined by where they reside, and for every country, "energy security is like a Rorschach inkblot test—you can see whatever you want to see in it."[10]

Understanding Energy Security in the Indian Context

The term 'energy security' varies in meaning across various regions due to its comprehensive character. Countries that depend significantly on oil and gas imports prioritise energy security through continuous supply. On the other hand, countries reliant on oil and gas exports perceive energy security as a matter of sustained demand. The issue of energy security, as documented in previous literature, emerged during World War I with supplying oil for the British military when Churchill changed the power sources of the Royal Navy's ships to oil from coal. As a result, diversification became the key to energy security during Churchill's tenure. Academics pursuing energy security emerged in the 1960s and 1970s and re-emerged in the 2000s along with increased demand in Asia.[11]

With the emergence of the idea of energy security in the 1970s, Willrich observed that "energy security is a matter of greatest concern to international politics"[12] and that it was solely concerned with crude supply. The concept of energy security broadened as a policy reaction to the Arab oil blockade of 1973. The Second Arab-Israeli War and Western backing for Israel led Arab nations to place energy embargoes on the U.S. and its allies in 1973. Many Arab countries and members of the Organization of the Petroleum Exporting Countries (OPEC) nationalised the U.S.' oil holdings. Although the oil embargo was only temporary, oil prices skyrocketed during and after the crisis, prompting the major oil-importing countries to implement a variety of countermeasures, such as energy investment, diversification of energy resources and import destinations, and energy efficiency and stockpiling measures. Further, the Organisation for Economic Cooperation and Development (OECD) countries created the IEA in 1974 to exert more influence over the global energy consumption market. Consequently, energy security became a top priority in the agenda-setting and policy-making of numerous countries. The IEA, established in the wake of the 1973 oil crisis, suggested a national energy security model centred on stabilising crude oil prices and ensuring continuous supply.

The concept of energy security is elusive because it has evolved in the last several decades to keep pace with the changing global energy milieu. Historically, the concept was associated with the security of oil supplies. The 'oil-centric' definitions of energy security have varied depending on whether the country is a net oil producer or a net consumer. For instance, energy security for the European Union (EU) and China means the security of oil supply, while for Russia and Saudi Arabia, it means the stability of global demand. Today, the term is more of an umbrella of definitions that countries pick and shape to suit their circumstances. With changes in the global energy landscape and growing worries about energy security amongst countries and organisations, the definition of energy security has extended beyond oil, and scholars have evaluated energy security from various viewpoints, considering the differences in economies. Today, the concept of energy security embraces issues such as climate change and sustainable development.

Energy security in the Indian context: The notion of energy security in its present shape includes specific definitions as well as broader viewpoints. The field of energy security has undergone significant advancements and now encompasses a wide range of concerns. India began to prioritise energy security as a critical domestic and foreign policy concern during Prime Minister Vajpayee's tenure. His administration regarded energy security as the primary catalyst for India's endeavours to diversify its energy sources and suppliers. Energy security remained a significant policy objective throughout Prime Minister Manmohan Singh's tenure. He highlighted energy security as the second most crucial security concern, following food security. In 2005, President Abdul Kalam emphasised the significance of achieving 'energy security' as a step towards achieving 'energy independence'. India's pursuit of energy security began in 2006, as evidenced in the Planning Commission's strategic plan for ensuring energy security:

> "We are energy secure when we can supply lifeline energy to all our citizens irrespective of their ability to pay for it, as well as meet their effective demand for safe and convenient energy to satisfy their various needs at

competitive prices, at all times and with a prescribed confidence level considering shocks and disruptions that can be reasonably expected."[13]

Prime Minister Modi's government continued prioritising energy security as a key focus of domestic and foreign policy agenda, acknowledging the evident connections between energy security and economic growth. For India's energy security, Union Minister Hardeep Singh Puri presented a '4-plank strategy': "(a) Diversification of energy supplies; (b) Increasing India's exploration and production footprint; (c) Using alternate energy sources; (d) Meeting energy transition through the gas-based economy, green hydrogen, and EVs."[14] One of the key points emphasised was India's increased international oil suppliers from 27 in 2006-07 to 39 in 2021-22, including new suppliers.[15] It is within the context of supply diversification and exploration and production strategies that India's energy security through regional energy cooperation in the Caspian states will be examined.

Union Minister Hardeep Puri's portrayal implies that India is actively taking measures to strengthen its energy security. The strategy focuses on diversity across several areas. The expansion of international oil suppliers from 27 to 39 demonstrates a deliberate effort to diversify import reliance. This decreases dependence on any individual country and its possible political or economic volatility. Here, the focus on domestic exploration and production demonstrates a strategic plan to reduce dependence on imports in the long run. Furthermore, the advocacy for alternative energy sources, such as renewables, demonstrates a dedication to sustainability and a decreased susceptibility to changes in fossil fuel prices. India's intention to transition towards a more secure and environmentally responsible energy future is seen in its exploration of cleaner alternatives, such as a increased use of natural gas, green hydrogen, and electric vehicles. This strategy tackles both the immediate need for energy and the long-term goal of sustainability. India's energy future is being made more secure and sustainable through the combination of diversification and domestic production, as well as the use of renewables and clean technologies.

Energy security has become a basic component of a country's economic and political success, as well as a significant factor in deciding its position.

The pursuance of India's progressive goals and the viability of its economic growth are both reliant on a continuous supply of energy. Despite India's attempts to expand green and alternative energy sources and the recent push for domestic oil and gas exploration and production, hydrocarbons and their imports continue to play a major role in its energy basket, accounting for the lion's share of India's energy mix, necessitating the need to turn overseas for these resources as domestic reforms may only facilitate bridging supply and demand imbalances in the short term. In summary, inferences from the '4-plank strategy' conclude that the notion of energy security for India encompasses four key dimensions: affordability, acceptability, availability, and accessibility of energy sources.

Energy and Geopolitics in the Caspian Sea Region

The Caspian Sea riparian states—Azerbaijan, Russia, Kazakhstan, Turkmenistan, and Iran—came into existence after the dissolution of the Soviet Union. Here, three more neighbours now share the Caspian Sea, a water body whose boundaries were once shared by the Soviet Union and Iran. Since 1991, the region has gained attention for two main reasons: oil and gas production and reserves and transit potential. In the last three decades, the region has witnessed an increasing role of non-regional actors, which includes the U.S., the EU, and China. At the same time, Russia, as a major power, has been attempting to maintain its influence over the neighbouring littoral states.

Agha Bayramov, in his work, provided a meticulous evaluation of the notion of the 'New Great Game' in the Caspian Sea region. He analysed the prominent actors in the region and the various ideas proposed as alternatives to the New Great Game concept. His work states that the primary contenders in the Caspian Sea region's New Great Game are the EU, the U.S., Russia, and China. These external actors are perceived as the predominant participants in the game. In addition, there are other significant regional actors, such as Turkey, Iran, Pakistan, Kazakhstan, Turkmenistan, and Azerbaijan, and observers note that regional actors align themselves with the established dominant actors to form temporary coalitions and pursue their own objectives.[16]

Dayyan Janbaaz and Mehrdad Fallah assessed the influence of regional and trans-regional actors on the establishment of the legal framework for the Caspian Sea. Russia's policy has effectively fostered strong relationships with coastal and trans-regional countries surrounding the Caspian Sea. Following the dissolution of the Soviet Union, the U.S. made significant efforts to establish a global order under the dominance of a single power. It regarded the Caspian Sea and the Middle East as significant sources of global energy for the 21st century. The primary objective of the U.S. strategy in the Caspian region was to exert control over the region's energy resources. This has led to the U.S. gaining influence and political dominance in the region while also facilitating the development of plans against China, Russia, and Iran.

The U.S. also plays a significant role in Europe's approach to Central Asia, the Caspian region, and the Black Sea. The U.S. backs the EU by focusing on countering Russian energy transit initiatives through the Caspian Sea to Europe. As the EU holds a small portion of the global supply of crude oil and natural gas, it was earlier projected that the EU would rely on imports for 90 per cent of its crude oil needs and 70 per cent of its natural gas requirements by 2020, taking into account both short-term and long-term aspects. Most of these resources come from the Persian Gulf, Russia, and northern Africa. Due to the fragility and geographical remoteness of energy resources in the Middle East, as well as the declining domestic production, the EU has intensified its attention to the Caspian region.

Multiple issues affect China's energy diplomacy in the Caspian region. Beijing's objectives are: firstly, to mitigate reliance on oil from the Persian Gulf; second, to actively engage with oil producers that are less susceptible to the impact of the U.S.' policies in order to mitigate the extent of American influence on the transportation of energy resources; third, to forge bilateral ties with the Caspian countries to mutually address the challenges that arise from production variations; and fourth, to provide funding for Caspian energy production, which, in turn, encourages Chinese enterprises to invest in the development of untapped oil and gas assets.[17]

Russia's special military operation in Ukraine since February 2022 has deeply impacted the energy politics of the Caspian Sea region. Tatiana Mitrova assessed Russia's reactions to the prospects of Caspian joint gas projects for the European market, the role of Turkey, Russia's strategy in Central Asia, and the Southern Gas Corridor. Russia places a higher importance on maintaining positive relationships with countries in the Caspian region rather than focusing on prospective competition in the EU gas market. Russia maintains friendly relations with these countries, using regular talks and enhanced economic collaboration in many sectors, notwithstanding their shared Caspian gas projects. Russia is actively seeking to capitalise on the remaining prospects to make cash from gas exports to countries such as Turkey and Azerbaijan. Additionally, it has expressed its objective to impede the construction of the Trans-Caspian pipeline and align itself with regional countries with new proposals. For instance, it is focusing on forming a tripartite gas union with Kazakhstan and Uzbekistan while also strengthening its relationship with Iran and agreeing to create an energy hub.

The EU views the Caspian region, particularly the Southern Gas Corridor (SGC), as a strategy to lessen its reliance on Russian energy. However, the EU's initiative will likely face challenges due to Russia's growing influence in the region, which creates geopolitical uncertainty. For example, Azerbaijan's cooperation with Russia and Iran in gas supply, especially considering the SGC's future expansion[18], will likely put the EU in a precarious position.

On similar lines, Vlad Kondratiev argued that the ongoing conflict between Russia and Ukraine will have a substantial influence on the geopolitical landscape of the Caspian region. Before the conflict, Ukraine aspired to become a pivotal trading ally for the countries of the Caspian region. Ukraine sought to establish alternative transportation lines that circumvented Russia and fostered closer collaboration with Iran and Turkmenistan. Nevertheless, the conflict has impeded these endeavours. On the other hand, the sanctions on Russia are likely to strengthen its ties with Caspian countries. Despite the Caspian littoral states' neutral position on the war, it is anticipated that Russia will continue to retain strong links with its traditional partners, Azerbaijan and Kazakhstan. In addition, Russian enterprises may seek out new economic prospects in the Caspian region. Iran has conveyed its endorsement of Russia, and there is potential for a substantial boost in bilateral trade between the two countries. Despite the ongoing conflict in Ukraine, Russia will emerge as the dominant power in the Caspian region. The conflict will foster collaboration between Russia and other littoral states of the Caspian Sea.[19]

After becoming independent, the Caspian Sea countries' interactions with each other and with non-regional actors have been affected by various factors, such as oil resources, strategic location, transition to democracy, and balance of power in the region. Over the last three decades, numerous global and regional actors have been vying for a portion of the region's oil and gas riches. While earlier research has explored Russia's dominance, Western interest, and energy export routes, it has largely neglected the potential for India's energy cooperation with the Caspian's littoral countries. Academicians have paid little attention to exploring the possibility of projects, for example, the International North-South Transport Corridor (INSTC) for energy transit. Additionally, existing studies have not adequately explored the potential for energy cooperation through regional frameworks like the Shanghai Cooperation Organisation (SCO) and Brazil, Russia, India, China, and South Africa (BRICS), which offer platforms for energy cooperation between Caspian states and India. Given the Caspian region's proximity to India, it is necessary to assess India's potential and propose a future course of action.

With regard to India's cooperation with Central Asian countries, Ramakrushna Pradhan highlighted that despite India's cultural and other aspects of its relations having flourished since 1991, its economic engagement with the region has been quite weak. Although the Central Asian countries view India as a potential substitute for the Chinese monopoly in the region, India's lack of enthusiasm and unimpressive economic profile in the region is worrisome. India's trade and economic contacts with the Central Asian states are very small, in contrast to its developing trade relations with China and Russia. India's energy security can be strengthened by utilising Central Asian hydrocarbon resources, which can, in turn, contribute to the eradication of poverty and fuel economic growth in the country. Given India's current economic expansion and the potential for future growth, its energy demand is expected to increase significantly in the coming years.[20]

This reason for India's lack of presence in the Caspian region can be understood by examining Sanjay Pradhan's *India's Quest for Energy Through Oil and Natural Gas: Trade and Investment, Geopolitics, and Security*. India faces three continental or marine challenges that hinder its efforts to secure uninterrupted and protected access to energy resources, notwithstanding its expanding presence in Central Asia. India's geographical position restricts its direct access to Central Asia. To enhance trade and communication with this region, India has to pass through territories such as Afghanistan, Pakistan, and Iran. The dependence on intermediary countries is essential for fulfilling India's energy transportation requirements. However, there are numerous and highly intricate problems. First, India is profoundly apprehensive about the potential rulers of the country, namely the Taliban, the Islamic State, or any other terrorist organisation. If Afghanistan were to come under their control, it could lead to the Islamic radicalisation of the country. This, in turn, would have a destabilising impact on the entire Eurasian region, including South Asia, West Asia, Russia, China, and the Caspian belt. Second, Pakistan serves as the intermediary nation that links India to Central Asia via Afghanistan. The bloodshed perpetrated by the extremists from Pakistan and Afghanistan has a destabilising impact. Third, Iran serves as a secure and viable pathway to connect India with Central Asia, albeit being slightly costlier due to its greater distance. Nevertheless, the regular imposition of sanctions on Iran hinders India's efforts to establish connectivity with the region through Iran.[21] While Ramakrushna and Sanjay Pradhan's focus was on Central Asia, their work highlighted several questions in energy cooperation that require attention.

In recent times, several estimates projected an increase in India's consumption of oil and gas. The IEA predicts that India's demand for oil will reach 6.6 million barrels per day by 2030, compared to 5.5 million barrels per day in 2023. Additionally, to fulfil this requirement, India is projected to increase its refining capacity by 1 million barrels per day (bpd) over the course of seven years. This would result in a further increase in India's crude oil imports to 5.8 million barrels per day by 2030.[22] When it comes to natural gas, the government aims to raise the proportion of natural gas in the country's primary energy mix to 15 per cent by 2030, up from a little over 6 per cent. The U.S. Energy Information Administration (EIA) predicts that India's net imports of natural gas will experience an annual growth rate of 4.9 per cent from 2022 to 2050.[23] These multiple energy forecasts clearly demonstrate the paramount significance of the Caspian region and its potential for imports in the upcoming years.

Assessment

The concept of energy security is dynamic and has conceptual ambiguity. It is because the concept's interpretations differ across countries and regions and are shaped by various factors, such as availability of domestic resources, geographical location, and economic development. Earlier, concerns regarding oil supply moulded the notion of energy security, but later, it evolved and encompassed other factors, such as climate change and environmental concerns and roles of non-state entities. Further, the interconnectedness of the international energy market and the rise of renewable energy have also facilitated shaping the notion. In the Indian context, the notion of energy security can be viewed as an umbrella concept encompassing the following sub-concepts: availability, accessibility, acceptability, and affordability. In the end, as India's appetite for oil and gas continues to grow, it needs to explore avenues for energy cooperation.

Notes

1. Raj Verma and Björn Alexander Düben, "Russia's Invasion of Ukraine: Cementing US Global Pre-eminence", *Journal of Indo-Pacific Affairs*, Vol. 3, No. 3, 2023, pp. 74–91.
2. Charles K. Ebinger, *Energy and Security in South Asia: Cooperation or Conflict?* (Washington, D.C.: Brookings Institution Press, 2011), p. 2.
3 International Energy Agency, "Energy Security", https://www.iea.org/topics/energy-security/. Accessed on April 16, 2022.
4. Ibid.
5. Aleh Cherp and Jessica Jewell, "The concept of energy security: Beyond the four As", *Energy Policy*, Vol. 75, 2014, pp. 415-421.
6. International Energy Agency, "Contribution of Renewables to Energy Security", IEA Information Paper, https://iea.blob.core.windows.net/assets/682ee8e1-a423-4775-bcd1-38bf4c18717f/so_contribution.pdf. Accessed on March 16, 2022.

7. World Economic Forum, "Global Risks 2009: A Global Risk Network Report", https://www.preventionweb.net/files/9102_globalrisks20091.pdf. Accessed on March 16, 2022.
8. Benjamin K. Sovacool and Marilyn A. Brown, "Competing Dimensions of Energy Security: An International Perspective", *Annual Review of Environment and Resources,* Vol. 35, 2010, pp. 77-108.
9. Aliaksandr Novikau, "Energy Security: Evolution of a Concept", in Scott N. Romaniuk and Peter Marton, ed., *The Palgrave Encyclopaedia of Global Security Studies,* (Switzerland: Palgrave Macmillan, 2020).
10. Benjamin K. Sovacool, "Introduction: Defining, measuring, and exploring energy security", in Benjamin K. Sovacool, ed., *The Routledge Handbook of Energy Security,* (New York: Routledge, 2011).
11. Daniel Yergin, "Ensuring Energy Security", *Foreign Affairs,* Vol. 85, No. 2, 2006, pp. 69-82.
12. Willrich M., *Energy and World Politics,* (New York: The Free Press, 1978).
13. Bala Bhaskar, *Energy security and economic development in India: A holistic approach,* (New Delhi: The Energy and Research Institute, 2013).
14. "Increased E&P, import diversification, biofuels part of India's four-plank energy security strategy", *The Hindu Business Line*, January 22, 2023, https://www.thehindubusinessline.com/economy/increased-ep-import-diversification-biofuels-part-of-indias-four-plank-energy-security-strategy/article66419965.ece. Accessed on March 28, 2023.
15. "India will contribute 25% of global demand by 2040 and achieve 20% ethanol blending in petrol by 2025: Hardeep Singh Puri", *Press Information Bureau (India),* January 10, 2023, https://www.pib.gov.in/PressReleasePage.aspx?PRID=1889967. Accessed on March 28, 2023.
16. Agha Bayramov, "Conflict, cooperation or competition in the Caspian Sea region: A critical review of the New Great Game paradigm", *Caucasus Survey,* Vol. 9, No. 1, 2020, pp. 1-21.
17. Dayyan Janbaaz and Mehrdad Fallah, "Energy Resources of the Caspian Sea: The Role of Regional and Trans-regional Powers in Its Legal Regime", in Mansoureh Ebrahimi et al., *The Dynamics of Iranian Border: Issues of Contention,* (Switzerland: Springer, 2019).
18. Tatiana Mitrova, *"Q&A: The Geopolitics of Caspian Gas",* Center on Global Energy Policy at Columbia University, School of International and Public Affairs, https://www.energypolicy.columbia.edu/qa-the-geopolitics-of-caspian-gas/. Accessed on December 17, 2023.
19. Vlad Kondratiev, "Ukraine conflict and the Caspian Sea regional geopolitics", *Special Eurasia,* Vol. 17, No. 2, 2022, https://www.specialeurasia.com/2022/03/06/ukraine-conflict-caspian-sea/. Accessed on March 17, 2022.
20. Ramakrushna Pradhan, *Geopolitics of Energy in Central Asia: India's position and policy,* (London: Routledge, 2021).

21. Sanjay Kumar Pradhan, *India's Quest for Energy Through Oil and Natural Gas: Trade and Investment, Geopolitics, and Security* (Singapore: Springer, 2020).
22. Sethuraman N. R. and Nidhi Verma, "India will be world's biggest oil demand growth driver through 2030, IEA says", *Reuters,* February 7, 2024, https://www.reuters.com/business/energy/india-be-largest-global-oil-demand-growth-driver-through-2030-iea-2024-02-07/. Accessed on February 16, 2024.
23. Rishi Ranjan Kala, "India's natural gas imports to grow at 4.9% annually till 2050: US EIA", *The Hindu Business Line,* February 15, 2024. https://www.thehindubusinessline.com/markets/commodities/indias-natural-gas-imports-to-grow-at-49-annually-till-2050-us-eia/article67849546.ece#:~:text=%E2%80%9CBy%202050%2C%20we%20project%20natural,per%20cent%2C%E2%80%9D%20it%20added. Accessed on February 16, 2024.

2

Caspian Energy: A Deep Dive into Oil and Gas

The Caspian Sea serves as both a bridge and a separator for the countries of the South Caucasus and Central Asia. In geological terms, the Caspian Sea is divided into three basins: the northern, central, and southern. The northern basin covers 27 per cent of the surface area and holds 0.6 per cent of the total volume of the sea. The central basin covers 38 per cent of the surface area and holds 36 per cent of sea volume. The southern basin covers 39 per cent of the surface area and holds 63 per cent of the total amount of water. Many transboundary rivers are the source of the Caspian Sea. The Volga, Ural, and Terek are the rivers of the northern coast that contribute 88 per cent of the total inflow. The Kura, Sulak, Samur, and a few other rivers that originate from the Caucasus Mountains account for 8 per cent of the total inflow. The remaining inflow occurs along the Iranian coast (Sefid-Rud and others). There is no river inflow from the eastern shore.[1]

The Caucasus Mountains divide the Caucasus region into north and south. The South Caucasus comprises Armenia, Azerbaijan, and Georgia, and the North Caucasus falls under the Russian territory, which comprises the ethnically defined regions of Adygea, Chechnya, Dagestan, Ingushetia, Kabardino-Balkaria, Karachay-Cherkessia, and Krasnodar Krai. Amongst the Caspian littoral states, Russia and Kazakhstan share the longest shorelines in the northwest and northeast, while southern shores are shared by Azerbaijan, Iran, and Turkmenistan.

On December 8, 1991, Russia, Ukraine, and Belarus made a unilateral declaration which marked the disintegration of the Union of Soviet Socialist Republics (USSR) and the formation of independent states in the Caucasus and Central Asia. In the Caspian region, Russia, Azerbaijan, Kazakhstan, and Turkmenistan overnight emerged as new littoral states, along with Iran. The Caspian littoral states hold significance for two reasons: first, their geostrategic position due to their hydrocarbon reserves; and second, as an important link between Central Asia and South Caucasus. The region's richness in hydrocarbons has become a point of contention among littoral states, while the transportation of energy resources in and around the region remains a sensitive issue for littoral states and external actors.

Against this backdrop, the chapter aims to understand the energy landscape of the Caspian region by answering the following questions: First, how has the oil and gas industry in the Caspian Sea states evolved? Second, what is the present status of reserves of hydrocarbons in Caspian Sea littoral states, and how do these profiles vary across the region? To address the aforementioned questions, the chapter is organised in the following fashion. The first section traces the development of the Caspian oil and gas industry. The second section outlines the hydrocarbon profile of the Caspian Sea states. The analysis includes a review of existing literature on the subject and statistical documents published by international agencies.

Development of the Caspian Oil and Gas Industry

Oil and gas played a significant role in the history of the Russian Empire and the Soviet Union. After the dissolution of the USSR, analysts compared the oil deposits in the Caspian region to those in the Persian Gulf and the Northern Sea. Since 1991, Caspian riparian states have linked their aspirations for economic recovery and their well-being to increased oil and gas output.

Evolution of the Oil and Gas Industry in the Russian Imperial Period

The use of the primitive methods of oil extraction was recorded by the German geophysicist, Engelbert Kampfer, in 1648. He stayed in Baku to explore the oil reserves of the Apsheron Peninsula and observed that the reserves of natural gas on the peninsula were abundant, and only a small fraction of those reserves was used for heating and cooking purposes. The oil was extracted from oil pits by using pumping installations powered by horsepower. In 1722, Russia, under Peter I, occupied the Persian-controlled eastern Transcaucasia, including Baku. One of Peter I's decisions in the region was to confiscate all oil wells and cancel the rights of the existing owners in favour of the Russian Crown. The Russian Empire further gained territory in the Caucasus region, surrounding present-day Azerbaijan, Georgia, and Armenia, when Persia signed the Treaty of Turkmenchay in 1828. In 1835, the military governorate was permitted by the Crown to lease oil-containing property on the condition that leases would remain limited to Russian officers. Consequently, Baku and its surroundings were declared a military zone, and access from the outer world was prevented. It was not until the mid-1840s that the strict military control was eased and the property rights were restored to the local Azeris.[2]

Azerbaijan became the world's first oil power in 1848 when the first oil well was drilled on the Absheron Peninsula, and Baku became the first place where an oil refinery was built. Gradually, this development led to widespread construction or drilling of oil wells across the region in the early 1870s.[3] After the discovery of oil, Russian firms used equipment to drill crude oil in the 1870s; by 1873, a few small refineries were operational in Baku.[4] Baku became the primary oil source for the Russian Empire as it provided 97.7 per cent of the oil in 1890, and later, in 1901, it produced almost half of the world's crude oil.[5]

One of the first developments observed in the Caspian-Caucasus oil industry was the renting out of oil fields by the state. In 1821, oil fields in Baku were rented out for four years by the state. The Crown Department of the Georgian administration rented out oil pits to individual contractors. However, oil production remained low because of the continuous use of primitive methods and obstructions caused by government monopolies in the growth of the Russian oil industry. The state monopoly was removed in 1872 when Tsar Alexander II agreed to auction oil fields to reduce the government deficit. Despite the abolition of state control, the government was cautious in lending oil fields to buyers.[6]

Together with the introduction of a policy to remove state monopolies, the treasury department levied excise duty on all petroleum products. During this period, many oil well owners lacked finance and innovation for drilling. Oil drilling was conducted manually, and oil was shipped off using horse-drawn carts, leather sacks, and barrels. The oil industry in Baku was inefficient due to a lack of technology. In 1876, the Baku oil industry encountered a serious crisis as the price of crude oil dropped, and in the following year, the government removed the excise tax based on Mendeleev's recommendations.

The removal of excise taxes enticed foreign and Russian investors in Caspian oil. The first foreign investment company that participated in the Azerbaijan oil industry was the Nobel Brothers Petroleum Production Company. By 1875, they purchased the Balakhany field and built the first modernised refinery and oil tanker in Russia. The company's oil wells produced 23 million barrels of crude oil per year by the late 1880s.[7] In the next 25 years, production rose by approximately 150 million barrels of oil.[8] The issue of oil transportation was solved in 1883 when a direct railroad was constructed from Baku to the Black Sea port of Batumi through the Caucasus. In 1883, Rothschild entered the oil industry and founded the Societe Commerciale et Industrielle de Napthe Caspienne et de la Mer Noire (Caspian and Black Sea Petroleum Company). Both Rothschild and the Nobel Brothers built streamer tanks for transporting oil across the Caspian Sea to Volga River barges, constructed a railroad from Baku to Batum, and built the pipeline, which was completed in 1905. Before World War I, the Nobel Brothers became the largest, and the Rothschild became the second-largest oil-producing enterprise in Russia.[9] Their involvement in the region facilitated the building of energy infrastructure.

Alongside Azerbaijan, oil was struck in Grozny, another section in the Caspian region, in the mid-1880s. Though ground pits were producing 36,000 tonnes of oil by 1890 in the region, the first two gushers were struck in 1893 by Alfred Stuart. Later, the region attracted many foreign investments. For example, the 'Societe de Grosnyi pour I'Industrie de Petroles sous la Firme J. A. Akhwerdoff et Cie', founded by Akhverdo (it went under the ownership of the Petroles de Grosnyi), played a vital role in the development of the oil industry in Russia.[10] It is evident that even though the Caspian-Caucasus region was blessed with oil reserves, the Russian Empire made minimal efforts to modernise the region. The abolition of state control undoubtedly increased oil production and modernised the Caspian oil industry. It was only after the entry of Nobel and later, Rothschild, that the region's oil industry saw developments in oil infrastructure. From 1888 to1901, Azerbaijan was the leading producer of oil in the world with approximately 11.5 million tonnes, and in the early 20th century, it accounted for 95 per cent of Imperial Russia's total oil production. It was in Azerbaijan that the foundation of the Soviet oil industry was laid and later expanded to other regions of the Soviet Union.[11]

Other regions, such as Turkmenistan and Kazakhstan, too, shared a history of oil production alongside Baku. In the 19th century, the region was known for its ozokerite oil deposits. Turkmen people also have a history of digging oil pits in the region and supplying oil to Persia and Astrakhan. Though the Nobel Brothers started drilling in 1887, oil production started in the early 20th century. A decade later, the Cheleken Peninsula (located in Western Turkmenistan) produced an oil output of 208,000 tonnes in 1911-12. In Kazakhstan, oil was first produced near Atyrau in 1911, and after securing concessions from the Tsar, Shell started its operations in the region.[12]

These accounts of history demonstrate that the region's oil infrastructure experienced rapid emergence and development only after foreign investments flowed into the region. The primary obstacle to the development of the oil sector was the state's control, coupled with a deficiency in technological know-how.

Evolution of the Oil and Gas Industry in the Soviet Union

After Imperial Russia, the role and contribution of Baku towards the development of the oil industry continued under the Soviet Union. Apart from its significance in oil production, the Caspian-Caucasus region was widely known for its revolutionary activities in Imperial Russia. In the early 20th century, oil workers in Baku frequently went on strikes to protest against the working conditions in the region. In 1903, revolts ignited in Baku and spread throughout Russia, which later led to the first general strike in the empire. The Revolution of 1905 in the Russian Empire was ignited in Baku, and during the revolution, oil workers intentionally set oil wells on fire, and by the end of 1905, the empire's entire oil export business was falling apart with unrecoverable production.[13] During the Russian Civil War period, recognising the significance of oil, Lenin ordered the Red Army from the North Caucasus to occupy Baku. He wrote, "We all know that our industries stood idle because of the lack of fuel. However, today, the proletariat of Baku has toppled the Azerbaijan government and is in charge of running the government. This means that now we own a basic economy that is capable of supporting our industries."[14] During World War I (1914-1918) and the Russian Civil War (1917-1922), oil production in the Baku region decreased due to the lagging domestic oil extraction technology compared to Western technology and a lack of equipment availability. Consequently, "between 1904 and 1913, the Russian share in global oil exports declined from 31 per cent to 9 per cent" (Ermolaev quoted Yergin)[15], and this trend continued till 1920 (Table 2.1).

Table 2.1: Russian Oil Output, 1912-1920 (in million barrels per annum)*

Years	Baku	Grozny	Cheleken	Kuban
1912	48.5	8.0	0.45	0.01
1915	43.0	10.5	0.35	0.08
1917	35.0	12.5	0.08	0.13
1919	22.5	5.0	0.09	0.21
1920	15.5	7.0	0.03	0.09

Source: Charles van der Leeuw, *Oil, and Gas in The Caucasus and Caspian: A History*, 2000, Curzon Press, England, p. 76.
* This paper employs both the U.S. Measuring System (e.g., barrels, million cubic feet) and the Indian Measuring System (e.g., metric tonnes, cubic metres) for oil and gas measurements. A conversion table between these units is provided in Appendix I.

In the formative years of the Soviet Union, the New Economic Policy (NEP) was launched under the leadership of Lenin towards the end of War Communism. Lenin justified the NEP as 'state capitalism' and saw it as the last stage of capitalism. E.H. Carr described it as an antidote to War Communism.[15] As the Bolsheviks found it necessary to acquire Western machinery and expertise, Lenin permitted concessions to foreigners and considered handing over the control of the Caspian-Caucasus petroleum industry to the Royal Dutch Shell Company. However, after Lenin's demise, Stalin abolished the NEP in 1928, bringing an end to the moderate policies introduced under it. The statistics on Russian oil production during the phase of the NEP are given below, presenting a significant rise in Russian oil production in the mid-1920s and showing oil trade surplus during the NEP (Table 2.2).

Table 2.2: Russian Oil Output, 1923-1925 (in thousands of tonnes)*

	1923	1925
Total Output	6500	10000
To France	112	180
To Germany	130	200
To Italy	60	880
To Britain	180	885
To The Netherlands	200	208

Source: Charles van der Leeuw, *Oil, and Gas in The Caucasus and Caspian: A History*, 2000, Curzon Press, England, p. 107.

* This paper employs both the U.S. Measuring System (e.g., barrels, million cubic feet) and the Indian Measuring System (e.g., metric tonnes, cubic metres) for oil and gas measurements. A conversion table between these units is provided in Appendix I.

The Soviet Union's First Five-Year Plan in 1929 authorised Moscow to control the exploration and production of petroleum. The primary aim was the rapid industrialisation of the Soviet Union. Despite discoveries in the Volga-Ural region, the Caspian-Caucasus region continued to account for 80 per cent of the USSR's crude oil output. During the industrialisation period, the Soviet government made various attempts to sustain Baku's output. For instance, the Petrochemical Academy, created in 1921, was able to draw experts and students from all over the world. The refinery was modernised, and its capacity was increased to 10 million tonnes a year. Many factories for the manufacture of drilling equipment, pipes, pumps, and oil production equipment were put into operation.[16]

During World War II, the Caspian oil resources were so significant that they were highlighted in Germany's wartime strategies. The German forces were ordered to move into the Caucasus-Caspian region as part of 'Operation Blue'. In 1942/43, Hitler refused to withdraw German troops from the area, as he told Field Marshal Erich von Manstein that, "… It is a question of the possession of Baku. Unless we get the Baku oil, the war is lost."[17] Though the forces retreated later, it shows how the region's oil resources were recognised as a major wartime necessity and the reason for continuing the war. During the war, drilling methods went through significant changes as the turbodrill system was adopted in the entire Soviet Union. Following the war, Soviet engineers came up with the first offshore oil rigs on the Baku coastline. This period saw increasing use of the turbodrill system, and the region became a primary focus for drilling during the Fourth, Fifth, and Sixth Five-Year Plans as oil discoveries were made in the region. The Seventh Five-Year Plan was drawn to increase the production of Baku to its pre-war level. An increase in the production of oil recorded in the post-World War II period shows that Stalin's industrialisation policy facilitated the efforts made during the NEP (Table 2.3).

Table 2.3: Post-Russian Revolution Caucasus-Caspian Oil Output (in million tonnes) *

	North Caucasus	Volga/ Ural	Azerbaijan	Kazakhstan	Turkmenistan	Total USSR
1930	7.35	0.006	10.6	0.35	0.012	18.45
1937	4.35	1.0	21.4	0.5	0.45	28.5
1945	-	2.8	11.5	0.8	0.63	19.45
1955	6.55	41.2	15.3	1.4	3.1	70.8
1965	20.7	173.6	21.5	2.0	9.65	242.9

Source: Charles van der Leeuw, *Oil and Gas in The Caucasus and Caspian: A History*, 2000, Curzon Press, England, p. 112.

* This paper employs both the U.S. Measuring System (e.g., barrels, million cubic feet) and the Indian Measuring System (e.g., metric tonnes, cubic metres) for oil and gas measurements. A conversion table between these units is provided in Appendix I.

At the beginning of the Eighth Five-Year Plan in 1966, the Ministry of Petroleum Industry was created, and the oil industry administration was returned to a centralised ministerial system. By the 1970s, the number of proven oil fields increased, and extensive pipelines allowed huge supplies of oil and gas to be available to many industrial centres. With oil production, Azerbaijan remained the main hub for manufacturing oil industry machinery for the entire Soviet Union, as its share in production was 70 per cent. Baku refineries were also used to refine crude oil brought from

Mangyshlak (Kazakhstan), Nebit-Dag (Turkmenistan), and western Siberia. By 1989, Azeri oil production was 13.8 million tonnes, and by the time of the disintegration of the USSR, it had dropped to 10 million tonnes.[18]

Along with Azerbaijan, there were oil fields in the Turkmen SSR and the Kazakh SSR that required similar attention. In the Turkmen SSR, oil production began in the oil fields of Nebit-Dag and Gum-Dag in 1949. In the Kazakh SSR, oil was first extracted near Atyrau in 1911. Shell extracted oil on behalf of the Ural Caspian Oil Corporation. During World War II, oil extraction reached 979,000 tonnes, and after the war, oil production reached 1.6 million tonnes as a result of the opening of fields in the Mangyshlak Peninsula and Emba region. Later, in 1954, proven oil reserves of 140 million tonnes were discovered in the Uzen oil field, and in 1979, the Tengiz oil field opened, with estimated reserves around 4.9 billion tonnes and recoverable oil reserves over 1.4 billion tonnes.[19]

Evolution of the Oil and Gas Industry in Iran

In the Caspian region, Iran is a country that was not a republic of the Soviet Union and geographically shares the south coast of the Caspian Sea. In 1901, William Knox D'Arcy signed an agreement with Muzaffar al-Din that provided the former the rights to explore and develop oil and gas fields in Iran. This agreement was Iran's first step toward developing an oil and gas industry in the country. Though many oil and gas fields were discovered between 1901 and 1904, their commercial viability was in doubt. In 1908, the Anglo-Persian Oil Company (APOC) was founded as a result of oil discovery in Masjid-I-Suleiman. The interests of the APOC and the British government aligned when the latter injected 2 million pounds into the oil company and acquired its majority shares. Later, in 1913, with the construction of an oil refinery at Abadan, the APOC became a major oil producer in the region. Undoubtedly, this development made the British government a direct partner in the Iranian oil and gas sector. The decision made by British Prime Minister Churchill to change energy sources for the Royal Navy's ships to oil from coal during World War I had significant repercussions on Iran's oil production. As a result, the Persian oil fields gained military status, and the APOC was required to cope with increasing military demand for its products.[20]

In 1951, the Iranian oil industry, dominated by the Anglo-Iranian Oil Company (APOC renamed), was nationalised.[21] However, it was short-lived as an international consortium agreement took effect in 1954. The development plans for the oil industry were pursued by the Ministry of Petroleum for renovation and reconstruction efforts through five major approaches: First, an expansion of the petrochemical industry because of its value-added products in world markets and necessities of local downstream industries. Second, giving priority to the expansion of gas connections to residential areas, industrial areas, and power plants. Third, an investment in the upstream sector and implementation of exploration projects to solidify Iran's position among OPEC countries. Fourth, to actively participate in OPEC and other international negotiations to bring stability to global oil markets. Fifth, to ensure financial resources required for the development projects and placing importance on the utilisation of local expertise, investments, and transfer of technology.[22] With the conclusion of the Iranian revolution led by Ruhollah Khomeini, the National Iranian Oil Company (NIOC) declared to end Iran's relations with consortium member companies. It cancelled all exploration and production contracts that had been signed with foreign companies based on the decision made by the Revolutionary Council in 1979.[23]

Hydrocarbon Profile of the Caspian Sea States

For a long period, hydrocarbons played different roles in the Soviet economy. Since 1991, countries such as Azerbaijan, Kazakhstan, and Turkmenistan have incorporated hydrocarbons as a crucial component in their economic growth. The Caspian countries have granted permission to international corporations to operate in the region's hydrocarbon sector through consortiums, allowing them to collectively invest in many projects. These consortiums include state-owned energy companies of the littoral states to ensure that governments maintain their involvement throughout the entire energy development process.

In the 1990s, the governments of the littoral states and many international institutions made predictions about the hydrocarbon potential in the region. The Caspian riparian governments independently valued the region's hydrocarbon resources. For example, the Azerbaijan International Operating Company (AIOC) estimated oil reserves on its Caspian shelf to be 4 billion barrels. Kazakhstan's Ministry of Energy estimated the oil reserves of the Caspian states to be 125 billion barrels. It was distributed to Azerbaijan (27 billion barrels), Iran (7.5 billion barrels), Kazakhstan (50-60 billion barrels), Russia (15 billion barrels), and Turkmenistan (16 billion barrels), despite agreeing to the fact that reserves are distributed unevenly. The Turkmen experts forecasted oil reserves in the Caspian region to be 161-202 billion barrels. Finally, Russian experts estimated the oil reserves of the Caspian region at 28-32 billion barrels and potential reserves at 250 billion barrels.[24]

The data on hydrocarbon potential has been assessed by other international organisations. These international institutions provided different estimations of the region's hydrocarbon reserves (Table 2.4). The findings of the United States (U.S.) Department of Energy on the vast oil reserves in the Caspian region were disputed by other organisations, such as the London Centre for Strategic Research, which dismissed the reports as speculation and an overestimate of the oil reserves. The absence of credible data on hydrocarbons in the region is attributed to limited geological knowledge and an overestimation by the littoral states to attract foreign investors.[25] Based on the data available, it is evident that there was a lack of consensus in the statistics released by these institutions.

Table 2.4: Forecasted Oil Reserves in the Caspian Sea Basin (billion barrels) *

Organisation(s)	Proven	Potential/ Possible	Forecast	Total Reserves
US EIA (1997)	15-29	178-191	-	-
Wood Mackenzie Consultant (1998)	28 (Explored)	-	-	-
Unocal Corporation (1998)	-	-	-	60
US Depart. Of Energy (1998)	20-36	200	-	-
London Centre for Strategic Research (1998)	-	-	-	60
CIS Institute (1998)	-	-	17.5	-
International Energy Agency (1998)	15-40	-	-	-

Source: Sergey S. Zhiltsov et al. (2016), "Hydrocarbon potential of the Caspian region", in Sergey S. Zhiltsov et al., eds., *Oil and gas pipelines in the Black-Caspian Sea region*, Springer: Switzerland, p. 39.

* This paper employs both the U.S. Measuring System (e.g., barrels, million cubic feet) and the Indian Measuring System (e.g., metric tonnes, cubic metres) for oil and gas measurements. A conversion table between these units is provided in Appendix I.

The latest comprehensive data was published by the U.S. Energy Information Administration (EIA) in 2013. It is estimated that 48 billion barrels of oil and 285 trillion cubic feet of gas are in proven and probable reserves, both from onshore and offshore fields (Table 2.5). In addition, the U.S. Geological Survey projected another 20 billion barrels of oil and 243 Tcf of gas as unexplored. As Caspian oil majorly comes from onshore fields, the offshore fields have prospects for future growth. The agency estimated 41 per cent of total Caspian oil and 36 per cent of total gas in offshore fields. The majority of offshore oil reserves lie in the northern portion of the Caspian Sea, while the majority share of gas reserves lies in the southern portion of the Caspian Sea. Further, 35 per cent of oil and 45 per cent of gas rest onshore in Russia's North Caucasus region, and 12 billion barrels of oil and 56 trillion cubic feet of gas are distributed onshore in the basins of Azerbaijan, Turkmenistan, and Kazakhstan[26] (Map 2.1). A comprehensive country-specific analysis of the hydrocarbon profile of the Caspian littoral states in the upcoming sections will provide an in-depth overview of the region.

Table 2.5: Caspian Basin Reserves

Country	Crude oil and lease condensate (billion bbl)	Natural Gas (Tcf)
Azerbaijan	8.5	51
Offshore Caspian	6.8	46
Onshore Caspian	1.7	5
Iran	**0.5**	**2**
Offshore Caspian	0.5	1
Onshore Caspian	(s)	1
Kazakhstan	**31.2**	**104**
Offshore Caspian	15.7	36
Onshore Caspian	15.5	68
Russia	**6.1**	**109**
Offshore Caspian	1.6	14
Onshore Caspian	4.5	95
Turkmenistan	**1.9**	**19**
Offshore Caspian	1.1	9
Onshore Caspian	0.8	10
Total	**48.2**	**285**
Offshore Caspian	19.6	106
Onshore Caspian	28.6	179

Source: U.S. Energy Information Administration Data, 2013.

Map 2.1: Caspian Region Oil and Gas Fields, Oil Refineries, and Gas Processing Plants

Source: U.S. Energy Information Administration, 2013.

Hydrocarbon Resources in Russia's Division

In 2020, Russia was the third largest oil producer and the second largest natural gas producer in the world. In its most recent *Energy Strategy to 2035*, the emphasis was on increasing energy exports, revenue, and expansion of gas infrastructure, mainly the midstream projects in eastern Siberia and Russia's Far East. From 2011 to 2020, revenue generated from oil and gas comprised approximately 43 per cent of Russia's total annual revenue. The overall proven oil reserves were at 80 billion barrels, and proven gas reserves were 1,688 trillion cubic feet as of 2021.[27]

The main companies operating in Russia's Caspian sector are state-owned Gazprom, Rosneft, and Transneft, as well as private firms like Lukoil, Yukos, and Sibneft. Three regions—Kalmykia, Daghestan, and Astrakhan—are littoral areas in the Russian sector. In the Astrakhan region, the continental part of the region is evaluated at 1 billion tonnes of oil, 6 trillion cubic metres of gas, and 1.2 billion tonnes of gas condensate. In Kalmykia, the oil reserves are estimated at 64 million tonnes and forecasted reserves at 200 million tonnes. According to the RAS Daghestan Research Centre, the hydrocarbon potential in Daghestan is estimated at 340 million tonnes for oil and 540 million cubic metres for gas.[28] Russia's oil production also came from onshore fields located in Krasnodar, Chechnya, and Stavropol. In 2010, Lukoil (a Russian private oil company) began production in the Yuri Korchagin field, which became the most profitable upstream project.[29] In the Russian sector, natural gas production is minimal. Gazprom operates in a gas-condensate field in Astrakhan and produces a minimal amount of gas from selected fields in the North Caucasus. Since the early 2000s, Russia has entered into both bilateral and plurilateral agreements with the littoral states to strengthen its presence in the Caspian energy sector.[30]

When it comes to energy transit, Russia possesses an extensive network of pipelines that it inherited from the former Soviet Union. Russia's two major energy firms, Lukoil and Gazprom, operate in the three main fields of Yuri Korchagin, Valery Grayfer, and Vladimir Filanovsky. The two main operating energy routes in the Russian Caspian sector are the Caspian Pipeline Consortium (CPC) and the Northern Early Oil pipeline. The former starts from the Tengiz field (Kazakhstan) and reaches its destination at Russia's Novorossiysk terminal, and the latter starts from Baku (Azerbaijan), passes through Dagestan, and terminates at the Novorossiysk terminal.

Hydrocarbon Resources in Azerbaijan's Division

Azerbaijan's overall proven oil reserves were estimated at 7 billion barrels in 2021 and produced approximately 716,000 barrels per day, and the overall proven gas reserves were estimated at 60 trillion cubic feet.[31] The majority of the country's oil production comes from the Azeri-Chirag-Guneshli offshore field (ACG) (Map 2.1). The Azerbaijan International Operating Company (AIOC), a consortium that includes the State Oil Company of the Azerbaijan Republic (SOCAR) along with international firms like British Petroleum, Japan's INPEX, and American Chevron, is presently operating in the area through production-sharing agreements.[32] Another main field is the Shah Deniz gas field (a part of the ACG group of fields), which is the most important gas-producing area. Approximately 75 per cent of the country's total natural gas production comes from this field. As per British Petroleum, the Shah Deniz has potential reserves of 30 trillion cubic feet of gas.[33]

To export energy, the country has many pipeline projects, such as the Baku-Tbilisi-Ceyhan pipeline (BTC), the South Caucasus pipeline, and the Baku-Supsa pipeline. Natural gas is transported through the Southern Gas Corridor (SGC). It bypasses Russian territory to transport resources from the Caspian Sea to European markets in Italy. The SGC comprises four projects: first, the operation of the Shah Deniz field; second, the operation of the South Caucasus pipeline; third, the operation of the Trans-Anatolian gas pipeline; and fourth, the operation of the Trans Adriatic pipeline. The SGC starts in Azerbaijan and runs through Georgia, Turkey, Greece, and Albania, and finally terminates in Italy.[34] The BTC pipeline links the Sangachal terminal (Azerbaijan) to the Ceyhan terminal (Turkey) through Georgia.[35] The South Caucasus pipeline transports gas from the Shah Deniz field (Azerbaijan) to Erzurum (Turkey) via Georgia.[36] Finally, the

Baku-Supsa pipeline runs from Baku in Azerbaijan to the Supsa terminal in Georgia.[37]

Hydrocarbon Resources in Kazakhstan's Division

Kazakhstan's proven oil reserves are estimated at 30 billion barrels, and proven gas reserves were estimated at 85 trillion cubic feet in 2019.[38] Tengiz, Karachaganak, and Kashagan are major oil and gas fields in the country, managed jointly by international firms and state-owned KazMunaiGaz. The Tengiz oil field, discovered in 1979, is the largest source of oil production in Kazakhstan (Map 2.1). The field is operated by the U.S.' Chevron, Russia's Lukoil, KazMunaiGaz, and ExxonMobil. Another oil discovery was made in the Kashagan field, and a consortium (Agip Kazakhstan North Caspian Operating Company) led by ENI, KazMunaiGaz, Shell, China National Petroleum Corporation (CNPC), Total, and INPEX operates in the area. Finally, the Karachaganak field is controlled by Chevron, Lukoil, and KazMuniaGaz.[39] (Table 2.6) It is evident that amidst enormous foreign investments in the country, the state has maintained its presence in all its assets.

Kazakhstan employed both Liquefied Natural Gas (LNG) carriers and pipeline means to transport energy. The Central Asia-Center Gas Pipeline system is used to supply energy to western markets. Additionally, hydrocarbons are shipped through LNG carriers to Baku, which are afterward forwarded to the BTC pipeline. On the eastern side, the main fields are Kashagan and Karachaganak.

Hydrocarbon Resources in Turkmenistan's Division

Turkmenistan's oil belt extends from west to east across a span of 200 km. It transverses the terrestrial region and partially extends into the Caspian Sea near the Apsheronian Peninsula. The Turkmenistan sector of the Caspian Sea has two geological blocks: the Depression shelf of the South Caspian Sea and the Central Caspian Sea, covering a total area of 70,000 km^2.[40] Turkmenistan is overall estimated to have 600 million barrels of proven oil and 265 trillion cubic feet of proven gas in 2016.[41] The country has massive volumes of gas, which come from either the Caspian Basin (onshore) or the Caspian Sea (offshore). In its Caspian sector, the Turkmen government declared 12 billion barrels of oil,[42] located mainly in the Garashyzlyk region (Map 2.1). The hydrocarbon resources, production, and transportation are administered by Turkmengas and Turkmenneft, both state-owned companies. As these companies control oil and gas production, there is limited access to international firms, except China's CNPC and the UAE's Dragon Oil[43] (Table 2.6). As a landlocked region, the country relies on pipelines for hydrocarbon exports.

Turkmenistan's hydrocarbon exports are directed towards both eastern and western markets. For exports to western markets, it relies on the Central Asia-Center Gas pipeline. The pipeline also carries gas from Kazakhstan and Uzbekistan to Russia and further to western markets. For exports to eastern markets, the main connection is the Central Asia-China Gas Pipeline. It passes through Uzbekistan and Kazakhstan territory to reach its destination in Xinjiang (China). The pipeline carries gas from the Tengiz field (Kazakhstan) along with gas from the Galkynysh field (Turkmenistan). Finally, for South Asian markets, significant progress is required for the Turkmenistan-Afghanistan-Pakistan-India Gas Pipeline (TAPI) project to materialise.

Hydrocarbon Resources in Iran's Division

In 2020, Iran was ranked as having the world's third largest oil reserves and second largest gas reserves. However, the country's production started diminishing in 2017 as a consequence of international sanctions, and by the end of 2020, Iran accounted for 12 per cent of global oil production. Its overall proven natural gas reserves were estimated at 1,200 trillion cubic feet and proven oil reserves at 208,600 million barrels.[44] Iran's oil and gas fields are mainly located in the southern part of the country. Though there is no significant production in the Iranian sector of the Caspian Sea, it has claimed the discovery of oil and gas in Sardar Jangal, which is presently in the exploration phase[45] (Map 2.1).

Table 2.6: Oil and Gas Projects in the Caspian Sea Region

Country	Project	Location	Commissioning Year	Firms Involved
Azerbaijan	Azeri-Chirag-Guneshli (ACG)	Caspian Offshore	1997	AIOC (BP, Chevron, Devon Energy, StatoilHydro, TPAO, Amerada Hess, SOCAR, ExxonMobil, Itochu)
	Shah Deniz	Caspian Offshore	2006	BP, StatoilHydro, SOCAR, TPAO, Total, NICO, LUKOil
	Araz-Alov-Sharg	Caspian Offshore	-	SOCAR, BP, ExxonMobil, StatoilHydro, EnCana, TPAO
Kazakhstan	Kashagan	Caspian Offshore	2013	North Caspian Operating Company (ENI, Shell, Total, ExxonMobil, KazMunaiGaz, ConocoPhillips, Inpex)
	Tengiz	Caspian Onshore	1991	Tengizchevroil (Chevron, ExxonMobil, KazMunaiGaz, Lukoil)
	Karachaganak	Caspian Onshore	PH 1 -1985, PH 2- 2000	Karachaganak Petroleum Operating (BG Group, ENI, Chevron, Lukoil)
	Kurmangazy	Caspian Offshore	-	Rosneft, KazMunaiGaz
Turkmenistan	Galkynysh	Onshore*	2006	Turkmengaz/CNPC
	Dauletabad	Onshore*	1983	Turkmengaz
	Cheleken	Caspian Offshore	1950	Dragon Oil, Turkmenneft
Russia	Yury Korchagin	Caspian Offshore	2010	LUKOil
Iran	-	-	-	-

Source: U.S. Energy Information Administration Data, 2013.

* Although not geologically part of the Caspian basin, these projects are included because they link up to the Caspian region infrastructure.

The geology of hydrocarbons has posed a twofold challenge for the Caspian states: the first is the need for investments in the development of upstream, midstream, and downstream infrastructure, while the second is their dependence on neighbouring countries for energy transit. These challenges resulted in the participation of both state and non-state actors in the development of upstream (exploration) and midstream (transportation) projects of Caspian hydrocarbons. To diversify energy supply routes, the Caspian littoral states adopted different policies and started to align with external actors, which led to a clash of interests in the region.

The hydrocarbon profiles of all littoral states can be compared to draw the following conclusions: First, Azerbaijan and Kazakhstan have allowed foreign investments, which brought foreign firms, such as Gazprom, Lukoil, British Petroleum, and Chevron, into the development of upstream and midstream projects. On the contrary, Turkmenistan has a minimal amount of foreign investment, mainly from China and the United Arab Emirates, and the government maintains its control over hydrocarbon assets through state-owned companies. Second, the market orientations of the littoral states are different from each other. Azerbaijan's main focus is on European markets, as the majority of its energy lines bypass Russia and go to Europe. Kazakhstan, on the other hand, exports energy to both Russia and eastern markets—China. Turkmenistan is the main supplier of gas to China in the east and also a key contributor of energy to the CAC pipeline, which goes to Russia. Here, Russia remains a key partner in Kazakhstan and Turkmenistan's energy transportation. Third, Iran does not play any significant role in the transportation of Caspian energy and relies mainly on its Persian Gulf resources. However, the significance of its territory as a potential transit route for Caspian hydrocarbons has been highlighted in many studies.

Assessment

The Caspian region has a complex history of the development of the oil and gas industry. The region's oil and gas industry has been moulded by a confluence of various factors, such as technological advancements, international competition, and shifts in political regimes, since its formative years of rudimentary extraction. The entry of foreign firms like Nobel and Rothschild aided the development and production of oil and gas despite state control and technological restrictions in the Russian Empire. The industrialisation push and centralised planning in the Soviet period expanded production. Simultaneously, conflict and instability also impacted the development of the oil and gas industry, for instance, civil wars in Russia, the World Wars, and political upheavals in Iran. The Soviet dissolution ushered the newly formed Caspian littoral countries into an age of competition and cooperation.

Notes

1. Stolberg, F. et al., "Caspian Sea, GIWA Regional assessment 23" , 2006, https://citeseerx.ist.psu.edu/viewdoc/download?doi=10.1.1.214.2882&rep=rep1&type=pdf. Accessed on April 15, 2022.
2. Nasib Nassibli, "Azerbaijan: Oil and Politics in the Country's Future", in Michael P. Croissant and Bulent Aras, ed., *Oil and Geopolitics in the Caspian Sea region*, (Westport CT: Praeger Publishers, 1999).
3. Ibid.
4. Bulent Gokay, "History of oil development in the Caspian basin", in Michael P. Croissant and Bulent Aras, ed., *Oil and Geopolitics in the Caspian Sea region*, (Westport CT: Praeger Publishers, 1999).
5. Ibid.
6. Firouzeh Mostashari, "Development of Caspian oil in Historical Perspective", in Hooshang Amirahmadi, eds., *The Caspian Region at a Crossroad: Challenges of New Frontier of Energy and Development*, (London: MacMillan Press, 2000).
7. Gokay, n. 4, p. 4.
8. Gokay, n. 4, p. 5.
9. Gokay, n. 4, p. 8.
10. Charles van der Leeuw, *Oil and Gas in the Caucasus and Caspian: A History*, (England: Curzon Press, 2000).
11. Sergey S. Zhiltsov, "Introduction", in Sergey S. Zhiltsov et. al., eds., *Oil and Gas Pipelines in the Black-Caspian Seas Region*, (Switzerland: Springer, 2016).
12. Gokay, n. 4, p. 44.
13. Gokay, n. 4, p. 4.
14. Michael P. Croissant and Bulent Aras, eds., *Oil and Geopolitics in the Caspian Sea Region*, (Westport CT: Praeger Publishers, 1999).
15. Sheldon L. Richman, "War Communism to NEP: The Road from Serfdom," *The Journal of Libertarian Studies*, Vol. 5, No. 1, 1981, pp. 89-97.
16. Charles, n. 10.

17. Lutz Kleveman, *The New Great Game: Blood and Oil in Central Asia*, (United States: Grove Press, 2004).
18. Gokay, n. 4, p. 8.
19. Sergey S. Zhiltsov et al., "Hydrocarbon potential of the Caspian region", in Sergey S. Zhiltsov et al., ed., *Oil and Gas Pipelines in the Black-Caspian Seas Region*, (Switzerland: Springer, 2016).
20. Farzin Nadimi, "The role of oil in the outcome of the Iran-Iraq War: Some important lessons in historical context", in Nigel Ashton and Bryan Gibson, ed., *The Iran-Iraq War: New International Perspectives*, (United Kingdom: Routledge, 2013).
21. Nasib Nassibli, "Azerbaijan: Oil and Politics in the Country's Future", in Michael P. Croissant and Bulent Aras, ed., *Oil and Geopolitics in the Caspian Sea region*, (Westport CT: Praeger Publishers, 1999).
22. Petroleum Iran, "Heroic reconstruction and development Campaigns", http://petroleumiran.com/index.php?option=com_content&view=article&id=66:-heroic-reconstruction-and-development-campaigns&catid=29:past&Itemid=57. Accessed on April 5, 2022.
23. Petroleum Iran, "The Islamic Revolution and the end of the Contracts", http://petroleumiran.com/index.php?option=com_content&view=article&id=64:-the-islamic-revolution-and-the-end-of-the-contracts&catid=29:past&Itemid=57. Accessed on April 5, 2022.
24. Sergey S. Zhiltsov, n. 19.
25. Sergey S. Zhiltsov, n. 19.
26. U.S. Energy Information Administration, "Caspian Sea", https://www.eia.gov/international/analysis/regions-of-interest/Caspian_Sea. Accessed on April 15, 2022.
27. U.S. Energy Information Administration, "Russia", https://www.eia.gov/international/analysis/country/RUS. Accessed on May 28, 2022.
28. Sergey S. Zhiltsov, n. 19.
29. U.S. Energy Information Administration, "Caspian Sea", https://www.eia.gov/international/analysis/regions-of-interest/Caspian_Sea. Accessed on April 15, 2022.
30. Ibrayeva, et al., "Importance of the Caspian Countries for the European Union Energy Security", *International Journal of Energy Economics and Policy*, Vol. 8, No. 3, 2018, pp. 150-159.
31. U.S. Energy Information Administration, "Azerbaijan", https://www.eia.gov/international/analysis/country/AZE. Accessed on May 28, 2022.
32. U.S. Energy Information Administration, "Caspian Sea", https://www.eia.gov/international/analysis/regions-of-interest/Caspian_Sea. Accessed on April 15, 2022.
33. Sergey S. Zhiltsov, n. 19.
34. Southern Gas Corridor, "What is Southern Gas Corridor?" https://www.sgc.az/en. Accessed on June 2, 2022.

35. British Petroleum, "Baku-Tbilisi-Ceyhan Pipeline", https://www.bp.com/en_az/azerbaijan/home/who-we-are/operationsprojects/pipelines/btc.html. Accessed on June 2, 2022.
36. British Petroleum, "South Caucasus pipeline", https://www.bp.com/en_az/azerbaijan/home/who-we-are/operationsprojects/pipelines/scp.html. Accessed on June 2, 2022.
37. British Petroleum, "Western route export pipeline", https://www.bp.com/en_az/azerbaijan/home/who-we-are/operationsprojects/pipelines/wrep.html. Accessed on June 2, 2022.
38. U.S. Energy Information Administration, "Kazakhstan", https://www.eia.gov/international/analysis/country/KAZ. Accessed on May 28, 2022.
39. U.S. Energy Information Administration, "Caspian Sea", https://www.eia.gov/international/analysis/regions-of-interest/Caspian_Sea. Accessed on April 15, 2022.
40. Justyna Misiągiewicz, "Geopolitics and Energy Security Policies in the Caspian Region", (Brill-Nijhoff: The Netherlands, 2024).
41. U.S. Energy Information Administration, "Turkmenistan", https://www.eia.gov/international/analysis/country/TKM. Accessed on May 28, 2022.
42. Sergey S. Zhiltsov, n. 19.
43. Ibid.
44. Organization of the Petroleum Exporting Countries, "Iran facts and figures", https://www.opec.org/opec_web/en/about_us/163.htm. Accessed on May 28, 2022.
45. U.S. Energy Information Administration, "Caspian Sea", https://www.eia.gov/international/analysis/regions-of-interest/Caspian_Sea. Accessed on April 15, 2022.

3

Energy Politics in the Caspian Sea Region

While global powers continue to focus their attention on the Ukraine conflict and related security issues in Europe since Russia's military operation, a series of events in the neighbouring Caspian Sea region have gone unnoticed. First, in July 2022, amidst the ongoing Ukrainian crisis, the European Union (EU) signed a deal with Azerbaijan to double its gas imports. The deal aims to import approximately 20 billion cubic metres[1] of gas in a year for 15 years to reduce Europe's dependency on Russian energy, and the Southern Gas Corridor (SGC) pipeline will play a key role in it. This action has highlighted the need for diversification of energy imports for Brussels.[2] Second, at the 6th Caspian Sea Summit meeting held in July 2022, President Vladimir Putin described the International North-South Transport Corridor (INSTC) route as a link between Russia and India via Iran. The route witnessed a surge in trade volume as the Iran Shipping Lines transported around 3000 tonnes of goods and 114 containers between May and July, 2022.[3] Third, in June 2022, Azerbaijan, Kazakhstan, and Turkmenistan agreed to strengthen regional connectivity and capitalise on the potential of the Trans-Caspian East-West Middle Corridor (also known as the Middle Corridor), which starts in Southeast Asia and China, passes through Kazakhstan, Turkmenistan, the Caspian Sea, Azerbaijan, and Georgia, and further to Europe. The route will enable Caucasus and Central Asia states to gain benefits from Europe-China trade.[4] Fourth, on August 24, 2022, the State Oil Company of the Republic of Azerbaijan (SOCAR) and the QazaqGaz of Kazakhstan signed a Memorandum of Understanding aimed at the implementation of joint gas projects. It includes the exploration and development of hydrocarbon deposits in Kazakhstan and the search for alternative transit routes for oil exports.[5]

The shared components in all of these events can be classified into the following:

(a) Increased focus on energy security: The events underscore a prioritisation of discovering alternate energy supplies and transit pathways in order to decrease dependence on Russia, especially in light of the Ukraine conflict. This is seen in the gas agreement between the EU and Azerbaijan, as well as the keenness on the INSTC and Middle Corridor routes.

(b) Regional cooperation: The significance of collaboration among the states bordering the Caspian Sea appears to be increasing. This is evident in the agreements entered into force among Azerbaijan, Kazakhstan, and Turkmenistan to enhance regional connectivity, as well as the signing of the memorandum of understanding between SOCAR and QazaqGaz.

(c) Diversification: The various advancements indicate a shift towards expanding the range of energy sources (EU-Azerbaijan accord) and transport routes (INSTC, Middle Corridor) in the Caspian Sea region. As the conflict in Ukraine has extended into 2023, it is uncertain as to how the events on the ground will unfold.

Against this backdrop, the reverberations that the new developments will have on the future of energy politics in the Caspian Sea region mandate examination. The Caspian states' energy politics can be better understood by answering the following critical questions: First, what is the status of ownership and control of oil and gas resources in the Caspian region? Second, how does the current legal status of the Caspian Sea hinder or facilitate the energy sector in the region? Third, what are the objectives of major actors—Russia, China, the United States (U.S.), and the EU—in the region? Fourth, how do connectivity approaches and initiatives, such as transport corridors and pipelines, influence energy politics in the Caspian Sea region? Fifth, how has conflict shaped the regional energy dynamics? Sixth, what does the current Ukraine conflict mean for the future of Caspian geopolitics?

To answer the aforesaid questions, the chapter is organised as follows: Section 1 discusses the oil and gas industry of the Caspian riparian states. Section 2 deals with the status of the Caspian Sea. Section 3 analyses power play in the region. Section 4 examines the connectivity approaches and initiatives undertaken by the Caspian littoral states and external countries. The section will also analyse how the Caspian states' connectivity objectives either align or compete with those of other major actors in the region. Section 5 outlines pipeline politics in the region. Section 6 explores the ongoing conflict's impact on regional energy dynamics. Section 7 focuses on forecasting the geopolitical competition in the Caspian region.

Ownership and Control of Oil and Gas Resources: An Overview

After the disintegration of the Soviet Union, the Caucasus and Central Asia region emerged as a 'grand chessboard' for regional and international actors as it offered opportunities in the form of untapped oil and gas resources and energy routes. The extraction and transportation of hydrocarbons have emerged as a major source of geopolitical tug of war. The struggle for oil and gas compelled global actors to adopt an assertive foreign policy in the region, which is referred to as the 'New Great Game', and it is not only limited to controlling oil and gas resources but also administering them. The region has witnessed an increasing role of regional actors, such as Russia, Azerbaijan, Kazakhstan, and Turkmenistan, (littoral countries) and non-regional actors, such as China, the EU, and the U.S.

Unlike the 'Great Game', where only Russia and Britain were engaged over territorial control, the 'New Great Game' includes control over oil and gas resources and connectivity routes, such as corridors and pipelines. Due to the abundant hydrocarbon resources in the Caspian littoral countries, the hydrocarbon sector plays a crucial role in their economic growth. For example, in Kazakhstan, oil contributes 8 per cent of the GDP and approximately 25 per cent of industrial production. In Azerbaijan, oil makes up more than 10 per cent of the GDP and 50 per cent of industrial production. In Turkmenistan, gas contributes 15-18 per cent of the GDP and 50 per cent of industrial production. Oil-related or linked activities also make significant contributions to the GDP of the Caspian littoral countries.[6]

Different sets of scholars have provided varying assessments of the key players of the 'New Great Game'. The first set of scholars mostly perceives the rivalry as being centred on major global powers, such as the U.S., Russia, and China. The second set of scholars perceives the region as a venue for 'small games' involving three major powers (the U.S., Russia, and China), as well as other influential countries (the EU, Japan, India, and South Korea). The third group of researchers perceives power dynamics in the region as a struggle for balance of power, considering the growing might of the Caspian littoral states in the region. Lastly, a fourth group of researchers has contended the importance of international organisations and multinational enterprises in the region. They emphasised the importance of incorporating non-state entities, in addition to state actors, into the power dynamics of the Caspian region.[7]

Ownership and Control in Russia

The current Constitution of the Russian Federation, adopted in 1993, contains two pertinent clauses on natural resources. One pertains to the ownership of natural resources, while the other focuses on their possession, use, and disposal. The Constitution stipulates that land and other natural resources are utilised and safeguarded inside the Russian Federation as the foundation for the existence and endeavours of its citizens. The ownership of natural resources may be classified as private, state, municipal, or other types (Art. 9). In this context, natural resources encompass land, subsoil, water supplies, forests, and other botanical resources. According to the Russian Constitution, ownership of oil and gas lies with the state and is a subject of joint jurisdiction of the federal government and regional government.[8]

From a legislative standpoint, the exploration and production of subsoil resources, including oil and gas, are managed by issuing subsoil use licenses. This process is governed by the Law on Subsoil and the accompanying Regulations on the Licensing of Subsoil Use, which are issued in accordance with that law. In Russian subsoil legislation, there are three categories of licences for the use of subsoil in relation to natural resource development: exploration licences, production licences, and combination licences (which cover both exploration and production).[9]

The Russian production sharing regime is outlined in the Law on Production Sharing Agreements. Since the enactment of this law in 1995, there has not been a single PSA executed in accordance with its provisions. As of now, the only PSAs that exist in Russia are the ones that were made before the PSA law was implemented. These include Sakhalin-I (involving ExxonMobil, Rosneft, SODECO, and ONGC), Sakhalin-II (involving Gazprom, Shell, Mitsui, and Mitsubishi), and Kharyaga (involving Zarubezhneft, Total, Statoil, and Nenets Oil Company).[10]

In the oil sector, Transneft (a government-controlled company) specialises in the transportation of crude oil and processed products and handles more than 90 per cent of the total oil produced in Russia. In order to export oil, access rights to the pipeline and sea terminals are distributed among oil producers and major oil retailers based on the amount of oil produced and supplied to the Transneft pipeline system, rather than just on oil production volumes.[11] Transnefteprodukt, a state monopoly, is responsible for transporting oil products throughout Russia. Since the transportation of oil and oil products is classified as a monopolistic activity under the Law on Natural Monopolies,[12] both Transneft and Transnefteprodukt are designated as natural monopolies. The export of oil and oil products from Russia is regulated by the government through the imposition of export duties.

In the gas sector, the Law on Gas Supply and the Natural Monopolies Law establish the regulatory framework for the supply and transportation of natural gas. According to these laws, transportation of natural gas through pipelines is classified as a monopolistic activity, and the entities or organisations involved in it are recognised as natural monopolies.[13] The majority state-owned company, Gazprom, is the key player in the distribution and conveyance of natural gas. The Unified Gas Supply System (UGSS) is the centralised infrastructure responsible for the extraction, conveyance, storage, and distribution of natural gas across Russia. Gazprom is the proprietor of the UGSS and bears the responsibility for overseeing its operation, maintenance, and safety. The ownership of the entity operating the UGSS (i.e., Gazprom) shall always be held by the state or state-owned firms, with a minimum ownership stake of 50 per cent plus one share. According to the Law on the Export of Gas, Gazprom, the operator of the UGSS, or its wholly owned subsidiary, Gazpromexport, has the sole authority to export natural gas outside of Russia.[14]

On foreign investment, the Law on the Procedure for Foreign Investments in Companies having Strategic Importance for the National Security and Defense of 2008 mandates that foreign investors obtain approval from the Governmental Commission, headed by the Russian prime minister, before gaining control over a strategic company.[15]

The Russian oil and gas industry has gone through decentralisation and transition to the market in the 1990s to a greater level of state control in the 2000s. The state directly controls around half of Russia's oil production through its ownership in Gazpromneft, Rosneft, and Bashneft. In the gas sector, while Gazprom leads the gas pipeline business, Novatek has gained the reputation to establish Russia as one of the major global LNG players.[16]

Ownership and Control in Kazakhstan

According to the Constitution of Kazakhstan and the Subsoil Code, the ownership of the subsoil is vested in the citizens of Kazakhstan. The state, acting on behalf of the people of Kazakhstan, holds ownership rights and allows the use of subsoil resources in accordance with legal regulations, terms, and restrictions.

Private companies, both domestic and international, have the ability to acquire the subsoil use right, which grants them the authority to investigate and/or exploit natural resources. According to a subsoil use contract, a subsoil user is granted the privilege to conduct exploration and/or extraction activities for oil and gas resources. Consequently, the natural resources obtained by a subsoil user through the exercise of their subsoil use rights are regarded as the possessions of that subsoil user. Therefore, minerals that have been extracted are the rightful property of the subsoil user according to ownership rights.[17] As the ownership of subsoil and natural resources is vested in the citizens of Kazakhstan, the state has the authority to engage in oil and gas exploration and production activities, in addition to subsoil users. It is typically carried out by creating a national company that focuses specifically on hydrocarbons. This corporation is established through a governmental decree, and its ownership and management are under the jurisdiction of the state or the national authority responsible for overseeing the extraction and utilisation of hydrocarbon resources.[18] KazMunaiGas is an exemplary company in the contemporary oil and gas industry. QazaqGaz is a state-owned gas company that engages in all aspects of the gas industry, including exploration, production, and the sale of finished goods.[19]

In order to engage in exploration or production activities, a company must acquire a subsoil use right (SUR), which is legally established through the signing of a subsoil use contract (SUC). The SUCs can be employed for both the exploration and production of hydrocarbons. According to the Subsoil Code, only a company that is owned by the state can acquire rights for exploration or production through direct talks, such as KazMunaiGas for oil and gas fields or QazaqGas for gas and gas condensate resources. Individual parties who are interested can acquire these rights alone by successfully bidding in an online auction. A SUR for the exploration or production of hydrocarbons in the Caspian Sea or the Aral Sea can only be awarded if KazMunaiGas is given a minimum 50 per cent stake in the corresponding SUC. If a joint operation or operator is established for the SUC, KazMunaiGas must have an initial participation share of at least 50 per cent. As a result, the operator's stake in the SUC and charter capital may be decreased, as long as KazMunaiGas maintains control over the decision-making process by subsoil users in the SUC.[20]

On December 28, 2023, a new set of changes to the Subsoil Code was signed, which took effect on February 28, 2024. One of the key provisions specifies that when a Special Use Right (SUR) is granted for a large field—defined as having geological reserves exceeding 100 million tonnes of oil or 50 billion cubic metres of gas—KazMunaiGas must hold a 50 per cent ownership stake in the Special Use Contract (SUC).[21]

Kazakhstan chose a balanced approach, considering the interests of major powers by allowing access to the international oil and gas companies. Nazarbayev was aware of the fact that respecting the interests of major powers would enhance stability in Kazakhstan's energy sector. In the beginning, Kazakhstan entered into energy agreements that benefitted international oil companies, but soon, the need for unrestricted Western investment declined, and Kazakhstan developed policies to retain its control over hydrocarbon resources gradually. In 2004, Kazakhstan enacted legislation that gave the state preferential rights to purchase or participate in energy projects that are available for sale. Kazakhstan has revised its tax code to raise the income tax for oil companies from 25-30 per cent to 60-85 per cent. In 2005, the state imposed limitations on the transfer of subsoil use rights and interests in mining companies. For example, Article 71 of the Subsoil Law grants the state the 'right of first refusal' to acquire energy assets and prohibits investors from transferring their mining rights for a period of two years after signing a contract. In 2007, Nazarbayev approved amendments to the Law on Subsoil Resources that allowed the government to unilaterally reassess, rewrite, and evaluate contracts with subsoil users. Based on these regulations, the government possesses the power to nullify any agreement that it perceives as a threat to national security or detrimental to its economic interests.[22]

Kazakhstan involved private foreign ownership in the oil sector by selling off the shares of the state energy companies. To begin with, the government created KazMunaiGas to manage oil enterprises inherited from the Soviet period in the Caspian basin. The government did not transform KazMunaiGas into a fully established national oil company, but instead it sold off its assets to international corporations. In October 2008, Kazakhstan entered into an arrangement with foreign companies to establish a new joint operating company known as the North Caspian Operating Company (NCOC). This consortium includes equal shares of KazMunaiGas, TOTAL, ENI, Royal Dutch Shell, and Exxon Mobil, with smaller shares controlled by other partners, for example, ConocoPhillips and INPEX.[23]

Kazakhstan's hydrocarbon sector attracted approximately US$ 8.9 billion in investment during the first half of 2023, representing a 10 per cent growth compared to the corresponding period in 2022. The exploration expenses during that period amounted to US$ 416 million, which is more than the total of approximately US$ 295 million for the entire year of 2022.

The process of conducting online auctions for the allocation of subsoil use rights has been enhanced, leading to a growing number of investors showing interest in acquiring these rights.[24]

Ownership and Control in Azerbaijan

Hydrocarbons have been and remain the driving force of Azerbaijan's economic development. After the dissolution of the Soviet Union, the oil and gas industry started to decline, but soon, foreign investments in the upstream sector facilitated Azerbaijan to revive its industry and economy. Under the Constitution of Azerbaijan, natural resources belong to the state, and legislations, such as the Law on Subsoil and Law on Energy, enforce the state's rights of ownership over oil and gas resources. The Law on Subsoil oversees the exploration, use, protection, safety, and supervision of the use of subsoil resources. The Law on Energy aims to complete the legal framework for the utilisation of subsurface resources, such as oil and gas. It is a comprehensive legislation that governs the regulation of the energy sector. In order to engage in energy activities, individuals must acquire explicit authorisation from the Ministry of Energy. This can be done by either entering into an energy contract or by filing an application directly with the ministry. The Law on Gas Supply governs the entire spectrum of activities related to the storage, distribution, sale, production, processing, transportation, and utilisation of various forms of gas, including natural gas.[25]

Oil and gas exploration and production in Azerbaijan is governed by two main regulatory systems: one established by the Law on Energy and executed through energy contracts and the other tailored to each instance formed by production sharing agreements (PSAs). The PSAs provide contractors with the unique and absolute authority to carry out upstream oil and gas activities in the specific area mentioned in the PSA.[26]

Most of Azerbaijan's hydrocarbon production is export-orientated, and the government has actively endeavoured to establish a favourable investment environment for foreign investors. In this regard, the government's objectives were laid out in the State Programme for the Development of Fuel and Energy Sector as follows:

> "Determining the minimum directions of the development of the fuel and energy complex of the Republic of Azerbaijan in accordance with modern requirements; Carrying out relevant scientific, technical and organisational measures to increase the efficiency of the industry; Ensuring the implementation of advanced technological measures for the production, processing, transportation, storage, accounting and consumption of energy resources; Establishing a fair competition environment in the fuel/energy sector; Attracting more investments for the development of the fuel/energy complex ..."[27] (Valiyev and Eminova quoted the State Programme for the Development of Fuel and Energy Sector)

Most of the international oil firms operate under PSAs in Azerbaijan. The PSA prevails over any local laws, except the Constitution. Through a series of PSAs inked in the 1990s, Baku was able to attract significant foreign investment from many international oil companies, and Azerbaijan's state oil company, the SOCAR, was able to own stakes in all PSAs.[28]

In Azerbaijan, upstream developmental projects and pipeline constructions are developed jointly, but midstream (except export pipelines) and downstream projects remain under state control through the SOCAR. Only state firms or joint-stock companies, with the state holding the majority stake, are authorised to engage in oil and gas production and processing. The SOCAR, established in 1992, engages in many operations within Azerbaijan's borders. This encompasses the investigation of both onshore and offshore oil reserves, planning, utilisation, and conveyance of oil, gas, and condensate and their by-products; the refining process; sales; meeting the consistent energy needs of consumers; and securing equitable compensation for their services. Azerbaijan is linked to its neighbouring countries, as well as European and global markets, by oil pipelines. The country is transversed by three major pipelines, all of which are owned by either British Petroleum or SOCAR.[29]

The role of the SOCAR has been increasing as an investment partner, both domestically and internationally. It played a significant role in energy projects, such as the Baku-Tbilisi-Ceyhan Pipeline (BTC) and the South

Caucasus Pipeline (SCP). Lately, the SOCAR has been actively promoting its initiatives with a focus on their commercial aspects. For example, the SOCAR is engaged in commercial involvements, such as TANAP, TAP, and the construction of offshore drilling rigs in the Caspian Sea.[30]

Ownership and Control in Turkmenistan

In Turkmenistan, according to the Law on Hydrocarbon Resources, which took effect in 2008, the State Agency for Hydrocarbon Resources Management and Use under the President of Turkmenistan has authority over almost all aspects of the industry's administration. The law essentially establishes a system of direct presidential governance in the oil and gas sector. The agency is accountable for licensing, negotiating, and forming PSA agreements and determining the gas transit tariff. The Ministry of Oil and Gas Industry and Mineral Resources oversees the operations of the oil and gas industry. Turkmengas, the largest gas company of Turkmenistan, focuses on the exploration and extraction of natural gas and gas condensate in several gas fields around the country. Additionally, it facilitates the transportation of gas throughout Turkmenistan and carries out its exportation. Turkmenneft (Turkmennebit) is involved in the exploration and extraction of oil from fields around Turkmenistan, as well as the production of gas in the western region of the country. It facilitates the transportation of petroleum and natural gas. Turkmenneftegasstroy is responsible for the building and development of all oil and gas facilities in the country. TurkmenNefteGaz participates in downstream operations in the oil and gas industry, which encompass the processing, transportation, and distribution of natural gas and oil products.

In 1992, Ashgabat declared the state's right to develop petroleum resources and formed two state-owned oil and natural gas companies: Turkmengaz (a natural gas company) and Turkmenneft (a national oil company). The government launched a ten-year development plan in 1993 and restricted foreign companies' investments, except for joint venture contracts. Several international energy corporations are engaged in the exploration and extraction of oil and gas in Turkmenistan's upstream sector, facilitated by PSAs with the government. The majority of foreign investment is in the country's oil and gas industry. In the gas industry, Turkmenistan has a natural gas production sharing agreements for the Bagtyyarlyk territory with the China National Petroleum Corporation (CNPC). It is the sole foreign entity permitted by Turkmenistan for onshore gas production. In the oil industry, there are two onshore production sharing agreements: the Nebitdag contractual area managed by Italy's ENI and the Hazar project, jointly controlled by Turkmennebit (state oil firm) and Austria's Mitro International. Furthermore, there are five PSAs for offshore operations: Block I, operated by PETRONAS of Malaysia; Block II (Cheleken Contractual Territory), operated by Dragon Oil (the UAE); Block III, operated by Buried Hill (the UK); Blocks 19 and 20, operated by ENI (Italy); and Block 21, operated by Areti (Russian-owned, headquartered in Switzerland).[31] Last year, President Berdimuhamedov urged the new Mejlis of Turkmenistan to enhance the legislation concerning 'On Foreign Investments' and 'On Hydrocarbon Resources' to facilitate the attraction of foreign investment and technology.

As part of its energy diversification strategy, Turkmenistan is hopeful about two significant energy projects aimed at reducing its dependence. The Trans-Caspian Gas Pipeline (TCP) aims to deliver Turkmen gas to Europe, while the TAPI pipeline is projected to transport Turkmen gas to India through Afghanistan and Pakistan. Turkmenistan is clearly pursuing a balanced approach to lessen its reliance on Gazprom while maintaining careful relations with both Moscow and Beijing.[32]

Ownership and Control in Iran

The Iranian Constitution, particularly Article 45, specifically prohibits foreign or private ownership of natural resources. Consequently, oil and gas reserves are jointly owned by the general public. The Ministry of Petroleum possesses ownership rights and control authority over natural resources, conferred by the people. It oversees the investigation, extraction, production, and transportation of petroleum and natural gas. It is responsible for supervising the exploration and production of oil and gas resources and has granted its jurisdiction to the National Iranian Oil Company (NIOC). This state-owned entity in Iran is tasked with the exploration, development, and production of oil and natural gas resources and has sole responsibility for the exploration, production, distribution, and export of oil and natural gas.[33]

While Iran prohibits foreign or private ownership of natural resources, foreign firms are allowed to invest in certain regions through contractual agreements. The international oil companies have the opportunity to participate by entering into risk service contracts with the NIOC. Until 2016, Tehran only allowed buyback contracts, which permitted foreign oil companies to ink contracts for exploration and development through an Iranian subsidiary. In late 2016, Iran approved and implemented the Iranian Petroleum Contract Resolution. The goal was to attract international investment and technology to help accelerate the development of oil and gas upstream projects. The terms of the new contract were a hybrid of those in buyback contracts and PSAs, and international energy companies were allowed to participate in exploration and development through Iranian petroleum contracts. The international oil companies have the opportunity to engage in the production phases, including the option of expanding into the Enhanced Oil Recovery (EOR) phases. This marks a significant break from Iran's previous use of the buyback system for nearly 20 years.[34]

The Ministry of Petroleum has granted authorisation and responsibility to the NIOC to participate in upstream oil and gas projects on behalf of the Iranian nation. Further, international companies have the opportunity to invest in the exploration and production of oil and gas by entering into contractual agreements and signing risk service contracts with the NIOC, thereby gaining access to the Iranian oil market. The responsible enterprises are the National Iranian Oil Company (NIOC), the National Iranian Gas Company (NIGC), and the National Oil Refining and Distribution Company (NIORDC). The NIOC controls oil and natural gas upstream projects through its eleven subsidiaries. It is responsible for all upstream oil and natural gas projects. Private companies have the autonomy to select countries for oil exports under the supervision and approval of the NIOC. Export destinations cannot be picked from countries that are in rivalry with other exporters, especially the NIOC. The NIGC has authority over the progression of natural gas projects in the downstream sector. The company has the authority to undertake the processing, provision, and distribution of natural gas for residential consumption. The National Iranian Gas Export Company (NIGEC) is a government-owned organisation involved in the exportation of natural gas. Furthermore, the Ministry of Petroleum has the authority to grant permission for private businesses to export natural gas, including liquefied natural gas. The latest ratified statute, known as the Instruction on Modification and Improvement of Export, Import, Transit, and Swap of Crude Oil and Natural (Liquefied) Gas and Petroleum Products in Customs of 2022, aims to control the export of natural gas and transactions that occur across borders. The NIORDC is responsible for all crude oil and petroleum product refining and distribution activities, including the development of refining and storage facilities, oil pipelines, and operations.[35]

Iran's vast hydrocarbon reserves did not lead to an increase in oil production between 2012 and 2016 due to the impact of sanctions related to its nuclear programme. The sanctions targeted Iran's energy sector, which negatively impacted upstream projects in both oil and gas sectors. In January 2016, after the sanctions were lifted as a result of the Joint Comprehensive Plan of Action, production and exports rose to pre-2012 levels.[36] In 2018, after the U.S. announcement of withdrawal from the Joint Comprehensive Plan of Action, Iran planned to sustain production capacity through the development of new wells and revamping existing ones. Due to international sanctions, the decline in foreign investment in recent years has prompted Iran to rely on domestic companies for its energy projects. Unfortunately, these local companies lack the necessary capital and technology to sustain production.[37]

The Status of the Caspian Sea

After the Soviet dissolution and emergence of new littoral states, the legal status of the Caspian Sea became one of the contentious issues. During the Soviet period, there were only two littoral states: Iran and the Soviet Union. Concerning the Caspian Sea, they signed the Treaty of Friendship (1921) and the Treaty of Establishment, Commerce, and Navigation (1935). A boundary treaty concluded in 1954 determined the land boundaries without marking sea boundaries. The Soviets declared the Caspian as a 'closed sea' along with the Black Sea and the Baltic Sea.

Iran, too, recognised the Caspian as a 'closed sea'. However, after 1991, this position on the Caspian Sea was not acceptable to the newly emerged littoral states.[38] Under Soviet and Iranian control of the Caspian Sea, the countries used the resources falling within their territorial waters; however, the central portion of the Caspian Sea was open to both for the exploitation of resources. In 1970, the Soviet Ministry of Oil Industry divided the Soviet portion of the Caspian Sea amongst the Russian SFSR, Azerbaijan SSR, Kazakh SSR, and Turkmen SSR. However, concerns amongst Caspian Sea countries grew over oil and gas resources after the Soviet dissolution.

Between 1991 and 1999, the littoral countries did not share a common position on the Caspian Sea. For Iran, the international law of the sea does not apply to the Caspian Sea, and therefore, until the littoral states come up with a new legal framework, the sea must be governed by the Soviet-Iranian Treaties of 1921 and 1940. In 1998, Iran accepted the principle of sectoral division of the sea on the condition of a single division scheme to be applied on the waters and the seabed, and that such division must be equal, i.e., each littoral state's share of waters and seabed must be 20 per cent.[39] Iran opposes any unilateral exploitation of resources, particularly those found in the seabed, and considers it undesirable. It has refuted bilateral agreements and expressed opposition to the ones between Kazakhstan and Russia, as well as Russia and Azerbaijan. Iran has always asserted its claim to a 20 per cent portion of the sea since the initial discussions on its division, despite opposition from Azerbaijan and Turkmenistan. Iran opposed any partition that was based on coastal length due to its small and concave coastline. The debate over whether the Caspian Sea is classified as a sea or a lake reinforces Iran's position in leveraging its oil and gas reserves.

Russia saw the Caspian Sea as a landlocked body of water and hence, never recognised international maritime law standards, such as the exclusive economic zone, continental shelf, and territorial sea. Russia reiterated that the status of the Caspian Sea was to be governed by the Soviet-Iranian treaties of 1921 and 1940 and asserted that the Caspian Sea is not subject to the 1982 United Nations Convention on the Law of the Sea (UNCLOS). However, as a result of Lukoil's involvement in the 'Deal of the Century',

Russia began adopting different policies regarding delimitation. In 1998, the Russian government supported the sectoral division of the Caspian seabed, and later, Russia and Kazakhstan divided the northern sector of the Caspian between themselves as per an equidistant line.[40] Russia, for its part, chose to view the legal framework governing the Caspian Sea as having two distinct aspects: one focused on the division of the seabed for the extraction of oil and gas and the other centred on the shared use of the sea for transportation, fisheries, and environmental protection.[41]

Azerbaijan advocated the division of the seabed and waters by means of an equidistant line. It maintained that the Soviet-Iranian treaties of 1921 and 1940 are limited to guarding and fishing and therefore, do not pertain to the legal status of the sea or the exploitation of natural resources. For Baku, the Soviet sector of the Caspian Sea was divided at the inter-republic level amongst Azerbaijan, Russia, Turkmenistan, and Kazakhstan, which was approved by then Russian Prime Minister, Viktor Chernomyrdin. Additionally, the Constitution of Azerbaijan has enshrined the country's sovereignty over its portion of the Caspian Sea. In 1998, Azerbaijan agreed on the division of the seabed according to an equidistant line.[42] Azerbaijan asserts that the Caspian Sea is an international sea with a seabed and coastal waters that belong to each state and so, should be partitioned to grant each state complete jurisdiction over its respective portion. The divide should be established according to the principles of international division, namely using a median line. As for other countries, their concept of division is based on the demarcation set by the Soviet Union Oil Ministry in 1970. This demarcation was primarily intended for oil exploration and extraction activities in the former Soviet republics. From Azerbaijan's perspective, if it acknowledges the validity of the Russian-Iranian treaties, it is believed that they do not grant authorisation to extract oil and gas.[43]

Kazakhstan argued that the status of the Caspian Sea was to be determined by the United Nations Convention on the Law of the Sea (1982). It supported the delineation of internal and territorial waters and an exclusive economic zone. Kazakhstan asserts that the Caspian Sea possesses the characteristics of a high sea due to its connections with the Baltic and Black Seas via the Volga and Don Rivers. Therefore, it argues that the legal framework outlined by the Convention on the Law of the Sea should apply. This entails delineating boundaries of 12 nautical miles as territorial waters, 24 miles in surrounding regions, and 200 miles as exclusive economic zones on the continental plateau. Kazakhstan maintains that the Caspian Sea is classified as a 'high sea' according to international standards that regulate the unrestricted movement of ships and aircraft, as well as the installation and positioning of pipelines and cables. Further, Kazakhstan asserts that the treaties signed in 1921 and 1940, prior to the dissolution of the Soviet Union, are null and void and no longer hold legal validity. Both Azerbaijan and Kazakhstan are considered to have unilaterally partitioned the Caspian Sea. Nevertheless, Kazakhstan's perspective is different from that of Azerbaijan. It is important to highlight that approximately 30-40 per cent of Kazakhstan's oil reserves are located in the Caspian Sea. Kazakhstan can only access these resources if the countries bordering the sea agree to a division of its territory.[44]

Finally, Turkmenistan has enacted a law asserting its jurisdiction over a 12-mile territorial sea and a marine economic zone, making it the first government to do so. Like Azerbaijan, Turkmenistan agreed on the principle of an equidistant-line division of the Caspian region.[45]

In the absence of a comprehensive agreement, a few states entered into bilateral agreements to explore and harvest Caspian energy. Between 1998 and 2004, Russia, Kazakhstan, and Azerbaijan negotiated agreements that included, in addition to sectoral delimitation, agreements to use resources in the northern Caspian. They split the northern Caspian region amongst themselves by employing median lines. The agreement between Russia and Kazakhstan in 1998 established states' rights to explore and exploit resources within their respective sectoral limits in the northern part of the Caspian Sea. Both parties also reached a consensus on having exclusive common rights to explore and utilise resources that span across the median line established by the treaty. Since 2005, Russia and Kazakhstan have been working on production sharing in the offshore Kurmangazy fields. The disputed fields of Kurmangazy, Khvalynskoe, and Tsentralnoe, situated at the median line between Russia and Kazakhstan, were developed commonly on a 50:50 basis. The second agreement was concluded between Kazakhstan and

Azerbaijan in 2001. They agreed on rights to explore and exploit resources within their respective sectoral limits. In a situation where a new energy field extends across the median line, both states would need to conclude a separate agreement. The third agreement was concluded between Russia and Azerbaijan in 2002. The agreement permitted the states to explore and exploit resources and conduct economic activities as per the sectoral boundaries defined under the treaty.[46] Further, in 2003, Russia, Azerbaijan, and Kazakhstan signed a trilateral agreement that partitioned the seabed into national sectors as per the median line principle.

The breakthrough was achieved a quarter century later when the littoral states signed the Convention on the Legal Status of the Caspian Sea as part of the 5th Caspian Summit (2018). It focused on the delimitation of national zones, jurisdictions, and sovereignty; the exercise of rights to subsoil exploitation; transit; laying submarine pipelines and cables; and the protection of the environment and biological resources. It also aimed at security concerns in terms of countering modern threats and challenges, preventing and eliminating emergency situations, and military activities of the Caspian states.[47] The Convention is for 'unlimited duration'. It is not specified as to whether the Caspian Sea is a 'sea' or a 'lake', but the term 'body of water' is used. The Convention provides each littoral state exclusive control over an area extending up to 15 nautical miles from its shores for mineral and energy exploration and a further 10 nautical miles as the fishing zone. Further negotiations will determine the joint sharing of the remaining area[48] (Map 3.1 and Map 3.2).

The Convention has also left some issues unresolved. For instance, when it comes to the development of pipelines, Article 14 of the Convention allows the construction of submarine cables and pipelines. It confirms that a pipeline route needs agreement only between the states through which the line crosses. At the same time, compliance with environmental regulations and procedures, particularly the Tehran Convention (also known as the Framework Convention for the Protection of the Marine Environment of the Caspian Sea), is a critical prerequisite for pipeline development. Europe, which has been trying to tap into Turkmenistan's hydrocarbons through the proposed TCP, will have to wait as Article 14 of the Convention is likely to cause issues for its plan to be realised. Both Russia and Iran might invoke an environment clause in the future to prevent Western powers from strengthening their access in the region after the success of the BTC oil pipeline and the Southern Gas Corridor.

Map 3.1: Delimitation of the Caspian Sea Region

Source: Radio Free Europe/Radio Liberty, "The Caspian Summit", August 13, 2018, https://www.rferl.org/a/the-caspian-summit/29430597.html. Accessed on August 15, 2022.

Map 3.2: Oil and Gas Reserves in the Caspian Sea Region

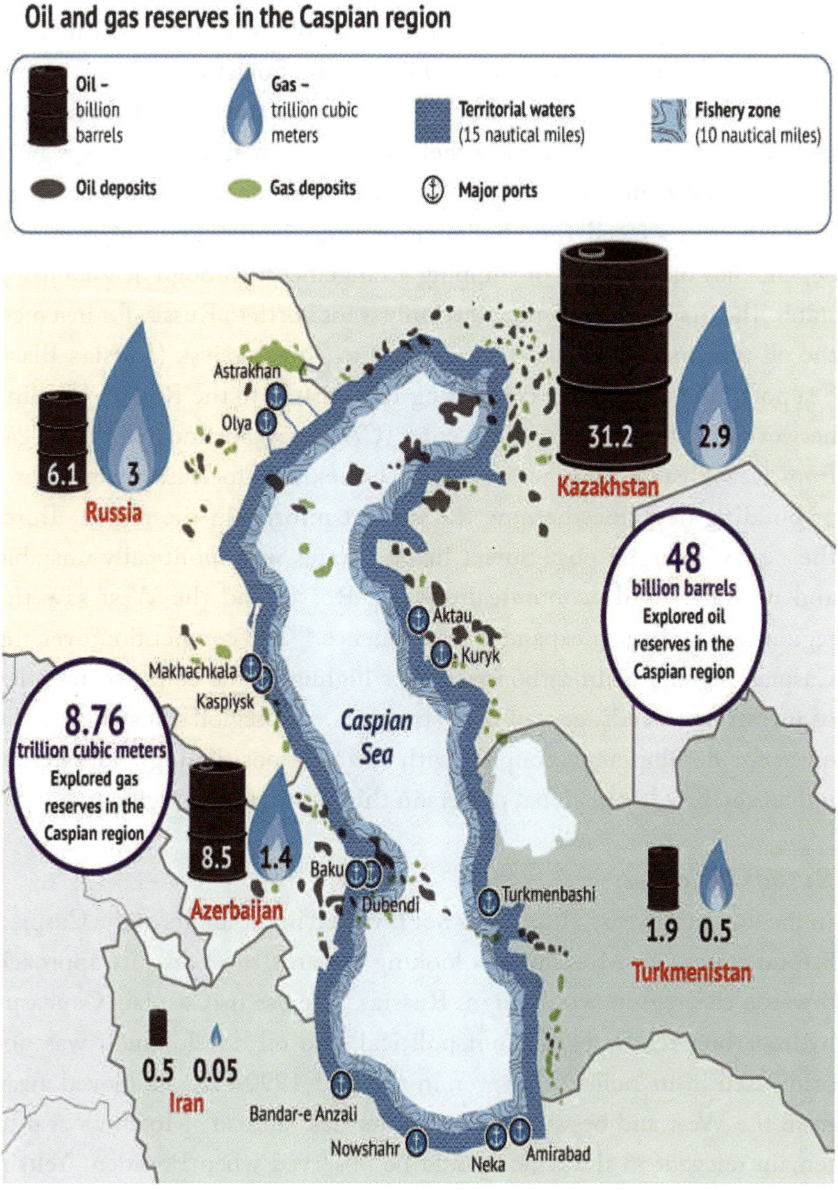

Source: Valdai Club, "Convention on the Legal Status of the Caspian Sea", August 28, 2018, https://valdaiclub.com/multimedia/infographics/convention-on-the-legal-status-of-the-caspian-sea/

Objectives of Major Powers in the Caspian Region

The Caspian region's hydrocarbon resources became a source of global economic and political competition for the following reasons: First, the region needed capital investment. During the Soviet period, the region suffered decades of abandonment. The littoral states needed capital and technical assistance to develop their hydrocarbon sector. In this regard, foreign investments were critical to its success. Second, the newly emerged Caspian states faced the challenge of their landlocked position and dependency on pipelines or shipping arrangements through neighbouring states. The majority of the pipelines only went north to Russia, for instance, the oil pipeline from Baku (Azerbaijan) to Novorossiysk (Russia's Black Sea port); the oil pipeline connecting Kazakhstan to the Russian pipeline network; and the Central Asia-Center (CAC) gas pipeline that carries gas from Kazakhstan, Turkmenistan, and Uzbekistan to Russia. Upgrading or building new lines became the utmost priority in the region. Third, the newly emerged post-Soviet littoral states were politically unstable and militarily and economically weak. Russia and the West saw the region as a sphere to expand their influence.[49] The competition over the Caspian region's hydrocarbon resources highlights the complex interplay of investment needs, geopolitical strategies, and regional instability. The quest for development, coupled with strategic positioning and external influences, has driven global powers in this resource-rich region.

Russia's Objectives

In the formative years, Russia was not involved in the affairs of the Caspian littoral states. As Moscow was looking towards the West, its approach towards the region was benign. Russia's interest in Caspian-Caucasus hydrocarbon resources was not political, and oil development was not prioritised in its policy. However, in the mid-1990s, Russia moved away from the West and began focusing on its 'near abroad'. Moscow's zeal to remain relevant in the region could be observed when President Yeltsin signed a secret order on 'Protecting the Interests of the Russian Federation in the Caspian Sea'[50], which stated that Moscow should maintain its influence in the region.

After Putin's accession as President in 2000, he prioritised the Commonwealth of Independent States (CIS) in Russian foreign policy. An increase in energy prices has made Russian foreign policy assertive in the Caspian region. Russian energy giants—Lukoil, Yukos, and Gazprom—founded the Caspian Oil Company to explore new oil and gas reserves on the Russian shelf in the Caspian Sea and adjacent littoral states. To prevent the establishment of alternative energy lines, Putin recommended increasing oil and gas supplies from the region through Russian pipelines.[51] After 2000, Russia developed strong geostrategic interests in the region, aiming towards: (a) safeguarding Russian territorialities from destabilising factors; (b) protecting the Russian population in the region; (c) exercising greater control over energy production and transportation to international markets; and (d) limiting the influence of non-regional actors in the region. To accomplish its purposes, Russia has come up with various organisations and is promoting greater cooperation with post-Soviet countries. Examples include the Eurasian Economic Community (EurAsEC); the Customs Union between Russia, Belarus, and Kazakhstan; and the Collective Security Treaty Organization (CSTO).[52]

Russia's relationship with Azerbaijan is shaped by the former's energy cooperation with Europe and its support for Armenia on the issue of Nagorno-Karabakh. The construction and success of the Baku-Tbilisi-Ceyhan (BTC) oil pipeline have become a point of contention between both countries. Russia viewed the success of the BTC pipeline as a direct challenge to its control, and Azerbaijan viewed it as a means to raise its energy profile internationally and gather support for the Nagorno-Karabakh conflict. Despite their diametrical relations, the first supply of natural gas to Russia started in 2010 as a result of the agreement signed between Russia and Azerbaijan in 2009. Baku has agreed to provide an annual supply of 500 million cubic metres of gas via the Mozdok-Makhachkala-Kazi Magomed pipeline. In subsequent years, Russia imported less gas at higher prices, which shows its interest in influencing the energy supply of Azerbaijan. This transaction was more political than economic in character.[53]

Russia has close energy ties with Kazakhstan. The latter has exported energy across Russian territory since the Soviet era and also plays an important role as a transit country for natural gas exports from Turkmenistan and Uzbekistan through the Central Asia-Center (CAC) gas pipeline. The pipeline is controlled by Gazprom and was constructed during the Soviet period. Both countries have a common interest in the development of upstream and downstream developmental projects in the region. For instance, Russian Lukoil has a 10 per cent share of Kazakhstan's entire oil production.[54]

Russia and Turkmenistan share a complex relationship. In the 1990s, Russia employed a barter system as a means of payment for Turkmenistan's gas. As Turkmenistan's gas exports increased through the CAC pipeline, Russia agreed to make 40 per cent of the payment in hard currency and the remaining in barter trade. In 2003, Gazprom entered into a 25-year arrangement to enhance the import of Turkmen gas from 5-6 billion cubic metres per year in 2004 to 70-80 billion cubic metres per year by 2028. However, Moscow restricted imports to up to 45 billion cubic metres per year. In 2007, Russia, Kazakhstan, and Turkmenistan agreed to upgrade the CAC pipeline and construct a new Caspian gas pipeline. However, the plan did not materialise due to disagreements over the pipelines' transit routes. Another point of contention between Moscow and Ashgabat was the disagreement over gas prices. For example, in the mid-2000s, Turkmenistan's demand for a price increase for its gas exports was denied by Russia.[55]

In the face of ongoing sanctions, Russia and Iran are strengthening their commercial and economic ties. Bilateral trade turnover between the two countries increased by 45 per cent between January and July 2022, reaching US$ 2.8 billion. The key sector that has grown significantly between Russia and Iran is energy cooperation. In October 2022, both countries entered into a Memorandum of Understanding (MoU), valued at US$ 4 billion, to enhance the gas business and construct infrastructure worth US$ 40 billion, including pipelines and liquefied natural gas facilities. Earlier, in July 2022, Iran's National Iranian Oil Company and Russia's Gazprom signed a MoU to develop the Kish and North Pars gas fields. Both are presently working on oil and gas swaps and supply of Russian gas through Turkmenistan.[56]

United States' Objectives

The U.S. involvement in the region can be traced back to the early 1990s, when American energy companies began exploring new sources of non-OPEC oil and the U.S. government decided to support energy lines bypassing Russian and Iranian territory. The U.S. support for the BTC pipeline and the EU's support for the SGC initiative are such examples. The U.S. prioritised the construction of new energy lines bypassing Russia in its foreign policy. Its interest is not restricted to controlling energy resources and infrastructure in the region; it seeks to compete with Russia and China. It wants to prevent Russia from geopolitically dominating the region by highlighting its own significance in the region's development. For instance, according to the National Security Strategy Document of 1998:

> "Stability and prosperity in the Caucasus and Central Asia will contribute to security in the area extending from the Mediterranean to China and facilitate the dynamic development of the transportation of the vast oil and gas resources from the Caspian region to international markets with the involvement of the US" (Misiągiewicz quoted Iseri).[57]

Cooperation between the U.S. and Azerbaijan in the hydrocarbon field started in 1994 with a product-sharing agreement signed between the SOCAR and a consortium of 11 international oil companies from six different states for the development of the Azeri, Chirag, and Deepwater portions of the Gunashli field (ACG). It included two American firms, Exxon and Chevron. The ACG product sharing agreement was initially signed for 30 years; later, in 2017, the deal was extended until 2050. Washington has been supportive of Baku's role in Europe's energy security and has repeatedly stated its commitment to the SGC.[58] Both Exxon and Chevron have invested in infrastructure development in the South Caucasus Pipeline and the BTC oil pipeline.[59] Baku serves as the largest port on the Caspian Sea and plays a crucial role as a transportation hub for the movement of products between Europe and Central Asia.

The U.S.' energy engagement with Kazakhstan goes back to Soviet times. After the Soviet dissolution, the U.S. participated in promoting diversification plans of export pipeline routes in the Caspian region, ensuring energy security in Europe, and diversifying market opportunities. With Washington's support, Astana agreed to transport oil through the BTC pipeline in 2006, as it found this deal necessary as Russia refused to increase the transportation capacity of the CPC pipeline.[60] The U.S. is the most prominent investor in Kazakhstan. Chevron runs Kazakhstan's Tengiz oilfield near the Caspian Sea alongside another U.S. oil company, ExxonMobil, holding a 50 per cent stake in Tengiz-Chevroil and a 15 per cent stake in the CPC.[61] Here, the Energy Partnership Commission plays an important role in energy cooperation between the U.S. and Kazakhstan.

The U.S. viewed Turkmenistan as an important player in reducing Europe's reliance on Russian energy, but at the same time, it feared that Ashgabat could enter into an energy partnership with Tehran if pushed away. Despite Chevron and ExxonMobil's interest in Turkmenistan, their main hindrance was, first, the reluctance on the part of the U.S. government to support U.S. commerce in the country, and second, the existence of many gas contracts with Russia and China, which cover all available gas.[62]

China's Objectives

China's initial interest in the region was moderate and related to security, mainly preventing terrorism and fundamentalism in its Xinjiang region. China's earliest engagement can be traced back to 1997, when the China National Petroleum Company (CNPC) agreed to construct an 1800-mile pipeline that would transverse Kazakhstan and end in Xinjiang, and later, in 2003, when Chinese energy firms inked their first deal with the State Oil Company of the Republic of Azerbaijan.[63] Experts have identified two primary reasons for China's active participation in the region: First, China is concerned about its growing need for energy security. At the domestic level, Beijing encourages oil and gas exploration and production, promotion of renewables, and energy conservation; internationally, it focuses on securing energy supply chains and transportation routes. Second, as China is dependent on the Strait of Malacca for LNG and oil imports from Africa and West Asia, its concern is focused on U.S. naval control of regional Sea Lines of Communication. To escape this dilemma, China started to focus on the construction of overland pipelines. Here, China's growing involvement in the Caspian region is linked to its objective of securing overland supplies.[64] China's involvement in the region can also be viewed through the prism of its "Belt and Road" initiative.

Among post-Soviet states, Kazakhstan is China's largest trading partner. Chinese firms are involved in more than a quarter of Kazakhstan's oil production and are the leading foreign investor in the country with an amount of US$ 30 billion.[65] Chinese energy corporations are projected to hold a 40 per cent stake in the oil business of Kazakhstan, with the Chinese CNPC being the dominant player. The CNPC, along with KazMunaiGaz, constructed the Kazakhstan-China oil pipeline and is presently working on the Kazakhstan-China gas pipeline. The CNPC owns 60 per cent of Kazakhstan's Aktobe Oil and Gas Corporation.[66]

China has successfully marked its presence in the Turkmen energy sector. In 2007, Beijing and Ashgabat started working on the Central Asia-China Gas Pipeline (CAC) by connecting Turkmenistan, Uzbekistan, and Kazakhstan with Xinjiang (northwest China). Currently, Turkmen gas is transported through the Central Asia-China pipeline and directly connected to China's domestic network. Ashgabat has received almost US$ 12 billion in loans from Chinese banks for the purpose of financing infrastructure development, gas exploration, and extraction.[67] For Ashgabat, the Chinese market is important to reduce the country's dependence on Moscow, increase revenue for its energy exports, and promote economic growth. Presently, the CNPC is one of the two foreign energy companies on Turkmen soil. Despite not being a member state of the Shanghai Cooperation Organisation, Turkmenistan has proposed the significance of the organisation for cooperation in the energy sector.[68]

China's energy engagement with Azerbaijan is very moderate, as most of its energy-related activities are concentrated in the Caspian states of Kazakhstan and Turkmenistan. Since 2002, China's CNPC has entered into a PSA with Azerbaijan, and its engagement is limited to providing technical support and services.[69]

From 1995 onwards, China began importing crude oil from Iran. In 2002, China and Iran signed a ten-year deal for oil commerce. By 2008, the entire volume of trade between the two countries had reached around 65 per cent. Between 2008 and 2010, Iran was the third largest exporter of oil to China. Iran permitted Chinese companies to exploit its oil and gas fields, and subsequently, the CNPC was given exploitation rights in 2004, while Sinopec signed an oil and natural gas agreement worth US$ 70 billion with Iran. In 2004, the Sinopec Group signed a memorandum of understanding with Iran in which they agreed to buy 250 million tonnes of liquefied natural gas over a period of 30 years. Additionally, they committed to developing the Yadavaran oil field. Iran has pledged to supply 150,000 barrels of crude oil per day to China for a duration of 25 years at the prevailing market price, following the commissioning of the oil field.[70] Iran viewed China as the main investor in its oil and gas fields, primarily in the downstream sector. On the other hand, Beijing's penchant for Caspian energy resources is linked to its aim to reduce reliance on maritime oil imports from Persian Gulf states.[71] China has also been an active player in Iran's Caspian Sea oil and gas development, as well as in modernising facilities in the Neka region. It also supports Iran's efforts to deliver Caspian oil and gas to southern Iranian ports for export to Europe and Asia via pipelines.

The European Union's Objectives

The EU, as a major energy importer, is also a prominent actor in the region. It has aimed to enhance collaboration with post-Soviet states and advocated for energy infrastructure initiatives stretching westward. The energy policy of the EU countries resembled that of the U.S., focused on diversifying energy sources while bypassing Russia and Iran. Till 2020, Russia accounted for 29 per cent of oil imports and 43 per cent of gas imports of the EU. Europe's reliance on Russian oil and gas was estimated to be 58 per cent. However, the EU, in February 2022, decided to reduce its dependency on Russian energy by two-thirds by December 2022, with the goal of being independent of Russian fuel by 2030. The EU has sought an alternative gas source by focusing on the Caspian Sea region.[72]

It is important to note that in the formative years after the Soviet disintegration, there were minimal energy ties between the EU and the Caspian littoral states. But, in the late 2000s, Europe's increasing demand for energy was entangled with gas disruptions during Russia-Ukraine gas disputes. Therefore, the EU developed the European Union Security and Solidarity Action Plan. The plan included developing new supply routes and gas import infrastructure in the Caspian Sea and Middle East regions.[73] The International Energy Agency's '10-Point Plan to Reduce the European Union's Reliance on Russian Natural Gas' indicated that non-Russian pipeline imports (including Azerbaijan) to Europe could increase by up to 10 bcm of gas compared to 2021. In the said plan, Azerbaijan is seen as a potential Caspian country to mitigate the EU's growing energy requirements. At present, the SGC is the only connection that transports energy to south-eastern European countries.[74] Clearly, despite the EU's interest in Caspian energy, its involvement in the region is very gradual. Due to the Western sanctions and Russia's military involvement in Ukraine, the EU believes that post-Soviet states, especially those in the Caspian Sea region and Central Asia, might facilitate dousing its appetite for hydrocarbons.

The EU signed a PSA with Azerbaijan in 1996 to promote commercial investment in the latter's energy sector. Both sides also inked MoUs on specific areas of energy cooperation in 2006, followed by the Joint Declaration on the SGC in 2011. Many European energy companies have engaged with Baku since the 1990s for upstream and downstream developmental projects. For example, British Petroleum is the largest investor in Azerbaijan, along with the Azerbaijan International Operating Company (AIOC).[75] European companies' engagements with Kazakhstan can be traced back to the early 1990s. They are involved in upstream developmental projects in Karachagnak fields and also hold shares in the North Caspian Operating Company (NCOC) consortium, which is developing the offshore Kashagan oil field.[76]

Since 1991, Turkmenistan has had limited foreign investments in its energy sector. The EU began its energy engagement with Turkmenistan when both parties signed a MoU in 2008 on technology exchange and development of oil and gas fields. Brussels has pinned its hope on the TCP as this proposed link will provide Europe with much-needed access to Turkmen gas. It is proposed to carry natural gas from Turkmenbasy (Turkmenistan) to Baku (Azerbaijan).[77]

Europe's energy engagement with Iran has a long history. Between 1996 and 2005, oil constituted 90 per cent of EU imports from Iran. Despite American sanctions, major European oil corporations, such as Eni (Italy) and Total (France), engaged in Iran's natural gas industry in the 1990s.[78] However, between 2010 and 2013, the EU imposed restrictive sanctions and an oil embargo on Iran in the aftermath of the UNSC sanctions in 2010. Later, the nuclear deal in 2016 permitted the EU and Iran to renew cooperation in oil and gas.[79] With the reimposition of sanctions after the U.S. withdrawal from the Joint Comprehensive Plan of Action (JCPOA), the EU is endeavouring to preserve the deal. Iran has recently expressed its willingness to export oil and gas to Europe to meet its energy needs if the U.S. lifts sanctions against Tehran as a result of the JCPOA.

Amidst the ongoing Ukraine conflict, the region will witness intense competition over Caspian resources. All four major powers will do their utmost to shape regional energy dynamics. The recent energy deal between the EU and Azerbaijan over doubling gas exports from Caspian fields and the Russian proposal for a 'trilateral gas union' with Kazakhstan and Uzbekistan are such endeavours.

Connectivity Approaches and Initiatives in the Caspian Sea Region

The Caspian region, once confined to the Soviet Union and Iran, has now transformed into an arena for regional and international actors to enhance their connectivity endeavours. This section attempts an analysis of the notion of the connectivity of Caspian Sea countries and external actors in the region. For centuries, the Caspian Sea region has been a locus of changing geopolitical dynamics. It has served as a platform for political rivalry, negotiations, commerce, and transportation. This multifaceted role of the region predates the establishment of the East-West dichotomy. For instance, highlighting the value of the Caspian region, Anthony Jenkinson (an English merchant) attempted to establish a trade route to the East through the Caspian region and provided a detailed account of his expedition, which he characterised as very arduous, perilous, and financially burdensome. Despite his regretful experience, he saw the Caspian routes as being potentially profitable and the trade, worthy of pursuit.[80] Today, connectivity initiatives are the latest geopolitical tool for advancing national interests.

Control over connectivity routes has always been critical for military and economic effectiveness. In general, land and maritime powers have long held opposing views on connectivity corridors. On the one hand, land powers prefer corridors that cross their own territory because they have more control over the flow of goods and people. On the other hand, maritime powers prefer corridors that cross international waters because they allow them to move their military troops and trade more freely. In recent years, these two different points of view have begun to converge in the Caspian Sea region. Landlocked states are gradually understanding the significance of maritime routes, while coastal states recognise the value of continental routes. This convergence in the Caspian region is due to the growing interests of global actors on the one hand and the interests of landlocked Caspian Sea littoral countries in accessing global markets on the other. Due to this convergence, it is essential to assess the connectivity initiatives in the Caspian Sea region.

Connectivity Approaches and Initiatives of the Caspian Sea Littoral Countries in the Caspian Sea Region

Historically, the South Caucasus and Central Asia regions have been geographically separated by the Caspian Sea, hindered by insufficient infrastructure, and by external forces, resulting in their division. Amidst the ongoing military operation in Ukraine, escalating tensions between China and the U.S., and evolving geopolitical reconfigurations in West Asia, the Caspian Sea littoral states are witnessing major shifts in terms of regional connectivity. As the economic and political viability of landlocked resource-rich countries in the Caspian Sea region is heavily dependent on their ability to reach markets, the littoral countries have engaged amongst themselves in various bilateral, trilateral, and multilateral connectivity project initiatives.

Azerbaijan has conditions that are different from those of other former Soviet republics in the region. The country gained global attention due to its history of energy resources and its role as an energy transit hub. Oil and gas play an important role in Azerbaijan's foreign relations. For instance, in its formative years, Elchibey's administration set a pro-Western approach in its foreign policy. Signifying the importance of oil and gas in Azerbaijan's foreign policy, Sabit Bagirov, former President of the State Oil Company of the Azerbaijan Republic, stated that "the only way to accomplish improving Azerbaijan's economic and political relations with the West was to resort to the 'oil card' and to offer the territory of Azerbaijan for the West's new strategic routes to Central Asia."[81] However, succeeding President Heydar Aliyev and President Ilham Aliyev adopted a balanced approach toward Russia and the West.[82] President Heydar allowed Lukoil to acquire 10 per cent of SOCAR's shares of the Azeri, Chirag, and Guneshli offshore fields. His strategy was to attract investments from multiple countries and corporations in the hydrocarbon sector to strengthen national security, as evidenced by the formation of the Azerbaijan International Operating Company (AIOC) in 1995.[83]

Azerbaijan considers connectivity to be a pivotal factor in its economic development, diversification, and integration within the region. Being a landlocked nation, Azerbaijan's transit approach is focused on the development of new infrastructure and the expansion of transport connectivity. The objective is to effectively utilise transit opportunities, offer state assistance for transport projects, align the legal and institutional framework with international standards, and implement comprehensive transport and logistical systems that streamline transportation operations and the movement of goods. Efforts are now underway to adopt new initiatives aimed at enhancing the transit capacity, as Baku has entered into many agreements in this region that facilitate the use of streamlined customs and border crossing protocols for international freight transit. The enhancement of transport infrastructure, which encompasses the establishment of international transport corridors that transverse the country's territory, plays a crucial role in augmenting its transit capacity.[84]

The following connectivity initiatives have been undertaken or are led by Baku:

(a) The East-West Transport Corridor or Trans-Caspian International Transport Route (TITR): This corridor connects Azerbaijan to Georgia, Turkey, and beyond, providing a link between the Caspian Sea and Europe.
(b) The North-South Transport Corridor: This corridor connects Azerbaijan to Russia, Iran, and beyond, providing a link between the Baltic Sea and the Indian Ocean.
(c) The Baku-Tbilisi-Kars Railway: This railway line connects Azerbaijan, Georgia, and Turkey, providing an alternative route for cargo transportation between Europe and Asia.
(d) The Astara-Astara railway: This 8.3-kilometre railway line connects Astara, Azerbaijan, with Astara, Iran. It is a section of the International North–South Transport Corridor.
(e) The Qazvin-Rasht-Astara Railway: This 164-kilometre railway line connects Qazvin, Iran, with Rasht, Iran, and Astara, Iran. It is part of the International North–South Transport Corridor.
(f) The Trans-Caspian International Transport Route: This route connects Azerbaijan to Kazakhstan and Turkmenistan, providing a link between the Caspian Sea and Central Asia (Table 3.1).

Russia is the third largest producer of crude oil in the world and the second largest producer of gas. Hydrocarbons play a significant role in the Russian economy, as revenue is generated from oil and gas production, and its exports constitute more than half of the country's federal budget revenue. The 'Energy Strategy of Russia', adopted in 2009, emphasised the significance of energy exports to Europe and Asian markets (China, South Korea, and Japan).[85] For example, the countries of Europe and Asia accounted for 72 per cent and 26 per cent of Russian crude oil exports, respectively. Russia is blessed with vast resources of oil and gas, which provide the leverage to influence its 'near abroad'. For many post-Soviet countries, such as Ukraine, Belarus, and the Baltics, Russia is the largest energy provider. Therefore, shaping hydrocarbon prices and interrupting energy supplies are measures for Russia to show its supremacy in the post-Soviet space. In this regard, Russia, in the past, made attempts to influence the implementation of any alternative pipeline connectivity projects that bypass Russian territory. Experts viewed Russia's approach towards its neighbours as 'petro-carrots'—using oil and gas to reward Moscow's allies—and 'petro-sticks'—using oil and gas to punish those states that stand against Moscow. For example, in Ukraine, both petro-carrots and petro-sticks strategies were used by Russia. Ukraine, under President Leonid Kuchma, received subsidised oil and gas from Moscow. Throughout Leonid Kuchma's tenure, the rate of gas was kept constant at US$ 50 per thousand cubic metres. However, Gazprom increased the rate of gas after Yushchenko's takeover.[86] Likewise, in Georgia, Russian sanctions were the repercussion of the 'Rose Revolution' of 2003, which removed President Eduard Shevardnadze from power.[87]

Russia's connectivity strategy, given its massive geography, focuses on three distinct geographic regions: Greater Eurasia, post-Soviet Central Asia, and the eastern region of the Russian Federation. Russia's efforts to promote connectivity in each of these three regions are guided by separate rationale. The connectivity frameworks advocated within the Greater Eurasian Partnership are intended to counter those promoted by the U.S. and ensure symbolic status parity with China.[88] With regards to the Caspian Sea region, inferences can be drawn by observing Russia's approach to connectivity with the Central Asian states. From 2000 onwards, Moscow has developed a growing inclination to maintain and, whenever feasible, enhance the current degree of connectivity between Russia and the Central Asian states. Since the mid-1990s, Moscow's overarching objective has been to play a role in the development of alternative infrastructure connections, particularly those that would transport natural resources from Central Asia to the European market. On the topic of connectivity in the region, Russia maintains a cooperative stance with the littoral states. Considering Russia's ongoing military operation in Ukraine and the EU's embargo on Russian oil and gas, Moscow is considering expanding its focus to Asian economies. Its renewed emphasis on the INSTC is one such example.

The connectivity initiatives that Russia has undertaken or is a member of are as follows:

(a) The INSTC: It is a multimodal transport corridor that connects India, Russia, Iran, and Central Asia. It aims to provide an alternative route for trade between India and Europe.
(b) The Greater Eurasian Partnership (GEP): It is a proposed connectivity initiative that would link Russia, China, India, and regions in Eurasia. It is still in its early stages, but its potential to be a major driver of economic integration in Eurasia cannot be negated. (Table 3.1).

Kazakhstan wants to contribute to regional and global energy security by achieving a balance of interests of transit countries, and energy-consuming countries and by establishing diversified, secure, and stable energy export routes.[89] In the last three decades, the country has employed a multivector approach to its foreign policy with the objective of maintaining its independent and sovereign character. Kazakhstan strategically interacts with various major countries by aligning mutual interests and reducing challenges linked to overdependence on a single partner. This multivector strategy of the country is reflected in its approach to connectivity. Kazakhstan, due to its strategic geographical position at the crossroads of Europe and Asia, has historically served as a pivotal hub for transportation and commerce. Kazakhstan still serves as a crucial transit hub for the transportation of products from China and Central Asia to Europe, with a significant proportion of over 80 per cent of these commodities traversing its territory. According to Murat Nurtleu, Deputy Prime Minister and Minister of Foreign Affairs of Kazakhstan, the connectivity strategy of Kazakhstan is driven by its objective to foster the development of a more equitable, environmentally conscious, and interconnected economy on a global scale. He asserted that the country's aspiration to enhance transcontinental trade routes should not be misinterpreted as the beginning of a 'new great game' defined by geopolitical rivalry.[90]

Kazakhstan's crucial objective is to foster positive and cooperative relationships with neighbours—Russia and China—to fully use the country's transport capabilities. The following connectivity initiatives have been undertaken or led by Kazakhstan:

(a) The Nurly Zhol Infrastructure Development Program: This ambitious programme aims to modernise and expand Kazakhstan's transport infrastructure, including roads, railways, ports, and airports. The programme is expected to cost over US$ 9 billion and is seen as a key driver of economic growth in Kazakhstan.
(b) The Trans-Caspian International Transport Route (TITR): It is a multimodal transport corridor that connects Kazakhstan with China, Georgia, Turkey, and Azerbaijan. The route is designed to provide an alternative to the traditional Suez Canal route for trade between Europe and Asia.
(c) The Western Europe-Western China International Transit Corridor: The project will increase transport efficiency on the road sections between Aktobe/Kyzylorda oblast border and Shymkent.
(d) Development of the Port of Aktau: The Port of Aktau is a major port on the Caspian Sea. The Kazakh government is investing in the development of the port to make it a major hub for trade between Kazakhstan and other Caspian Sea countries (Table 3.1).

Turkmenistan, a country that has included the principle of 'permanent neutrality' into its constitutional structure, seeks to engage in connectivity initiatives from a position of neutrality. Ashgabat believes that it has a strategically advantageous geographical position, enabling the country to serve as a pivotal junction for regional transportation networks. The country has some notable strengths, such as its strategic coastal location, well-developed railway systems, and a range of specialised infrastructure, and it is actively pursuing the enhancement of its transit capabilities. A transit corridor in Turkmenistan has important implications for the transportation and logistics sector of the region. As the discontinuation of conventional trade routes from the East to the West through Russia, Belarus, and Ukraine has prompted regional countries to explore alternative trade routes, the situation has also motivated Turkmenistan to actively participate in new initiatives, particularly due to the intensifying initiatives for transportation routes.[91] Turkmenistan has undertaken or is a member of the following connectivity initiatives:

(a) The INSTC: Turkmenistan is a key participant in the INSTC, a multimodal transport corridor that connects India, Russia, Iran, and Central Asia.
(b) The Ashgabat Agreement: Turkmenistan is a signatory to the Ashgabat Agreement, aims to link Central Asia and the Persian Gulf.
(c) The Lapis Lazuli Corridor: Turkmenistan is also involved in the Lapis Lazuli Corridor, a transport corridor that connects Afghanistan, Turkmenistan, Azerbaijan, Georgia, and Turkey. The corridor is expected to improve connectivity and trade between the countries involved.
(d) Turkmenbashi International Seaport: Turkmenistan has invested heavily in the development of the Turkmenbashi International Seaport, which is now one of the largest ports on the Caspian Sea and has connectivity with other major ports in the sea (Table 3.1).

For Iran, corridors serve not only as means of transportation but also as instruments for facilitating trade growth and enhancing the economic development at the national, regional, and global levels.[92] Tehran has made a commitment to mitigate the susceptibility of landlocked nations, aiming to facilitate commerce and enhance their access to global markets while decreasing associated costs. It attempts to fulfil the transit requirements of landlocked countries in the region, positioning itself as a developing transit country alongside other transit countries in the region.[93]

The significance of corridors in facilitating transportation routes within the Persian Gulf, the Gulf of Oman, the Indian Ocean, and the Caspian Sea has gained more prominence. The following corridors now play a crucial role in enabling the transit of commodities from their point of origin to the intended destinations of landlocked countries within the region:

(a) The INSTC: Iran is a key participant in the INSTC, a multimodal transport corridor that connects India, Russia, Iran, and Central Asia.

(b) The Ashgabat Agreement: Iran is a signatory to the Ashgabat Agreement, which aims to create a new transport and transit corridor linking the Central Asia and the Persian Gulf.
(c) The Persian Gulf-Black Sea Transport Corridor: Iran is also involved in the project, which connects Iran, Armenia, Georgia, and Greece. The corridor is expected to improve connectivity and trade between the countries involved.
(d) Chabahar Port: Iran has invested heavily in the development of Chabahar Port, which is strategically located on the Gulf of Oman. The port is expected to become a major hub for trade between Iran, India, and Central Asia.
(e) Development of the Port of Bandar Abbas: The Port of Bandar Abbas is a major port on the Persian Gulf. The Iranian government is investing in the development of the port to make it a major hub for trade between Iran and other Persian Gulf countries (Table 3.1).

Table 3.1: Connectivity Initiatives in the Caspian Sea Region

Country	Land	Sea
Azerbaijan	East-West Transport Corridor (TITR), North-South Transport Corridor, Baku-Tbilisi-Kars railway (BTK), Astara–Astara railway, Qazvin–Rasht–Astara railway	Trans-Caspian International Transport Route (TITR)
Russia	International North-South Transport Corridor (INSTC), Greater Eurasian Partnership (GEP)	International North-South Transport Corridor (INSTC)
Kazakhstan	Nurly Zhol Infrastructure Development Program, Trans-Caspian International Transport Route (TITR), Western Europe-Western China International Transit Corridor	Development of the Port of Aktau
Turkmenistan	International North-South Transport Corridor (INSTC), Ashgabat Agreement, Lapis Lazuli Corridor	Turkmenbashi International Seaport
Iran	International North-South Transport Corridor (INSTC), Ashgabat Agreement, Persian Gulf-Black Sea Transport Corridor	Chabahar Port, Development of the Port of Bandar Abbas

Source: Composed by the author.

The post-Soviet dissolution period witnessed the proliferation of several initiatives aimed at establishing transit corridors to link the South Caucasus and Central Asia countries. The signing of an agreement on 'Cooperation in the Field of Transport' by the Caspian Sea countries in 2018 is one such example of cooperation. Article 2 of the agreement emphasised that the purpose is to foster collaboration among the Caspian Sea countries to establish and enhance the Caspian Sea region as a prominent global hub for transportation and logistics. This includes the development of a robust infrastructure and a significant level of engagement in international transport activities.[94]

Connectivity Approaches and Initiatives of External Actors in the Caspian Sea Region

Russia's special military operation in Ukraine in 2022 has altered the strategies of world powers regarding the Caspian Sea region, which will be examined in this section. Currently, various global powers, mainly Russia, the EU, the U.S., and China, are driving many modern networking efforts. The West—the U.S., in partnership with its European allies—seeks to strategically shift the dynamics of regional relationships by reducing Russian influence. Washington strategically uses contemporary global processes to increase its influence in the domain of Russia's traditional interests. This is accomplished by increased engagement with post-Soviet countries in a variety of areas, including commerce, economics, politics, humanitarian initiatives, and security.[95] The U.S. significantly increased engagement with the countries in the region after the Soviet dissolution and after the events of 9/11. However, in 2017, the U.S. shifted its focus away from the region. The National Security Strategy of 2017 did not mention the term 'Caspian', and little emphasis was laid on Central Asia, with just a single phrase dedicated to counterterrorism in the region.[96] The U.S. lacks a coherent and coordinated strategy for increasing connectivity in the Caspian region. The geographical distance between the U.S. and the Caspian region and its minimal reliance on Caspian resources influence its attitude towards connectivity.

However, the U.S. considers the Caspian region strategically important for two interconnected reasons: first, the Caspian region is an important energy source for the U.S.' allies in Europe because of its potential to reduce Europe's dependency on Russian fossil fuels while also improving energy security in Europe. In this regard, the U.S. is willing to assist Central Asian and European countries in improving their ability to withstand and counter Russia's strategic energy tactics.[97] For instance, the U.S. National Security Strategy of 2022 reiterates its aim to "reduce Europe's dependence on Russian fossil fuels" and "strengthen European energy security."[98] Second, there is fierce competition for control in the region. Given the significant involvement of Russia and China in this region, the U.S. seeks to impede these countries from further strengthening their influence in the Caspian region. Considering the current surge in economic and security ties among Russia, China, and some Central Asian countries, the U.S. seeks to hinder or offset these alliances to the greatest extent possible.[99]

The European strategy, known as the Global Gateway-2021, focused on addressing difficulties within the present geopolitical landscape via the development of infrastructural solutions. The focal points of this framework include five key policy drivers, namely, digital, climate and energy, transport, health, and education and research. With regards to connectivity in the Caspian region, the European Union Strategy on Central Asia-2019 seeks to enhance the region's connectivity by expanding upon the existing Global Gateway strategic framework.[100] In 2007, the EU implemented its first strategy for Central Asia with the intention of addressing multiple objectives. However, several commentators expressed disapproval towards the union for allocating its resources too widely and for treating Central Asia as a unified area rather than recognising the distinct requirements of individual nations. The 2019 plan, named 'New Opportunities for a Stronger Partnership', considered these lessons and included three main areas of focus: resilience, prosperity, and regional collaboration.[101]

In recent years, there has been an increasing level of engagement by the EU in the Caspian Sea region. One of the primary motivations is to strengthen partnership with Central Asia in pursuit of Brussels' geoeconomic aspirations to enhance Euro-Asian connectivity. This entails the development of both physical and non-physical infrastructure that facilitates the unrestricted movement of commodities, people, and services. The EU has actively engaged in the domain of connectivity within the region. The establishment of energy and transport linkages between the two areas was identified as a priority in the 2007 Central Asia Strategy by the EU.[102] These two areas were reiterated by the EU foreign policy chief, Josep Borrell, in November 2022, when he said, "Connectivity is going to be the key word for the future."[103] This emphasis aligns with the EU's Global Gateway foreign policy strategy, which aims to enhance digital, energy, and transportation linkages. It is important to note that the EU's pursuit of alternative energy sources is a fundamental aspect of its involvement in the Caspian region. Amidst the ongoing military operation in Ukraine, the importance of the Caspian region for Europe has increased significantly. The EU and littoral countries' European Union-Central Asia Investment Forum, held in January 2024, focused on sustainable transport corridors that link Europe and Central Asia. This event highlights Europe's strong desire for enhanced connectivity.[104]

Connectivity Initiatives:

(a) The Southern Corridor: This is a major transport corridor that connects the Caspian Sea region with Europe via the South Caucasus. The corridor includes a railway, a road, and several oil and gas pipelines. The U.S. has been a strong supporter of the Southern Corridor, and it has been seen to reduce reliance on Russia for energy and transportation.

(b) The Transport Corridor Europe-Caucasus-Asia (TRACECA): This is a major transport corridor that connects Europe with Central Asia via the Caucasus. The corridor includes a railway, a road, and a number of maritime routes. The EU has been a major supporter of TRACECA, providing funding for a number of projects along the corridor.

In China, the concept of connectivity is seen through the prism of the famous adage, 'Better roads lead to better life.'[105] The Silk Road Economic Belt and the 21st Century Maritime Silk Road, which are today labelled as China's Belt and Road Initiative (BRI), aim to promote stronger ties among relevant nations to foster a harmonious and peaceful coexistence. At the beginning of Xi's administration, connectivity was not designated as the core principle of Chinese foreign policy. In his first addresses on the Belt and Road Initiative in Kazakhstan and Indonesia in 2013, Xi did not make any reference to connectivity.[106] The aim of the project was to provide new infrastructure and stimulate the rejuvenation and expansion of commerce and economic development across Asia and other regions. The initiative originally prioritised energy and infrastructure but then broadened its scope.[107] Nevertheless, connectivity has been the central focus of China's rhetoric on the BRI and its foreign policy. The inclusion of the Belt and Road Initiative (BRI) in the Chinese constitution underscores the importance of connectivity to national interests.

Connectivity Initiatives:

(a) China-Kazakhstan Railway: This transnational railway line connects China's western regions with Kazakhstan, spanning over 2,700 kilometres. It is a crucial component of the BRI and has significantly enhanced trade and transportation links between the two countries.

(b) China-Central Asia Gas Pipeline: This massive natural gas pipeline stretches from Turkmenistan through Uzbekistan and Kazakhstan before reaching China. It plays a vital role in transporting natural gas from Central Asia to China, meeting the latter's growing energy demands.

(c) China-Kazakhstan-Turkmenistan-Iran corridor: This project aims to facilitate the rapid movement of goods from China's east coast to the Persian Gulf and Middle East markets.

(d) Baku-Tbilisi-Kars Railway: This railway line connects Baku (Azerbaijan), Tbilisi (Georgia), and Kars (Turkey), providing an alternative route for transporting goods between Europe and Asia. Beijing has actively participated in the project.

(e) The Trans-Caspian International Transport Route (TITR): The corridor links China and the Europe through Central Asia, the Caucasus, Turkey, and Eastern Europe.

To conclude, in recent years, the Caspian littoral countries have been actively involved in initiatives to develop and facilitate intra-regional connectivity. Leaders are reaching out actively to non-regional actors to strengthen engagements on connectivity. For example, in October 2023, Mohammad Mokhber, the first vice president of Iran, expressed willingness to establish a transit corridor to connect the member states of the SCO. In a similar vein, Turkmenistan and Azerbaijan have expressed their readiness to augment the number of goods transported over the CASCA+ (Central Asia, South Caucasus, and Anatolia) multimodal transport route, as well as the Trans-Caspian International Transport Corridor. This proliferation of connectivity corridors serves as tangible proof of regional cooperation. As Russia is now strategically shifting its focus towards Asia due to the imposition of Western sanctions, there are chances of an increase in corridor cooperation among the littoral states. At the same time, the countries in the region also recognised Russia's shift as an opportunity to implement and strengthen their transit initiatives. It is possible that the situation will result in outcomes that are advantageous to all of the Caspian littoral countries.

Assessing Connectivity Initiatives in the Caspian Sea Region: Cooperation or Competition?

The paper authored by Stuart Coles et al., titled "Seven ways Russia's war on Ukraine has altered the world", elucidates seven specific ways in which Russia's military operation has brought about changes on a global scale. The areas of focus include realignment, security, nuclear weapons, energy and food, international law, Russia, and Ukraine.[108] Energy is highlighted as one of the seven areas that has been considerably changed. It confirms that the crisis has compelled Europe to seek alternative energy sources, while Russia has begun to focus on the East. However, the paper failed to recognise the importance of connectivity corridors in the Eurasian region amidst the ongoing conflict in Ukraine. The importance of connectivity corridors is seen in Russian President Putin's strong advocacy for the INSTC as the primary route for connectivity during the 6th Caspian Sea Summit.

With the crisis in Ukraine now in its third year and not a hint of resolution in sight, the prolonged dispute has brought forth difficulties and possibilities for the Caspian Sea littoral states. One of the challenges that Caspian countries have faced because of the conflict is escalating inflation and economic pressures. On the other hand, the breakdown in economic relations between Russia and the Western countries, along with the strategic positioning of the Caspian states, has emphasised the significance of these countries in promoting connectivity initiatives across Eurasia. This is particularly relevant in crucial sectors, such as energy and transportation.

Russia: Following Russia's special military operation in Ukraine, Moscow actively sought other trade partners due to the loss of access to European markets. In 2022, Russia saw a 50 per cent reduction in imports from Europe, while Europe's imports from Russia witnessed an even more significant decline. The global community has placed sanctions on Russia because of the conflict, thereby isolating Moscow from international trade routes for containerised freight. Prominent shipping companies have ceased operations in Russia and are no longer accepting reservations for ports. Consequently, Russia has experienced a state of isolation from international trade routes, resulting in a near cessation of cargo operations at its ports.[109] Similarly, the EU, the United Kingdom (UK), and the U.S. enforced sanctions on the Russian railway that have hindered Moscow's ability to expand. Therefore, for Moscow, the other four countries in the Caspian region serve to alleviate its economic load. President Putin's endorsement of a US$ 1.7 billion deal in May 2023 to finance the construction of a railway line that would link Iran and Azerbaijan, serving as a crucial component of the North-South Corridor, is one such example.[110]

Kazakhstan: In light of the current geopolitical situation in Ukraine, Kazakhstan is proactively pursuing new transportation routes to improve cross-border cooperation. The heightened regionalisation processes in Central Asia have led to a surge in commerce among the countries. The establishment of the Central Asia International Centre for Cross-Border Cooperation on the Kazakhstan-Uzbekistan border, along with the Kyrgyz-Kazakh industrial, commerce, and logistics complex at the Ak-Tilek and Karasu crossings, was a crucial measure taken in this direction.[111] As of now, Kazakhstan accounts for 60 per cent of the gross domestic product (GDP) of Central Asia and attracts 70 per cent of the Foreign Direct Investment (FDI) in the region. The Caspian Sea ports in Kazakhstan have achieved an unprecedented level of trade activity during the first half of 2022. For instance, according to Kazakhstan's Statistics Committee, the transportation of goods via domestic water transport infrastructure increased to US$ 0.97 million, which is more than five times the turnover compared to the same period in 2021. In June 2022, the Kazakhstan-Turkmenistan-Iran-Türkiye Corridor established a new connectivity initiative as the first goods train from Kazakhstan reached Iran en route to Türkiye and Europe, which shows growing connectivity amidst the conflict.[112] Likewise, significant progress has been made with regard to the Middle Corridor route (a.k.a. the Trans-Caspian International Transport Route) since February 22, 2022. Last year, cargo transportation through the Middle Corridor climbed 88 per cent, reaching 2 million tons by 2023.[113]

Turkmenistan: In the 5th Consultative Meeting of Heads of States of Central Asia on September 14, 2023, President Berdimuhamedow of Turkmenistan suggested the creation of a unified transport and logistics platform for Central Asia. Following the 5th Consultative Meeting, the foreign ministers of the Central Asian governments signed two new agreements, one of which was the 'Agreement on strengthening the connectivity of land transport in Central Asia', which underlined the increasing importance of intra-Caspian connectivity for Ashgabat. According to Berdimuhamedow, transport plays a crucial role in the ongoing negotiations among the littoral countries, and he saw the current circumstances as an opportune moment to enhance collaboration in this field, considering the advantages for both freight and passenger movement among the Central Asian republics. Ashgabat, with its abundant deposits of fossil fuel—natural gas—is actively pursuing more advantageous transportation links between the South Caucasus and Central Asia. Within the framework of the aforesaid agreement, the BTK railway aligns well with the strategic objectives of Turkmenistan to expand its presence in international markets.

Azerbaijan: In the case of Azerbaijan, its foreign policy advisor to the President, Hikmet Hajiyev, stated that Baku's geopolitics involve a multifaceted approach to foreign policy. It has prioritised balance in its endeavour towards connectivity initiatives. Azerbaijan has played a proactive role in developing regional connectivity. The country has allocated resources towards the advancement of transport infrastructure, encompassing the construction of roadways, trains, and ports, with the aim of fostering collaboration and facilitating novel commercial prospects. The construction of transport and communication infrastructure in Azerbaijan, such as the Baku International Sea Trade Port and the Baku-Tbilisi-Kars Railway, serves as evidence of the same. In another significant decision in 2022, Baku signed an agreement with Tehran that aimed to create new transport networks that will connect the western region of Azerbaijan's main territory with its Nakhchivan Autonomous Republic via northwest Iran.[114]

Iran: The conflict in Ukraine has prompted Iran to engage in unprecedented levels of connectivity and cooperation. For example, the INSTC is a major connectivity project through which Tehran aims to establish itself as a pivotal link between the Economic Cooperation Organization (ECO), ASEAN, EAEU, GCC, India, Central Asia, and West Asia regions. Further, the INSTC, together with the Ashgabat Agreement of 2018 (which involves India, Oman, Iran, Turkmenistan, Uzbekistan, and Kazakhstan), has the potential to streamline the movement of goods between Central Asia and West Asia. Since the beginning of the Russia-Ukraine conflict, the strategic significance of the INSTC has gained relevance for Moscow and Tehran, as both countries are now subject to economic restrictions and wish to enhance the efficiency of the corridor. As Tehran joins the SCO and BRICS, Iran's intra-regional connectivity efforts are expected to intensify.

Overall, after facing sanctions from the West, Russia has been compelled to seek new economic partners. As a result, trade with the neighbouring Caspian states has expanded. The conflict has underlined the Caspian republics' relevance in pushing connectivity initiatives across Eurasia. This is especially important in critical industries like energy and transportation. Correspondingly, sanctions on Russia have opened new commercial prospects for Caspian countries, such as Azerbaijan and Kazakhstan, as these countries can now export their goods to Russia at a time when they are in high demand. The conflict has led to increased collaboration among the Caspian republics.

Connectivity initiatives in the Caspian Sea region are a complex interplay of cooperation and competition. While there is a shared desire to enhance regional connectivity, there are also significant geopolitical and economic rivalries that shape the development of these initiatives. The connectivity initiatives in the region—north-south and east-west— converge in terms of their reach and sophistication. Therefore, these developments cannot be construed as one initiative gaining an edge in a competitive environment, and hence, are completely a matter of geopolitical speculation.

Energy Pipeline Politics in the Caspian Sea Region

Energy pipelines are one of several facets of energy security that remain a top concern for all economies; therefore, pipeline politics over how to exert control over energy routes remains a competitive issue. The term 'pipeline politics' can be defined broadly as "a process where producers, transit countries, and importers engage in strategic competition to increase their energy security based on their respective interests and priorities."[115] Based on this conceptual framework, this section will attempt to address the primary question: How are regional and non-regional actors attempting to dominate Caspian resource export routes?

Historically, oil and gas producers in the Caspian lacked export infrastructure. The main reason was linked to Moscow's position that the Caspian Sea was an internal lake of the USSR with no necessity to link the region to international markets. It was only after World War II that Moscow laid further emphasis on the exploration and production of Caspian oil.

During the post-Soviet period, Caspian littoral governments took a variety of approaches to international participation. Azerbaijan and Kazakhstan, for example, were able to enhance oil export capacity by building the CPC and BTC pipelines.[116]

The Caspian region witnessed intense geopolitical rivalry because of its oil and gas reserves. Hooshang Amirahmadi observed and attributed the following reasons for rivalry: first, huge hydrocarbon reserves claim over these resources by littoral countries; second, route options for pipelines; third, ethnic strife; and fourth, the environment. Here, the struggle over pipeline routes for hydrocarbon transportation is identified as one of the key reasons for regional rivalry. Securing control over the routes for hydrocarbon transportation has been a critical aspect of the struggle for supremacy in the Caspian region. Since the late 1990s, the U.S. and the EU have supported the Nabucco project. Despite political support from the West, the Nabucco project was unable to take off because of matters concerning financial feasibility and limited supply commitments from the Caspian littoral states.

For years, Moscow maintained a monopoly over export routes for Caucasus-Central Asian hydrocarbons, as it inherited the Soviet-built pipeline network infrastructure. For Moscow, the U.S.-Europe strategy represents a threat to its traditional position in the Caspian region. To maintain its control in the Caspian region, it is important for Russia to ensure that pipelines pass through its territory. Though oil and gas production has increased year after year, the growth of export capacity has been sluggish. Regional and non-regional countries desire control of the Caspian oil resources and transit routes in order to expand their position in the region, minimise reliance on the Persian Gulf, and ensure economic prosperity.[117]

The spatial distribution of oil and gas reserves across the region necessitates the construction of pipelines. Considering Caspian resources' geographical limitations or remoteness, several transportation routes are identified by experts. Hooshang Amirahmadi distinguished transport routes in four directions: Northern routes, Southern routes, Western routes, and Eastern routes.[118] All five Caspian littoral and non-regional governments endorse and promote different routes in accordance with their respective interests.

Northern routes: The post-Soviet period witnessed a rise in competition in the region over the export routes. The Russian approach towards pipelines in the Caspian was shaped in 1991, when the CIS was formed. Moscow, in order to control the exports from the Caspian region, insisted that the littoral states supply hydrocarbons to Russia or via its territory. In the first decade after the Soviet dissolution, Moscow was able to consolidate its position as the main transit country because the new littoral states did not have their own energy pipeline network. Moscow has earlier used the unresolved international legal status of the Caspian Sea to guard its interest by preventing the littoral countries from going ahead with unilateral decisions on hydrocarbon pipelines. Russia signed an agreement with Kazakhstan in1992 to establish the Caspian Pipeline Consortium (CPC) to transport Caspian oil from the Tengiz field to the Russian Black Sea port of Novorossiysk. Another important route is the Atyrau-Samara oil pipeline. This line was developed to deliver oil from Kazakhstan to the Russian ports of Novorossiysk, Primorsk, and Ust-Luga. The Russian state-owned gas company, Gazprom, has played an important role in fulfilling Moscow's ambitions in the Caspian region. In the past, there are instances where Gazprom purchased gas from Caspian and Central Asian countries at low prices to sell at a higher price in Europe.

Later on, it has become increasingly difficult for Moscow to continue to maintain its grip on the region. For Moscow, the success of the Baku-Tbilisi-Ceyhan oil pipeline and the South Caucasus Pipeline is a contentious issue. To ensure its presence, Moscow has employed legal and commercial means: first, ensuring Russian firms' participation in developing the region's natural resources, by allowing regional oil and gas exporters to continue with Russian pipelines; second, minimising the involvement of western companies in joint ventures in the region; third, intimidating prospective foreign competitors by announcing alternative pipelines favourable to Moscow; and fourth, promoting bilateral energy ties with countries in the region under the umbrella of multilateral security.[119]

Russia promotes the Northern route/Russian route to protect its interests. It claims that the northern routes offer the most affordable and technically possible solution for exporting oil and gas from the region. These lines go from Baku (Azerbaijan) to Novorossiysk, Atyrau (Kazakhstan) to Samara (Russia), and from the Tengiz oil field (Kazakhstan) to Novorossiysk.[120] Presently, the northern routes comprise the Caspian Oil Pipeline Consortium (CPC) (Map 3.3), the Uzen-Atyrau-Samara oil pipeline, the Baku-Novorossiysk oil Pipeline (also known as the Northern Route Export Pipeline and Northern Early Oil Pipeline), and the Central Asia-Center gas pipeline system (CAC) (Map 3.4).

Map 3.3: Caspian Oil Pipeline Consortium

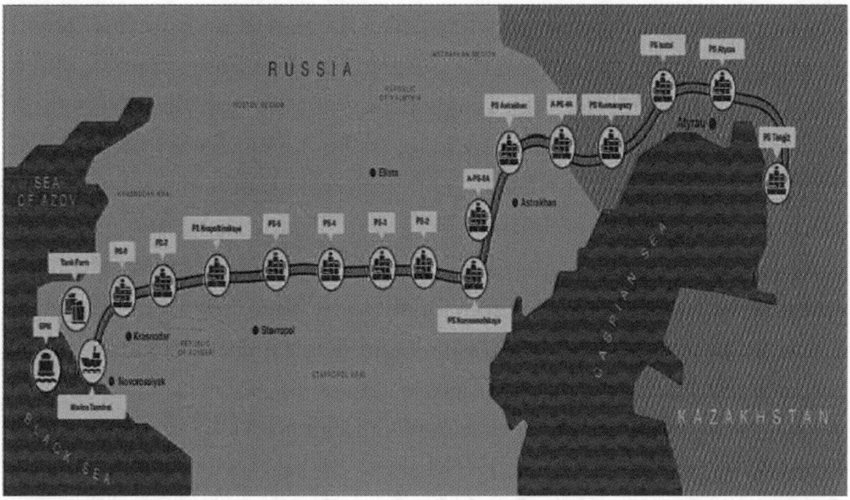

Source: Justyna Misiągiewicz, *Geopolitics and Energy Security Policies in the Caspian Region*, (Leiden: Koninklijke Brill BV, 2024).

Western routes: The routes in the western direction focuses on European markets. The history of western routes can be traced back to the building of the Baku-Batumi pipeline in 1907, followed by pipelines constructed during the Soviet period. After the Soviet dissolution, Azerbaijan saw foreign investments in export routes as an opportunity to become independent of Russian influence.

Map 3.4: Northern Routes

Source: United States Energy Information Administration Data, 2013.

Further, the importance of western routes can be examined through the lens of the U.S. and the EU approaches. The U.S. is not interested in Caspian and Central Asian energy because it needs a fresh source of imports. Washington already has strong relationships with other suppliers, and with the exception of Russia, none of the Caspian states were among Washington's top five import partners in 2021. The U.S. is mainly interested in stopping Russia from monopolising energy supplies and manipulating prices, as well as preventing Iran from profiting. As a result, the U.S.' backing for the Baku-Tbilisi-Ceyhan oil pipeline is unequivocal.[121]

When the Soviet Union disintegrated, the EU prioritised political collaboration alongside cooperation in the petroleum sector and building of pipelines. During the Cold War and after 1991, Russian exports met Europe's demand for oil and gas. However, with the discovery of hydrocarbon riches in the littoral countries and energy disputes between Ukraine and Russia, the dynamics have shifted dramatically. The EU began extending active support for the energy corridor going westward as it wants hydrocarbon transit routes to Europe from Azerbaijan.

During the 2000s, the EU focused on attaining energy security as the main objective of its strategy in the Caspian region. The goal was to connect the littoral states' gas markets to the European internal energy market. With increasing amounts of hydrocarbon extraction in the region, the EU planned to diversify energy lines.[122] It sees the TCP as a potential energy line, along with the ongoing Southern Gas Corridor. As a result, the U.S., the EU, and Azerbaijan favour the Western route, which intends to transfer oil and gas from the Caspian region while avoiding Russian and Iranian territory. The western route includes the Baku-Tbilisi-Ceyhan (BTC) oil pipeline and the South Caucasus (Baku-Tbilisi-Erzurum) gas pipeline, and hopes are pinned on the TCP from Kazakhstan and Turkmenistan to Azerbaijan[123] (Map 3.5).

Map 3.5: Western Routes

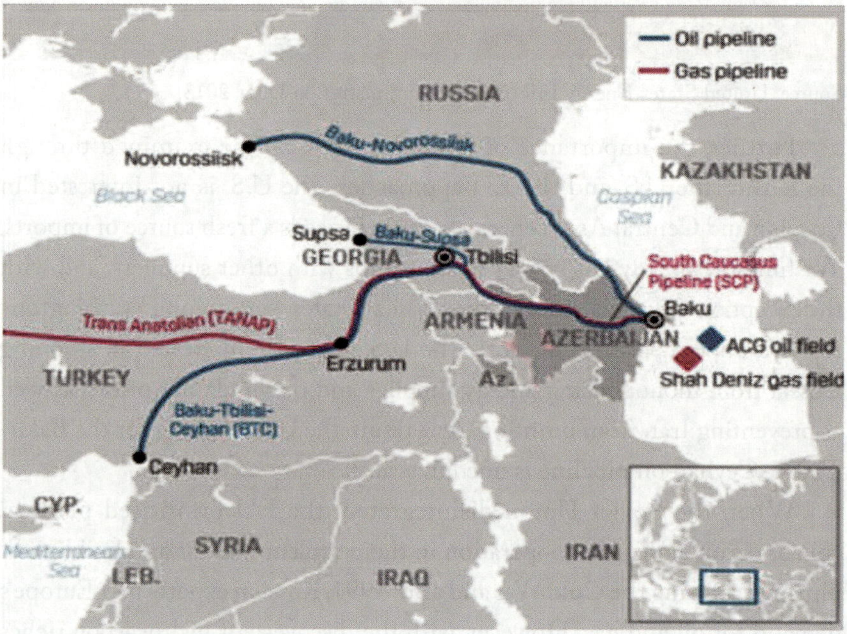

Source: Seymur Mammadov, "Azerbaijan doubles down by expanding gas exports to Europe", *bne IntelliNews*, 2024.

Eastern Routes: The eastern direction has gained significance for both Kazakhstan and Turkmenistan, as well as for China. China began to engage in Caspian oil and gas production as a result of its explosive increase in oil and gas consumption. Kazakhstan was the first Caspian littoral country to provide China with hydrocarbons. The latter half of the 2000s, witnessed the development of specific trends in China's energy policy. First, China-Kazakhstan ties advanced to the level of strategic cooperation. Second, Kazakhstan became the Chinese economy's raw material supplier. Third, China actively participated in the 'oil and gas game' among geopolitical actors in the Caspian and Central Asian regions. Finally, China provided financial aid to Central Asian countries. Beijing did not limit itself to hydrocarbon delivery contracts, but instead, began pursuing agreements on collaboration in the development and shared ownership of hydrocarbon resources. Through these agreements, Beijing ensured it would safeguard itself from abrupt swings in world energy costs and diversify its energy supplies. It has signed oil transportation agreements with Kazakhstan, for which Beijing built the Kazakhstan-China pipeline, and to import gas, China built the Central Asia-China (CAC) pipeline, which connects China with Turkmenistan, Uzbekistan, and Kazakhstan in Central Asia.[124]

China favours the Eastern route/Chinese route due to its proximity to hydrocarbon deposits in the Caspian countries of Kazakhstan and Turkmenistan. The route now includes the Central Asia-China Gas Pipeline, which transports gas from Amu Darya (Turkmenistan) via Uzbekistan and Kazakhstan before terminating in Xinjiang (China), and the Kazakhstan-China oil pipeline, which begins in Atyrau (Kazakhstan) and ends in Xinjiang (China) (Map 3.6).

Southern Routes: Iran advocates the Southern route/Iranian direction as energy lines would go through Iranian territory and terminate on the Persian Gulf. The route is economically beneficial for both exporter and importer countries because it provides the shortest, cheapest, and fastest routes for the transport of hydrocarbon resources. However, this route is opposed by the U.S., and since 1995, American companies are prohibited from engaging in business activities with Tehran. Furthermore, as the Iran

Sanctions Act (ISA) imposes sanctions on non-US companies engaging with Iran's oil and gas sector, it has discouraged the Caspian states from doing business with Iran.[125] Iran's geographical access, swap arrangements with other littoral states, and low transit fees provide an advantage for the Caspian littoral states to export their hydrocarbons. Most importantly, Iran has extensive export facilities in the Persian Gulf region and an established domestic energy transit network. Both Neka and Bandar-e-Anzali ports in the Caspian Sea are well equipped to receive swapped oil by sea[126] (Map 3.7).

Map 3.6: Eastern Routes

Source: Jack Farchy and James Kynge, "Connecting Central Asia", *Financial Times,* 2016.

Map 3.7: Southern Routes

Source: Oil and Gas 360^0, 2016.

While the western route has been the more successful option so far in terms of volume and reliability, India cannot ignore the urgency to explore the potential of the southern route for energy transportation.

Ongoing Conflict in Ukraine and Regional Energy Dynamics

After the Soviet dissolution, the Caspian littoral states of Kazakhstan, Azerbaijan, and Turkmenistan adopted multivector foreign policies, which have become a guiding principle of their foreign, security, and economic relations. All littoral countries have adopted their versions of the multivector policy as they aim to balance Moscow's influence by establishing relations based on national interest. Kazakhstan was the first state to pursue a multivector policy. Along similar lines, Turkmenistan adopted a stance of strict neutrality and refused to join any sort of alliance. Azerbaijan refrains from joining both the Collective Security Treaty Organization (CSTO) and the North Atlantic Treaty Organization (NATO) and engages in many regional cooperation frameworks.[127] In simple terms, multivector foreign policy is observed as "developing relations that are based on non-ideological and pragmatic foundations, which are shaped by the interplay of external and domestic dynamics, to foster short or long-term benefits."[128] Iran, since 2021 onward, has prioritised ties with non-Western powers—Russia and China.

Amidst the ongoing conflict, Azerbaijan initially provided humanitarian aid and sent over 100 tonnes of fuel to ambulances and other emergency service vehicles in Kyiv. Baku abstained from voting in the United Nations General Assembly resolution that condemned Moscow's invasion of Ukraine and demanded immediate withdrawal. Likewise, it abstained from the UNGA resolution to suspend Russia from the United Nations Human Rights Council. It has not recognised the sovereignty of Donetsk and Luhansk as a result of a joint declaration signed with Kyiv in January 2022. Baku's silence on the situation can be viewed as a strategy to avoid upsetting Moscow while simultaneously pursuing its energy ties with Western powers and the Caspian states.

Kazakhstan has urged for a peaceful settlement of the conflict and offered to mediate talks in March 2022. It attributed the failure to implement the Minsk agreements as the cause for the military operation. In an article written by President Tokayev, titled "Turbulence Across Eurasia Will Not Slow Kazakhstan's Progress", he highlighted Kazakhstan and Russia's special relations of cooperation and traditional relations with Ukraine. On the present conflict, he wrote, "…we hope for a swift and just resolution of the conflict in accordance with the UN Charter."[129] Almaty has been cautious not to condemn Moscow. At the same time, it has upheld the inviolability of international borders and declined to recognise the self-proclaimed independence of Donetsk and Luhansk.

Turkmenistan chose to remain silent, as its position is directly aligned with its official stand of 'permanent neutrality'. Despite its neutrality at the international level, it has been reported that internally, at the domestic level, officials are vilifying the West and whitewashing Moscow's image.[130] Finally, given Iran's history of distrust with the West, the former has been very vocal about the conflict. Supreme Leader Ayatollah Ali Khamenei held the U.S. and Western powers responsible, as he said, "The root of the crisis in Ukraine are the U.S. policies that create crisis, and Ukraine is one victim of these policies."[131] Further, during Putin's visit to Tehran, Khamenei said, "...if you had not taken the helm, the other side would have done so and initiated a war" and referred to NATO as a 'dangerous entity'. Similar thoughts were shared by President Raisi when he said, "The expansion of NATO is a serious threat to the stability and security of independent countries in different regions."[132] Tehran abstained from voting in the UNGA resolution that condemned Moscow's invasion and demanded immediate withdrawal. Similarly, it voted against the UNGA resolution to suspend Russia from the UN Human Rights Council.

The Caspian littoral states are treading carefully to pursue their interests. None of them have condemned Russia or supported its military operation in Ukraine. They have either abstained or not voted on the UNGA resolutions. As the littoral states are either members of Moscow-led alliances or have a strong bilateral partnership with it, it can be inferred that the littoral states would take Russian interests into their foreign policy considerations henceforth. For instance, Kazakhstan is a member of the CSTO and the Eurasian Economic Union; Turkmenistan and Azerbaijan are members of the CIS; and Moscow and Tehran have strong military cooperation. As they have maintained their neutrality, it is clear that there is "... no prospect for a collective démarche"[133] from riparian states.

For Caspian states, Russia has been and remains their closest partner and ally, and they cannot disregard decades of multilevel cooperation with it when formulating their positions. This is demonstrated by the aforementioned political postures. Compared to political positioning, things are dynamic when it comes to energy.

In the recent past, Azerbaijan has decided to double its gas supply to Europe. In July 2022, during her visit to Azerbaijan, European Commission President Ursula von der Leyen signed a MoU on a 'Strategic Partnership in the Energy Field' that would double Baku's gas supply to Europe by 2027. Subsequently, in October 2022, President Aliyev inaugurated the Greece-Bulgaria Interconnector (IGB) gas pipeline that will allow the supply of natural gas from the Caspian Sea to Bulgarian markets.

When it comes to oil exports, Kazakhstan relies on the Caspian Pipeline Consortium (that passes through Russia) for 53 million tonnes of oil exports out of 68 million tonnes of total oil exports. In October 2022, Kazakhstan announced to increase trans-Caspian shipments tenfold to 20 million tonnes in the years to come. This is a clear sign of Kazakhstan's move towards diversification, as highlighted by Prime Minister Smailov: "We have developed a roadmap to diversify (oil) exports … work is underway to expand and increase oil export capabilities in all directions."[134] The reason for diversification is not Russia but rather a technical one. For instance, in mid-2022, Kazakh oil supplies were disrupted several times due to production suspensions and repairs. The Novorossiysk terminal broke down on several occasions, which hindered the transportation of oil. Under sanctions, Russia is currently facing inconveniences related to repairs, which, in turn, have given rise to the need to diversify supply.[135]

In terms of natural gas, Turkmenistan is one of the top four countries. Its reserves are estimated to be around 13.6 trillion cubic metres.[136] In October, Turkmenistan announced plans to double gas exports to China and increase gas exports to 65 billion cubic metres per year after building a fourth gas pipeline between the two states,[137] consequently making China the largest buyer of Turkmen gas. In a recent agreement between Azerbaijan and Turkmenistan, the latter emphasised the TCP bypassing Russian territory.

In June, Iran and Azerbaijan signed an agreement to increase the volume of gas swaps between Azerbaijan and Turkmenistan. As per an earlier gas swap agreement signed amongst three littoral states in November 2021, Iran delivers 1.5 to 2 billion cubic metres of Turkmen gas to Azerbaijan. From January 2022 onwards, the supply volume rose to 5-6 million cubic metres of gas per day. Iran receives Turkmen gas and then delivers an equal amount to Azerbaijan.[138] Amidst the ongoing conflict, Iran also signed a US$ 40 billion energy cooperation deal with Russia in July. This rising energy cooperation was endorsed by Kazem Jalali, Iranian Ambassador to Russia, when he said, "Iran welcomes foreign investors, especially from friendly countries such as Russia, to implement relevant projects."[139] Finally, the Caspian states met for the 2nd Caspian Economic Forum on October 5–6, 2022, and the key focus was on increasing energy ties. The riparian countries emphasised increasing oil and gas swaps on the shores of the Caspian Sea, settlements based on national currencies, and cooperation in the energy field to counter sanctions.[140]

On the energy front, the littoral states will benefit from the increasing attention of Russian and European energy companies as they are looking for new investment avenues. Amidst the Ukrainian conflict, the littoral states are increasing regional cooperation amongst themselves and endeavouring to access alternative markets for their oil and gas. For instance, Russia is looking toward east and south Asian markets; Azerbaijan, Kazakhstan, and Turkmenistan are looking toward European markets; and Iran is hoping to become a regional hub for energy.

Forecasting Geopolitical Competition in the Caspian Region

This section is an attempt to forecast Caspian geopolitics in light of emerging realities in Eurasia. As a result of Russia's incorporation of the Crimean Peninsula in 2014, the transit routes between Ukraine and other post-Soviet states were disrupted. The transit blockade of Ukraine by Moscow compelled the former to explore new routes for trade. Around the same period, sanctions were lifted against Iran as a result of the JCPOA. It permitted Iran (a Caspian littoral country) and Ukraine to forge ties. Both countries started taking interest in transport corridors, such as the South-West corridor created by India, Iran, Azerbaijan, Georgia, Ukraine, and Poland, and Ukraine took steps to become a member of the Trans-Caspian International Transport Route (TITR). It involves the development of trade and economic ties between China and the EU by transit through Caspian states, such as Kazakhstan and Azerbaijan. However, the events of February 2022 annulled all efforts toward the development of a transit corridor between the Caspian littoral states and Ukraine for the foreseeable future.

The most important question in the context of the ongoing Russian-Ukrainian conflict is the future of the Caspian region and the Caspian countries' relationship with Russia. At the moment, three events are intertwined in Eurasian geopolitics: (a) international sanctions imposed on Russia in response to its ongoing military operation in Ukraine; (b) international sanctions imposed on Iran due to its nuclear programme; and (c) Europe's growing interest in the Caspian region. With resentment growing against the US and Europe for their roles in the aforementioned incidents, three key regional players—Russia, Iran, and China—are likely to take an assertive attitude in reaction to the West's growing footing in the Caspian region.[141]

Previously, Russia prioritised enhancing its control in overseeing the production and transportation of energy from the region to international markets, while also seeking to restrict the impact of external actors like the US and the EU. Russia even saw China's rise in the Caspian as a challenge.[142] However, the situation has drastically changed in the recent past. U.S. House Speaker Nancy Pelosi's visit to Taiwan has left China fuming. This incident occurred amidst Russia's 'special military operation' in Ukraine. As a result of these incidents, Russia and China have turned to one another for support. For instance, President Xi Jinping stressed his willingness to collaborate with Russia in order to achieve the status of major global powers. Putin reiterated Moscow's support for China's claims over Taiwan.[143] Sharing a common anti-West position, China and Russia would not hesitate to confront Western powers in the Caspian region.

The SGC's success has sparked a renewed interest in the TCP project. The heightened involvement of the EU in the area is expected to intensify the contentious issue of the TCP among the involved parties, namely, Russia and Iran. The EU endorses the TCP due to its objective of expanding the diversity of energy imports. In the past, the EU and the U.S. have shared a common approach in promoting the establishment of various energy transportation routes.[144] However, both Moscow and Tehran are not in favour. Moscow is wary of attempts to strengthen the energy exports of Caspian countries as it would undermine its dominance in the region. Russia's ongoing military operation is one illustration of how Russia will not tolerate outsiders' involvement in its 'near abroad'. Any endeavour toward fulfilling the project will push Moscow and Tehran to join hands. Both are already growing closer due to their opposition toward the West. It can be witnessed in the recent energy MoU, worth US$ 40 billion, signed between Russia's Gazprom and Iran's National Iranian Oil Company on July 19, 2022.[145] In a statement, the Supreme Leader, Seyed Ayatollah Ali Khamenei, noted Iran's position to end the war in Ukraine but simultaneously tagged the US and its allies as the root cause of the crisis. He said, "The U.S. has brought Ukraine to its current state."[146] Undoubtedly, the extensive sanctions imposed on Russia will deepen relations between Moscow and Tehran in the Caspian Sea region. In the last three decades, regional and external players have weaved a tangled web in the Caspian region. In days to come, the Caspian region will witness polarised geopolitical competition, and Russia, China, and Iran will enter into an entente.[147]

Assessment

The ownership and control of hydrocarbon resources in the Caspian region remain complex and dynamic issues due to the various ways these resources are governed and exploited across the region. Russia, in spite of adopting some liberalisation policies in its formative years, has witnessed a resurgence of state control with the oil and gas sector dominated by state-owned entities, such as Rosneft and Gazprom. Kazakhstan has adopted a balanced approach. It has allowed foreign investment while also ensuring state role through companies such as KazMunaiGas. Turkmenistan continues a highly centralised system with strong state control over the hydrocarbon sector. Though the country has allowed some foreign investment through production sharing agreements, it is now endeavouring to attract further foreign investments. The recently concluded Turkmen Energy Investment Forum (TEIF) 2024, aimed at attracting foreign investment in the country's energy sector, is one such example. As the Iranian Constitution forbids foreign ownership of Iran's natural resources, the country has relied on state-owned companies, such as the NIOC, to manage its hydrocarbon sector. Despite policy adjustments in recent years focused on attracting foreign investment, the international sanctions continue to discourage its energy sector. Finally, among all the Caspian states, Azerbaijan has been successful in employing production sharing agreements to attract foreign investment for its oil and gas sector. The role of the SOCAR validates the state's crucial role in various aspects of the industry.

The Caspian region has become a coliseum for global and regional economic and political interests, fuelling both, competition and cooperation. Russia, the U.S., China, and the EU will likely continue to compete for securing energy supplies and gaining political influence within the Caspian region. Further, the ongoing Russian military operations in Ukraine will have long-term political, economic, and security implications for the Caspian states. In the coming years, Russia will try to strengthen ties with the littoral countries, and the latter would be reluctant to antagonise Moscow. For example, Russia and Iran, as sanction-hit states, will converge on challenges related to the Caspian Sea. Likewise, the ongoing Ukraine conflict did not prevent Russia and Azerbaijan from signing the 'Declaration on Allied Cooperation'.

With the Caspian region emerging and developing as a centre for connectivity, the ongoing conflict in Ukraine has underscored the importance of rethinking connectivity initiatives in the region. This conflict has escalated cooperation among the littoral states and non-regional powers to diversify energy routes. In this context, the renewed importance of connectivity initiatives, such as INSTC, serves as an example of this change. Though all littoral states share a common goal of augmenting connectivity in the region, conflicting interests between major actors and among the littoral countries will shape the trajectory of current and projected initiatives.

Disclaimer: Parts of this chapter appeared as the author's articles in Air Power Journal, Vol. 19, No. 2, (April-June, 2024); and Defence and Diplomacy Journal, Vol. 12, No. 2, (January-March, 2023).

Notes

1. This paper employs both the U.S. Measuring System (e.g., barrels, million cubic feet) and the Indian Measuring System (e.g., metric tonnes, cubic metres) for oil and gas measurements. A conversion table between these units is provided in Appendix I.

2. "EU agrees deal with Azerbaijan to double gas exports by 2027", *Euronews,* July 19, 2022, https://www.euronews.com/my-europe/2022/07/18/von-der-leyen-heads-to-azerbaijan-to-secure-new-gas-import-deal. Accessed on September 20, 2022.
3. Dipanjan Roy Chaudhury, "Amid curbs, India-Russia trade via INSTC booms", *Economic Times,* August 17, 2022, https://economictimes.indiatimes.com/news/india/amid-curbs-india-russia-trade-via-instc-booms/articleshow/93603407.cms?from=mdr. Accessed on September 20, 2022.
4. Ilham Karimli, "Azerbaijan, Kazakhstan join forces to tap into Middle Corridor's potential", *Caspian News,* August 25, 2022, https://caspiannews.com/news-detail/azerbaijan-kazakhstan-join-forces-to-tap-into-middle-corridors-potential-2022-8-25-1/. Accessed on September 20, 2022.
5. Aybek Nurjanov, "Kazakh, Azerbaijan energy giants sign cooperation deal", *Caspian News,* August 26, 2022, https://caspiannews.com/news-detail/kazakh-azerbaijani-energy-giants-sign-cooperation-deal-2022-8-25-0/. Accessed on September 20, 2022.
6. Chris Kushlis and Ben Slay, "Economic overview of the Caspian region", Belfer Centre, November 30, 2016, https://www.belfercenter.org/publication/economic-overview-caspian-region. Accessed on September 20, 2022.
7. Karen Smith Stegen and Julia Kusznir, "Outcomes and strategies in the 'New Great Game': China and the Caspian states emerge as winners", *Journal of Eurasian Studies,* Vol. 6, No. 2, 2015, pp. 91-106.
8. Government of the Russian Federation, "Constitution of the Russian Federation", http://archive.government.ru/eng/gov/base/54.html. Accessed on October 01, 2022.
9. Jennifer Josefson and Alexandra Rotar, "Oil and gas regulation in the Russian Federation: Overview", Morgan, Lewis & Bokius LLP, April 01, 2021, https://uk.practicallaw.thomsonreuters.com/0-527-3028?transitionType=Default&contextData=(sc.Default)&firstPage=true#co_anchor_a656860. Accessed on October 01, 2022.
10. King & Spalding, "Russian oil and gas sector regulatory regime: Legislative overview", https://www.kslaw.com/attachments/000/006/245/original/Russian_Oil__Gas_Legislative_Overview.pdf?1535466606. Accessed on October 01, 2022.
11. "Transneft: Russian oil exports via its network down 6.5% in 2023", *Reuters,* January 10, 2024, https://www.reuters.com/markets/commodities/transneft-russian-oil-exports-via-its-network-down-65-2023-2024-01-10/. Accessed on March 30, 2024.
12. World Trade Organization, "Federal Law No. 147-FZ of August 17, 1995 on the Natural Monopolies", https://www.wto.org/english/thewto_e/acc_e/rus_e/wtaccrus48_leg_67.pdf. Accessed on October 01, 2022.
13. Ibid.
14. Anatole Boute, "Shaping the Eurasian Gas Market: The Geopolitics of Energy Market Regulation", *Geopolitics,* Vol. 28, No. 5, 2023, pp. 2042-2073.

15. ALRUD Law Firm, "Strategic Investments regime in Russia", https://www.alrud.com/upload/alrud-brochures/Strategic_Investments_regime_in_Russia.pdf. Accessed on October 1, 2022.
16. Tatiana Mitrova and Vitaly Yermakov, "Russia's energy strategy-2035: Struggling to remain relevant", December 2019, *Institut français des relations internationals, Russie.Nei.Reports,* 28, pp. 11-12.
17. Kurmangazy Talzhanov et al., "*Oil & Gas Laws and Regulations Kazakhstan 2024*", February 13, 2024, https://iclg.com/practice-areas/oil-and-gas-laws-and-regulations/kazakhstan#:~:text=The%20main%20regulatory%20legal%20act,gas%20are%20recognised%20as%20hydrocarbons. Accessed on October 5, 2022.
18. CIS Legislation, "Code of the Republic of Kazakhstan of December 27, 2017 No. 125-VI ZRK, About Subsoil and Subsurface Use", 27.12.2017, https://cis-legislation.com/document.fwx?rgn=102988. Accessed on October 1, 2022.
19. Talzhanov, n. 17.
20. Ibid.
21. Talzhanov, n. 16.; and Erin Hopkins and Luke L. Burns, "Comparative Guides: Oil and Gas", *Mondaq,* https://www.mondaq.com/Guides/Results/38?jurisdiction=1110&mode=all. Accessed on March 1, 2024.
22. Ramakrushna Pradhan, *Geopolitics of energy in Central Asia: India's position and policy,* (New York: Routledge, 2021).
23. U.S. Energy Information Administration, "Caspian Sea", https://www.eia.gov/international/analysis/regions-of-interest/Caspian_Sea. Accessed on October 1, 2022.
24. Erin Hopkins and Luke L. Burns, "Comparative Guides: Oil and Gas", *Mondaq,* https://www.mondaq.com/Guides/Results/38?jurisdiction=1110&mode=all. Accessed on March 1, 2024.
25. Kamil Valiyev and Rena Eminova, "Oil and gas regulation in Azerbaijan: Overview", Natural Resource Governance Institute, https://www.resourcedata.org/dataset/rgi-oil-and-gas-regulation-in-azerbaijan-overview/resource/6d6cc12e-73dd-43fb-8026-efb9c0b584f5. Accessed on October 5, 2022.
26. International Energy Agency, "Azerbaijan 2021: Energy Review Policy", https://iea.blob.core.windows.net/assets/49662c46-575f-4561-a541-5541f5342b07/Azerbaijan2021EnergyPolicyReview.pdf. Accessed on October 1, 2022.
27. Kamil Valiyev and Rena Eminova, n. 24.
28. U.S. International Trade Administration, "Azerbaijan: Energy", https://www.trade.gov/country-commercial-guides/azerbaijan-energy. Accessed on October 5, 2022.
29. International Energy Agency, n. 26.
30. Aykhan I Asadov, "Azerbaijan", in Christopher B Strong, eds., *The Oil and Gas Law Review (1st Edition),* (United Kingdom: Encompass Print Solutions, 2013).
31. U.S. Department of State, "2022 Investment Climate Statements: Turkmenistan", https://www.state.gov/reports/2022-investment-climate-statements/turkmenistan/#:~:text=In%20the%20energy%20sector%2C%20

Turkmenistan,in%20Turkmenistan%20is%20government%20owned. Accessed on October 5, 2022.

32. Ramakrushna Pradhan, n. 22.
33. Anahita Asgari Fard and Hosna Hasavinia, "Oil and Gas laws and regulations Iran 2024", February 12, 2024, https://iclg.com/practice-areas/oil-and-gas-laws-and-regulations/iran. Accessed on March 1, 2024.
34. Ibid.
35. Ibid.
36. Kali Robinson, "What Is the Iran Nuclear Deal?", Council on Foreign Relations, October 27, 2023, https://www.cfr.org/backgrounder/what-iran-nuclear-deal. Accessed on March 1, 2024.
37. U.S. Energy Information Administration, "Country analysis executive summary: Iran", November 2022, https://www.eia.gov/international/content/analysis/countries_long/Iran/pdf/iran_exe.pdf. Accessed on October 5, 2022.
38. Kamyar Mehdiyon, "Ownership of oil and gas resources in the Caspian Sea", *The American Journal of International Law,* Vol. 94, No. 1, 2000, pp. 179-189.
39. Ibid.
40. Ibid.
41. Abbas Maleki, "The politics of natural resources in the Caspian Sea: A new great game in an ancient world", in Harry Verhoeven, eds., *Environmental politics in the Middle East,* (London: C. Hurst & Co. Ltd, 2018).
42. Kamyar Mehdiyon, "Ownership of oil and gas resources in the Caspian Sea", *The American Journal of International Law,* Vol. 94, No. 1, 2000, pp. 179-189.
43. Abdollah Baei Lashaki and Masoumeh Rad Goudarzi, "Evolution of the Post-Soviet Caspian Sea Legal Regime", in Mansoureh Ebrahimi et al., *The Dynamics of Iranian Borders Issues of Contention,* (Switzerland: Springer, 2019).
44. Ibid.
45. Mehdiyon, n. 42.
46. Barbara Janusz-Pawletta, *The legal status of the Caspian Sea: Current challenges and prospects for future development*, (Berlin: Springer, 2015)
47. Ministry of Foreign Affairs of the Republic of Kazakhstan, "Legal status of the Caspian Sea', October 16, 2019, https://www.gov.kz/memleket/entities/mfa/press/article/details/591?lang=en. Accessed on October 5, 2022.
48. President of Russia, "Convention on the Legal Status of the Caspian Sea", August 2018, http://en.kremlin.ru/supplement/5328. Accessed on October 5, 2022.
49. Paul Kubicek, "Energy politics and geopolitical competition in the Caspian basin", *Journal of Eurasian Studies,* Vol. 4, No. 2, 2013, pp. 171-180.
50. Sarah O' Hara, "Great game or grubby game? The struggle for control of the Caspian", *Geopolitics,* Vol. 9, No. 1, 2004, pp. 138-160.
51. Kubicek, n. 49.
52. Karen Smith Stegen and Julia Kusznir, "Outcomes and strategies in the 'New Great Game': China and the Caspian states emerge as winners", *Journal of Eurasian Studies,* Vol. 6: 2, 2015, pp. 91-106.

53. Lidiya Parkhomchik, "Azerbaijan and Russia: Prospects for Energy Cooperation", Eurasian Research Institute, https://www.eurasian-research.org/publication/azerbaijan-and-russia-prospects-for-energy-cooperation/. Accessed on October 15, 2022.
54. Stegen and Kusznir, n. 52.
55 Ibid.
56. Grzegorz Kuczynski, "Russia, Iran forge energy cooperation", 2022, Warsaw Institute, https://warsawinstitute.org/russia-iran-forge-energy-cooperation/. Accessed on October 15, 2022.
57. Justyna Misiągiewicz, *Geopolitics and Energy Security Policies in the Caspian Region,* (Leiden and Boston: Brill-Nijhoff, 2024).
58. Embassy of the Republic of Azerbaijan to the United States of America, "Economic relations", https://washington.mfa.gov.az/en/content/165/economic-relations. Accessed on October 15, 2022.
59. Stegen and Kusznir, n. 52.
60. Embassy of the Republic of Kazakhstan in the United States, "Energy Partnership", https://kazakhembus.com/us-relations/economic-cooperation/energy-partnership. Accessed on September 20, 2022.
61. Stegen and Kusznir, n. 52.
62. Ibid.
63. Kubicek, n. 49.
64. Karen Smith Stegen and Julia Kusznir, "Outcomes and strategies in the 'New Great Game': China and the Caspian states emerge as winners", *Journal of Eurasian Studies,* Vol. 6, No. 2, 2015, pp. 91-106.
65. Zorigt Dashdorj, "Russia's and China's quiet contest in Central Asia", Geopolitical Intelligence Services, April 17, 2018, https://www.gisreportsonline.com/r/chinas-interest/. Accessed on September 25, 2022.
66. Stegen and Kusznir, n. 52.
67. Zorigt Dashdorj, n. 65.
68. Stegen and Kusznir, n. 52.
69. Ibid.
70. Yu Guoqing, "China's foreign energy policy towards Iran", International Institute for Asian Studies, https://www.iias.asia/sites/default/files/nwl_article/2019-05/IIAS_NL62_27.pdf. Accessed on September 25, 2022.
71. John S. Park and Cameron Glenn, "Iran and China", *The Iran Primer,* October 11, 2010, https://iranprimer.usip.org/resource/iran-and-china. Accessed on October 20, 2022.
72. Ngangom Dhruba Tara Singh, "EU-Azerbaijan growing partnership and Caspian geopolitical competition", 04 October, 2022, *CAPS InFocus article,* 71/2022, https://capsindia.org/eu-azerbaijan-growing-partnership-and-caspian-geopolitical-competition/. Accessed on October 20, 2022.
73. Stegen and Kusznir, n. 52.

74. Ngangom Dhruba Tara Singh, "EU-Azerbaijan growing partnership and Caspian geopolitical competition", 04 October, 2022, *CAPS InFocus article,* 71/2022, https://capsindia.org/eu-azerbaijan-growing-partnership-and-caspian-geopolitical-competition/. Accessed on October 20, 2022.
75. Stegen and Kusznir, n. 52.
76. Ibid.
77. Ibid.
78. Thierry Coville, "EU and Iran towards a new partnership?" French Institute for International and Strategic Affairs, 2014, https://www.iris-france.org/44347-eu-and-iran-towards-a-new-partnership/. Accessed on October 25, 2022.
79. Hirah Azhar, "Iran and the European Union: Prospects and Challenges", Centre for Geopolitics and Security in Realism Studies, April 20, 2016, http://cgsrs.org/publications/55. Accessed on October 25, 2022.
80. Erika Monahan and Matthew P. Romaniello, "Early modern trade in the Caspian region", *Russian studies in History,* Vol. 60, No. 1-4, 2021, pp. 1-7.
81. Pinak Ipek, "Azerbaijan's Foreign Policy and Challenges for Energy Security", *Middle East Journal,* Vol. 63, No. 2, 2009, pp. 227-239.
82. Brenda Shaffer, "Foreign policies of the States of the Caucasus: Evolution in the post-Soviet period", *International Relations*, Vol. 7, No. 26, 2010, pp. 51-65.
83. Sergewi Ermalaev, "The formation and evolution of the Soviet Union's oil and gas dependence", Carnegie Endowment for International Peace, March 29, 2017, https://carnegieendowment.org/2017/03/29/formation-and-evolution-of-soviet-union-s-oil-and-gas-dependence-pub-68443. Accessed on April 15, 2022.
84. Office of the High Representative for the Least Developed Countries, Landlocked Developing Countries and Small Island Developing States, "National Reports on the implementation of the Vienna Programme of Action for Landlocked Developing Countries for the Decade 2014–2024 (2023) of Azerbaijan", https://www.un.org/ohrlls/sites/www.un.org.ohrlls/files/azerbaijan_national_report_assessment_of_the_implementatin_of_the_vpoa.pdf. Accessed on November 2, 2023.
85. Vladimir Kutcherov et al., "Russian natural gas exports: An analysis of challenges and opportunities", *Energy Strategy Reviews,* Vol. 30, 2020, pp. 1-10.
86. Randall Newnham, "Oil, Carrots, and Sticks: Russia's energy resources as a foreign policy tool", *Journal of Eurasian Studies*, Vol. 2, No. 2, 2011, pp. 134-143.
87. Steven Woehrel, "Russian energy policy towards neighbouring countries", 2006, Congressional Research Service.
88. Kristiina Silvan and Marcin Kaczmarski, "Russia's approach to connectivity in Asia: From cooperation and coercion", *East Asia,* Vol. 40, 2023, pp. 317-334.
89. Office of the President of the Republic of Kazakhstan, "Concept of the foreign policy of the Republic of Kazakhstan for 2020-2030", https://www.akorda.kz/en/legal_acts/decrees/on-the-concept-of-the-foreign-policy-of-the-republic-of-kazakhstan-for-2020-2030. Accessed on March 16, 2022.
90. Murat Nurtleu, "Kazakhstan is building more connections with the world", *Nikkei Asia,* September 20, 2023, https://asia.nikkei.com/Opinion/Kazakhstan-

is-building-more-connections-with-the-world#:~:text=Our%20new%20economic%20agenda%20places,China%20and%20Europe%20via%20the. Accessed on October 05, 2023.

91. Evgeniya Makhmutova, "Outlook for Turkmenistan as Eurasia's Transport Hub", Russian International Affairs Council, July 27, 2023, https://russiancouncil.ru/en/analytics-and-comments/analytics/outlook-for-turkmenistan-as-eurasia-s-transport-hub/. Accessed on November 05, 2023.
92. Office of the High Representatives for the Least Developing Countries, Landlocked Developing Countries and Small Island Developing States, "A transit country perspective – Remarks by Dr. Mahdi Safari Deputy Foreign Minister for Economic Diplomacy of the Islamic Republic of Iran", August 16, 2022, https://www.un.org/ohrlls/sites/www.un.org.ohrlls/files/h.e._mr._mahdi_safari_deputy_foreign_minister_for_economic_diplomacy_of_iran.pdf. Accessed on November 5, 2023.
93. Office of the High Representatives for the Least Developing Countries, Landlocked Developing Countries and Small Island Developing States, "Speech by Rostam Ghasemi, Honorable Minister of Roads and Urban Development of the Islamic Republic of Iran In the conference of developing landlocked countries", August 15-16, 2022, https://www.un.org/ohrlls/sites/www.un.org.ohrlls/files/ministerial_iran_text_rostam_ghasemi.pdf. Accessed on November 5, 2023.
94. Ministry of Foreign Affairs of the Russian Federation, "Agreement among the Governments of the Caspian Littoral States on Cooperation in the Field of Transport", August 15, 2018, https://www.mid.ru/tv/?id=1574918&lang=en. Accessed on December 4, 2023.
95. Vladislav Kondratyev, "Transformation of US geostrategy in the Caspian region", Caspian Institute for Strategic Studies, November 14, 2023. https://caspian.institute/product/kondratyev-vladislav/transformation-of-us-geostrategy-in-the-caspian-region-38596.shtml. Accessed on December 4, 2023.
96. Luke Coffey, "Time for a U.S. Strategy in the Caspian", The Heritage Foundation, August 19, 2019, https://www.heritage.org/europe/report/time-us-strategy-the-caspian. Accessed on December 4, 2023.
97. Vladislav Kondratyev, "Transformation of US geostrategy in the Caspian region", Caspian Institute for Strategic Studies, November 14, 2023. https://caspian.institute/product/kondratyev-vladislav/transformation-of-us-geostrategy-in-the-caspian-region-38596.shtml. Accessed on December 4, 2023.
98. Haley Nelson, "Biden Carries on the Cold War Paradigm in the Caspian Region", *Caspian Affairs Magazine,* Issue No. 7, 2023, pp. 34-36.
99. Eugene Chausovsky, "Strategic Connectivity: The U.S./China Competition in the Caspian Region", Caspian Policy Centre, November 2023, https://api.caspianpolicy.org/media/ckeditor_media/2023/11/02/the-uschina-competition-in-the-caspian-region.pdf. Accessed on December 4, 2023.
100. European Commission, "Global Gateway in the Middle East, Asia and the Pacific", https://international-partnerships.ec.europa.eu/policies/global-gateway/initiatives-

region/initiatives-middle-east-asia-and-pacific_en?page=0. Accessed on December 4, 2023.

101. Anna Matveeva, "A New Opening for EU–Central Asia Relations?" Carnegie Europe, April 23, 2023, https://carnegieeurope.eu/2023/04/13/new-opening-for-eu-central-asia-relations-pub-89454. Accessed on December 10, 2023.
102. Alouddin Komilov, "What Explains Growing European Engagement in Central Asia?" *The Diplomat,* November 22, 2022, https://thediplomat.com/2022/11/what-explains-growing-european-engagement-in-central-asia/. Accessed on December 10, 2023.
103. Anna Matveeva, n. 101.
104. Directorate-General for International Partnerships, "EU-Central Asia: 19th Ministerial meeting held in Luxembourg", European Commission, October 23, 2023, https://international-partnerships.ec.europa.eu/news-and-events/news/eu-central-asia-19th-ministerial-meeting-held-luxembourg-23-october-2023-2023-10-23_en. Accessed on December 10, 2023.
105. Chen Xu, "Connectivity for Common Prosperity", *Embassy of the People's Republic of China to the Kingdom of the Netherlands,* January 05, 2015, http://nl.china-embassy.gov.cn/eng/zhgx/201501/t20150105_10044916.htm. Accessed on December 10, 2023.
106. Nadine Godehardt and Paul J. Kohlenberg, "China's global connectivity politics: a meta-geography in the making", in Nadine Godehardt and Paul J. Kohlenberg, ed., *The multidimensionality of regions in world politics,* (New York: Routledge, 2021).
107. International Transport Forum, "Enhancing Connectivity and Freight in Central Asia", 2019, https://www.itf-oecd.org/sites/default/files/docs/connectivity-freight-central-asia_2.pdf. Accessed on December 10, 2023.
108. Stuart Coles et al., "Seven ways Russia's war on Ukraine has changed the world", Chatham House, February 20, 2023, https://www.chathamhouse.org/2023/02/seven-ways-russias-war-ukraine-has-changed-world#russia-the-pariah-state. Accessed on December 10, 2023.
109. Dennis Koegeboehn, "Impacts of the Russia-Ukraine War on Ports and Transport", TOC Europe Website, https://www.tocevents-europe.com/en/media/press/impacts-of-the-russia-ukraine-war-on-ports-and-transport.html. Accessed on December 10, 2023.
110. "Iran & Russia: New Land & Sea Networks", *The Iran Primer*, May 18, 2023, https://iranprimer.usip.org/blog/2023/may/18/iran-russia-new-network-land-sea-routes. Accessed on December 15, 2023.
111. Nurlan Kulbatyrov and Aida Haidar, "Five Trade Trends in Central Asian Connectivity", *The Astana Times,* June 26, 2023, https://astanatimes.com/2023/06/five-trade-trends-in-central-asian-connectivity/. Accessed on December 15, 2023.
112. Muhammad Rafiq, "Economic Gains of Kazakhstan in Wake of Shifting Supply Chains", *The Astana Times,* August 19, 2022, https://astanatimes.com/2022/08/economic-gains-of-kazakhstan-in-wake-of-shifting-supply-chains/. Accessed on December 15, 2023.

113. Assel Satubaldina, "Cargo Transportation Along Middle Corridor Soars 88%, Reaches 2 Million Tons in 2023", *The Astana Times,* December 28, 2023, https://astanatimes.com/2023/12/cargo-transportation-along-middle-corridor-soars-88-reaches-2-million-tons-in-2023/#:~:text=In%20the%20first%20nine%20months%20of%202022%2C%20the%20figure%20stood,million%20tons%20of%20cargo%20annually. Accessed on December 29, 2023.
114. Official website of the President of the Republic of Azerbaijan, "Ilham Aliyev received delegation led by Iran's Minister of Roads and Urban Development", March 11, 2022, https://president.az/en/articles/view/55603. Accessed on July 1, 2023.
115. Kerem Oge, "Understanding pipeline politics in Eurasia: Turkey's transit security in natural gas", *Geopolitics,* Vol. 26, No. 5, 2021, pp. 1510-1532.
116. Abbas Maleki, "The politics of natural resources in the Caspian Sea: A new great game in an ancient world", in Harry Verhoeven, eds., *Environmental politics in the Middle East,* (London: C. Hurst & Co. Ltd, 2018).
117. Barbara Janusz-Pawletta, *The legal status of the Caspian Sea: Current challenges and prospects for future development*, (Berlin: Springer, 2015).
118. Hooshang Amirahmadi, *The Caspian Region at a Crossroad: Challenges of a New Frontier of Energy and Development,* (United States: Palgrave Macmillan, 2000).
119. Ramakrushna Pradhan, n. 22.
120. Hooshang Amirahmadi, n. 118.
121. Ramakrushna Pradhan, n. 22.
122. Sergey S. Zhiltsov, "EU policy shaping the pipeline architecture in the Caspian region", in Sergey S. Zhiltsov et al., eds, *Oil and Gas pipelines in the Black-Caspian Seas region,* (Switzerland: Springer, 2016).
123. Hooshang Amirahmadi, n. 118.
124. Ramakrushna Pradhan, n. 22.
125. Sarah O' Hara, "Great game or grubby game? The struggle for control of the Caspian", *Geopolitics,* Vol. 9, No. 1, 2004, pp. 138-160.
126. Hooshang Amirahmadi, n. 117.
127. Fariz Imailzade, "Azerbaijan's foreign policy priorities and the role of the Middle East", Middle East Institute, May 12, 2020, https://www.mei.edu/publications/azerbaijans-foreign-policy-priorities-and-role-middle-east. Accessed on December 12, 2022.
128. Çağlar Kurç, "The puzzle: multi-vector foreign policy and defense industrialization in Central Asia", in Çağlar Kurç et al., eds, *Defence industries in the 21st Century: A Comparative analysis,* (New York: Routledge, 2021).
129. Kassym-Jomart Tokayev, "Turbulence across Eurasia will not slow Kazakhstan's progress", *The National Interests*, April 04, 2022, https://nationalinterest.org/feature/turbulence-across-eurasia-will-not-slow-kazakhstan%E2%80%99s-progress-201591. Accessed on December 16, 2022.

130. "Turkmenistan turns up pro-Russian propaganda, warns against western media, agents", *Radio Free Europe/Radio Liberty,* December 14, 2022, https://www.rferl.org/a/turkmenistan-pro-russian-anti-western/32176574.html. Accessed on December 17, 2022.
131. Garrett Nada, "Iran blames US, West for Ukraine war", *The Iran Primer,* March 03, 2022, and updated on July 19, 2022, https://iranprimer.usip.org/blog/2022/mar/03/iran-blames-us-west-ukraine-war. Accessed on December 17, 2022.
132. Ibid.
133. Yelnur Alimov, "Russia is using the Caspian Sea to launch strikes against Ukraine. So why are the Caspian countries silent?" December 02, 2022, *Radio Free Europe/Radio Liberty,* https://www.rferl.org/a/caspian-sea-ukraine-war-russia-peace-friendship-convention/32158822.html. Accessed on December 23, 2022.
134. Olzhas Auyezov, "Shocked by Ukraine war, Russian neighbour Kazakhstan looks west", *Reuters,* November 17, 2022, https://www.reuters.com/world/asia-pacific/shocked-by-ukraine-war-russian-neighbour-kazakhstan-looks-west-2022-11-17/. Accessed on December 18, 2022.
135. Aygerim Sarymbetova, "Kazakhstan temporarily reduces oil export through Russia", *The Caspian News,* August 04, 2022, https://caspiannews.com/news-detail/kazakhstan-temporarily-reduces-oil-exports-through-russia-2022-8-4-54/. Accessed on December 18, 2022.
136. Aygerim Sarymbetova, "Turkmen leader, Saudi foreign minister discuss energy and trade ties", *The Caspian News,* December 22, 2022, https://caspiannews.com/news-detail/turkmen-leader-saudi-foreign-minister-discuss-energy-and-trade-ties-2022-12-22-49/. Accessed on December 23, 2022.
137. Aybulat Musaev, "Turkmenistan to double natural gas exports to China", *The Caspian News,* October 18, 2022, https://caspiannews.com/news-detail/turkmenistan-to-double-natural-gas-exports-to-china-2022-10-17-1/. Accessed on December 23, 2022.
138. Aygul Ospanova, "Azerbaijan president, Turkmen official discuss energy, transport ties", *The Caspian News,* November 29, 2022, https://caspiannews.com/news-detail/azerbaijani-president-turkmen-official-discuss-energy-transport-ties-2022-11-29-53/. Accessed on December 23, 2022.
139. Nigar Bayramli, "Iran, Russia sign $40 billion energy cooperation deal", *The Caspian News,* July 19, 2022, https://caspiannews.com/news-detail/iran-russia-sign-40-billion-energy-cooperation-deal-2022-7-19-0/. Accessed on December 23, 2022.
140. "Increased energy ties key topic in Caspian talks", SHANA Petro Energy Information Network, October 11, 2022, https://en.shana.ir/news/462904/Increased-Energy-Ties-Key-Topic-in-Caspian-Talks. Accessed on December 23, 2022.
141. Ngangom Dhruba Tara Singh, n. 72.
142. Stegen and Kusznir, n. 52.

143. "Taiwan warns Russia, China ties 'harm' international peace", *The Hindu,* September 16, 2022, https://www.thehindu.com/news/international/taiwan-warns-russia-china-ties-harm-international-peace/article65898043.ece. Accessed on November 1, 2022.
144. Paul Kubicek, "Energy politics and geopolitical competition in the Caspian Basin", *Journal of Eurasian Studies,* Vol. 4, No. 2, 2013, pp. 171-180.
145. "A coalition of the sanctioned: On Russia and Iran", *The Hindu,* July 23, 2022, https://www.thehindu.com/opinion/editorial/a-coalition-of-the-sanctioned-the-hindu-editorial-on-russia-and-iran/article65666244.ece. Accessed on November 1, 2022.
146. Silvia Boltuc, "Caspian Sea summit geopolitical background", *Geopolitical Report,* September 27, 2022, https://www.specialeurasia.com/2022/09/27/caspian-sea-summit-geopolitics-2/. Accessed on November 1, 2022.
147. Ngangom Dhruba Tara Singh, n. 72.

4

Oil and Gas in India's Energy Profile

Amidst the ongoing conflict in Ukraine, Russia accounted for roughly 42 per cent of all crude oil imports by India in May 2023.[1] In response to the imposition of sanctions, Russia started the sale of oil at cheaper prices. Taking advantage of this opportunity, India has purchased a substantial quantity of oil since the start of the military operation in 2022. For India, an increase in oil imports is directly correlated to its growing energy consumption, necessitated by a growing population, and increased per capita income. Energy consumption has risen consistently across all sectors, such as agricultural, industrial, commercial, and residential, and is likely to rise further. India currently holds the position of being the third largest consumer of primary energy globally. According to the International Energy Agency's (IEA) World Energy Outlook of 2021, India accounts for 6.1 per cent of the world's primary energy consumption. Further, according to the projected policy scenario, this percentage is likely to increase to approximately 9.8 per cent by the year 2050.[2]

India's primary energy consumption is met mostly by coal, crude oil, and natural gas, followed by nuclear and renewable energy. Here, oil and gas play a crucial part in India's energy mix since they provide more than one-third of the energy required.[3] In 2020, coal remained the primary source of energy in India, accounting for 44 per cent of the country's total energy consumption. Petroleum and other liquid fuels accounted for 24 per cent of total energy use, while conventional biomass and waste accounted for 21 per cent. Alternative renewable fuel sources constituted a modest yet increasing proportion (1 per cent) of overall primary energy consumption. Despite natural gas currently constituting only 6 per cent of India's energy consumption, the country aims to raise its market share to 15 per cent by 2030. This objective is in line with India's commitment to reducing air pollution and transitioning to cleaner-burning fuels.[4] (Figure 4.1)

Figure 4.1: Total Primary Energy Consumption in India by Fuel Type, 2020

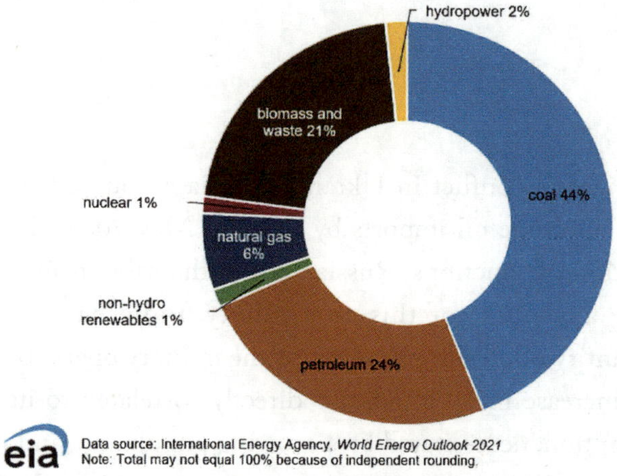

Source: US Energy Information Administration Data, 2022.

Prior research has ascribed the following concerns to India's energy security: economic growth (growth in real national income); changes in the nature of the economy (structural changes from agriculture to service sectors); demography (increase in population); growth in the transport sector (demand for oil and gas, increase in vehicle ownership); and incomplete or gradual energy transition (dependency of rural households on biomass and shortage in electrification).[5] In the context of India's developing economy and its growing energy demands, this chapter seeks to elucidate the significance of oil and gas in the country's energy mix. Using a descriptive approach, this chapter is organised as follows: Section 2 focuses on oil and gas in the present energy landscape and their significance in India's context. Sections 3, 4, and 5 offer insights into the upstream, midstream, and downstream sectors, respectively. Section 6 endeavours to understand certain government policies concerning oil and gas. Finally, section 7 sets out an assessment.

Oil and Gas in India's Energy Mix and their Significance

The term 'energy mix' refers to "the combination of the various energy types that are used to satisfy the energy requirements of a particular region."[6] In the last decade, the percentage of energy supply from oil and gas in India's energy mix has been fluctuating, while coal's contribution has been increasing. The share of nuclear and hydroelectric energy has stayed consistent, while that of renewables has increased (Table 4.1). Despite the slight reduction, oil and gas remain 2nd and 3rd in the country's primary energy supply. Their role in the energy mix has been anticipated to increase in the future. For instance, in the context of oil and gas in India, Ayed S Al-Qahtani, Director, OPEC's Research Division, highlighted that "oil will retain the largest share of the energy mix until 2045 despite a decrease in its share."[7] It will constitute 29 per cent in 2045, a drop in its share from 31 per cent in 2021. Concerning natural gas, he forecasted its share in the energy mix to increase to 24 per cent by 2045.[8]

Table 4.1: India's Primary Energy Supply, 2012-2023 (in per cent)

Year	Crude Oil	Natural Gas	Coal	Nuclear	Hydropower	Renewables
2012	29.1	9.8	57.6	0.5	2.0	0.8
2013	29.6	8.9	58.3	0.4	1.6	0.8
2014	29.0	7.9	59.5	0.4	1.9	0.9
2015	28.1	7.2	61.3	0.4	1.7	1.0
2016	30.1	7.1	59.5	0.4	1.5	1.1
2017	33.3	7.6	55.8	0.4	1.5	1.0
2018	32.4	7.7	56.4	0.4	1.5	1.2
2019	31.5	7.4	57.5	0.4	1.5	1.5
2020	30.7	7.5	57.7	0.5	1.7	1.6
2021	29.7	7.7	58.3	0.5	1.8	1.8
2022	29.3	7.7	58.6	0.5	1.7	2.0
2023	29.4	8.8	57.6	1.4	1.6	0.8

Source: Composed by the author using data from the India Climate Energy Dashboard (NITI Aayog).

Oil consumption in India has been increasing for decades across all industries, fuelled by rapid economic expansion. Since 2008, India's oil demand has grown rapidly, with an average annual growth of close to 160 thousand barrels[9] per day to 4.4 million barrels per day in 2017, accounting for 5 per cent of the global consumption. By 2024, India's oil demand is estimated to be approximately 6 million barrels per day.[10] The demand for crude oil climbed by 5 per cent in 2021 to 4.7 million barrels per day as India's economy recovered to pre-pandemic levels. India ranked as the third largest consumer of petroleum products in 2021, trailing only the United States and China. In India, diesel was the predominant oil product in terms of usage, representing 35 per cent of the overall consumption of petroleum products in 2021. Its primary application was in commercial transportation, with lesser usage observed in the industrial and agricultural sectors. Petrol usage accounted for 16 per cent of the total oil consumption in India. The illustration (Figure 4.2) below reveals a growing pattern of oil consumption over the last 20 years. It shows that from 2002 to 2021, the production of oil remained constant at 0.82 million barrels per day, whereas the consumption rate reached 4.65 million barrels per day by the end of 2021 from 2.2 million barrels per day in 2002. The gap between production and consumption has grown threefold in the last decade.

Figure 4.2: Pattern of India's Oil Production and Consumption, 2002-21 (in million barrels per day) *

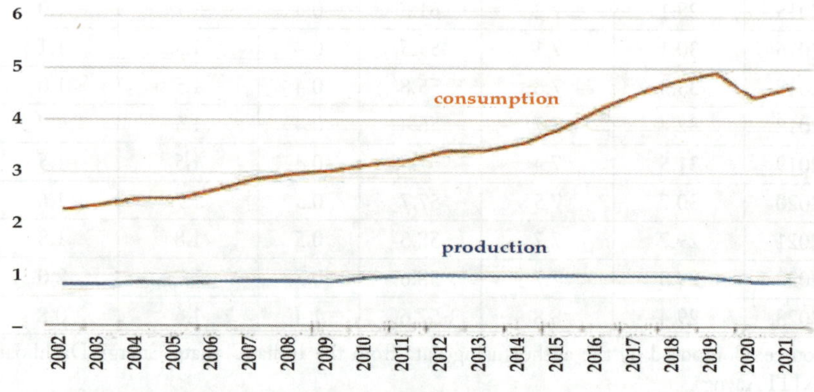

Source: U.S. Energy Information Administration Data, 2022.

* This paper employs both the U.S. Measuring System (e.g., barrels, million cubic feet) and the Indian Measuring System (e.g., metric tonnes, cubic metres) for oil and gas measurements. A conversion table between these units is provided in Appendix I.

Natural gas consumption is classified into 'energy purpose' and 'non-energy purpose'. The natural gas consumption for 'energy purpose' was 66 per cent in 2012-13 and reached 64 per cent in 2021-22. The natural gas consumption for 'non-energy purpose' was 34 per cent in 2012-13 with minimal growth of 35.9 per cent in 2021-22. Here, the fertiliser and power generation sectors hold a majority share of 28.29 per cent and 15.89 per cent, respectively.[11] The illustration (Figure 4.3) shows the share of natural gas production and consumption between 2010 and 2021. The production of gas declined from 1.8 trillion cubic feet[12] in 2010 to 1.1 trillion cubic feet in 2021. The consumption, on the other hand, remained constant with slight fluctuations between 2013 and 2017.

Figure 4.3: Pattern of Natural Gas Production and Consumption, 2010-21 (in trillion cubic feet) *

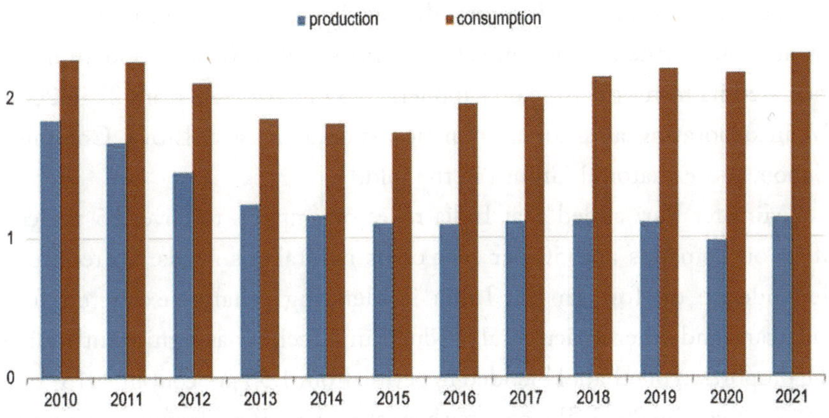

Source: U.S. Energy Information Administration Data, 2022.
* This paper employs both the U.S. Measuring System (e.g., barrels, million cubic feet) and the Indian Measuring System (e.g., metric tonnes, cubic metres) for oil and gas measurements. A conversion table between these units is provided in Appendix I.

With respect to natural gas, except for a 1 per cent decline in 2020, India's natural gas usage has increased every year since 2015, reaching 2.3 trillion cubic feet in 2021. In 2021-22, the fertiliser industry consumed the most natural gas (19.5 billion cubic metres), city gas distribution (12.5 billion cubic metres), and power (7.5 billion cubic metres). A substantial part of this increase can be attributed to the vast expansion of the infrastructure for distributing natural gas. The Indian government plans to allocate US$ 60 billion for expansion purposes, aiming to establish connectivity to the natural gas infrastructure for 70 per cent of the country's population.[13]

Although the proportion of oil and gas in India's total energy mix is fluctuating, they, nevertheless, play a vital role in the country's current energy situation. While renewable energy sources are becoming more popular, the need for oil is expected to increase in the future as a result of economic expansion, with a persistent dependence on imported oil.

Union Minister for Petroleum and Natural Gas Hardeep Singh Puri provided insight into India's diverse energy landscape. In the context of oil and gas, he emphasised the government's efforts to increase India's exploration area for hydrocarbon production to 0.5 million square kilometres by 2025 and 1.0 million square kilometres by 2030. Exploration across a larger region is expected to result in additional discoveries, increasing local oil and gas production. Further, in the context of energy supply diversification, India has increased its roster of crude oil suppliers to 39 in 2021-22 from 27 in 2006-07, incorporating additional countries, such as Russia, Libya, Colombia, Gabon, and Equatorial Guinea in the fold.[14]

Minister Puri added that India relies on imports to cover 85 per cent of its oil demands and 50 per cent of its natural gas needs. To reduce its dependence on foreign oil, India is blending ethanol extracted from sugarcane and other agricultural products into fuel. It has significantly raised the proportion of ethanol blended in petrol, from 1.53 per cent in 2013-14 to 10.17 per cent in 2022. The country has set a target of achieving a 20 per cent ethanol blended fuel by 2025. The introduction of E20 (20 per cent ethanol-mixed fuel) was also highlighted as an example.[15] The minister credited the country's successful navigation of the recent global energy crisis, the worst since 1973, to its robust '4-plank strategy' for energy security. It includes:

(a) Diversification of energy supplies;
(b) Increasing India's exploration and production footprint;
(c) Alternate energy sources; and
(d) Meeting energy transition through a gas-based economy, green hydrogen, and EVs.[16]

The 4-plank strategy demonstrates India's willingness to adapt to the changing energy landscape to secure its energy security. This strategy shows India's means of accommodating its concerns for climate change commitments, mitigating demand for hydrocarbons amidst growing economic development, and sustainable development. The relevance of oil and gas for India is reflected in its 4-plank strategy, which prioritises securing oil and gas from a wider range of sources and ramping up domestic exploration and production.

Despite India's vigorous advocacy for the utilisation of renewable energy sources to decrease its reliance on fossil fuels, it still considers oil and gas to be crucial in meeting its increasing energy needs. For example, despite the Oil and Natural Gas Corporation's (ONGC) goal to invest 2 trillion rupees in a variety of renewable energy projects in order to attain net-zero emissions by 2038, it reiterated that exploration and production of oil and gas will remain the cornerstone of its energy business.[17]

The IEA report anticipated that India's annual import bill for fossil fuels would quadruple by 2040, as the country is set to experience the world's largest rise in energy consumption over the next two decades. In the Stated Policies Scenario (STEPS), based on current policy settings, net dependency on imported oil will climb to more than 90 per cent by 2040, up from 75 per cent currently. Natural gas imports will double to 124 billion cubic metres in 2040, accounting for almost 60 per cent of domestic consumption. As per the IEA's key scenario, the country's refining capacity would increase by 50 per cent by 2040. In 2040, it is projected that in the country's primary energy mix, coal's share is expected to fall from 44 per cent to 34 per cent by 2040. Oil's share is to remain steady at 26 per cent, while that of natural gas is to increase to 11 per cent from 6 per cent. The share of renewables will increase from 1 per cent to 10 per cent, while that of hydro will remain at 2 per cent. Bioenergy's share falls from 20 per cent to 13 per cent, while nuclear energy's share rises from 1 per cent to 4 per cent.[18]

The aforesaid analysis forecasts an increase in India's dependence on fossil fuel imports, specifically oil and natural gas, to fulfil its escalating energy requirements. Although there is an anticipated growth in renewable energy sources, it is uncertain if this growth will be sufficient to counterbalance the increase in consumption of fossil fuels because of current policies. Hence, there is a need to strike a balance between the two.

To assess the significance of oil and gas for India, this section will employ the 4As framework—accessibility, availability, affordability, and acceptability—as a theoretical lens. This framework, developed by the Asia Pacific Energy Research Centre (APERC), provides a comprehensive approach for evaluating energy security.[19]

Availability: The availability of resources is a geological consideration. It refers to adequacy and access to energy. This means the availability of fuel reserves, both domestically and through external suppliers. If domestic demand exceeds production, the country needs to import energy.

Accessibility: It is a geopolitical notion that involves diplomatic relationships with other countries across the world. It opens the possibility of fuel diversity, which reduces risk.

Affordability: It is an economic angle. The terms relate to prices and paying ability. In many circumstances, the producers set the price since they have a monopoly. The price may be accessible to one segment of society while being unaffordable to another. As a result, a government is required to consider how inexpensive fuel is to various economic classes in the country. Here, subsidies play a significant role in domestic energy supply in the context of domestic energy security.

Acceptability: This is an environmental requirement that includes both environmental and social components. For instance, on the one hand, too much reliance on fossil fuels is unsustainable in the context of the environment. On the other hand, non-fossil energy forms lack volume. Alternatives, such as wind, hydro, and solar energy, involve the relocation of local residents, which is not socially acceptable.

This essence of the 4-As framework can be witnessed in the five enablers of energy justice, envisioned by former Union Minister for Petroleum and Natural Gas Dharmendra Pradhan (2014-21), which included "… availability and accessibility, affordability, energy efficiency, energy sustainability, and energy security."[20] Pradhan emphasised India's commitment to eradicating energy poverty through a major energy sector transformation. The strategy prioritises twin objectives: enhancing access to and affordability of clean fossil fuels and renewable energy sources. Pradhan acknowledged the significance of oil and gas by forecasting a twofold increase in India's demand for oil and a threefold increase in demand for gas by 2040.

Here, the APERC's 4-As framework closely corresponds to the objectives outlined by Dharmendra Pradhan, which prioritise availability and accessibility, affordability, energy efficiency, and energy sustainability. The upcoming sections will leverage this 4-As framework as a conceptual prism to analyse the ongoing relevance of oil and gas within the Indian energy landscape. By examining oil and gas through the lens of the 4-As framework, this section tries to systematically assess its ability to contribute to a robust and sustainable energy future for India.

Availability: India has been importing oil and gas from a variety of countries, with the majority of imports coming from West Asia, Latin America, Africa, and the United States. In recent times, India imported oil from Russia, which grew from 6 per cent in April 2023 to 40.4 per cent in May 2023.[21] New Delhi's intention to continue India's oil imports can be observed in Union Minister Puri's position to purchase oil from sources that offer the lowest price. Deep discounts offered by Russia ensured it became India's primary supplier of oil, and its market share increased to 24.2 per cent in 14 months, up from a meagre 2 per cent in the fiscal year 2022.[22] Iran's recent admittance to the BRICS and the Shanghai Cooperation Organisation (SCO), along with India's geographical proximity to the Caspian Sea countries, presents new opportunities for regional cooperation and availability of oil and gas.

Accessibility: As India is still hugely dependent on oil and gas for its domestic energy needs, it requires simple access to international oil and gas reserves. When it comes to oil and gas, accessibility refers to the ease of extracting oil and natural gas. This could be influenced by factors like geographical location (onshore vs. offshore), infrastructure, and technologies.

(a) Geographical distribution: Given the global dispersion of oil and gas deposits, India can gain access to them by diversifying its sources. This implies that an increasing number of countries possessing oil and gas resources are becoming a more feasible option for India.

(b) Infrastructure: Infrastructure enables the efficient movement of oil and gas from their source to their destination.
(c) Established technology: The energy business globally possesses firmly established technologies for extracting oil and gas. These technologies have undergone significant advancements over time and are highly efficient and economically viable when compared to other available options.

Affordability: It means that oil and gas are relatively affordable for the public. Affordability is driven by various factors, such as exploration and production, government policies, promotion of alternative fuel, and building next-generation infrastructure. For instance, the Indian government's measures are enhancing the accessibility and affordability of fuel gas for millions of households, catering to their cooking and heating requirements.[23]

Acceptability: This refers to the willingness of people to use oil and gas. Given the widespread reliance on oil and gas, it seems improbable that society will disregard its need for these fuels in the future. In reaction to climate change, the oil and gas companies have recently adopted innovative energy transition methods to maintain their acceptability. The oil and gas sector's social acceptability is at risk if it fails to address the need for climate and energy transition. As Dr. Fatih Birol, Executive Director, IEA, highlighted, "No energy company will be unaffected by clean energy transitions."[24] India's wide acceptance of oil, a reliable and cost-effective energy source that is easily accessible, guarantees its consumption for the foreseeable future. In recent times, the Indian government has set a target of blending 20 per cent ethanol with gasoline by 2025. Blending ethanol and petrol is the process of combining ethanol, a sustainable fuel generated from plant sources, with petrol. This blending programme has the potential to make petroleum more acceptable in the following ways:

(a) Lowers greenhouse gas emissions: Blending ethanol with petrol can cut greenhouse gas emissions by up to 40 per cent, according to the IEA.
(b) Improves energy security: According to the IEA, India may generate enough ethanol to cover 10 per cent of its petroleum needs by 2030.

Natural gas is becoming more popular due to growing concerns about climate change, an increase in natural gas supply, and its comparatively low cost. The role of natural gas as a bridge fuel in the transition to a greener energy future is expected to further shape its acceptability in the coming years. For instance, the Indian government's programmes, such as the Pradhan Mantri Ujjwala Yojana (PMUY) and the National Gas Grid Policy (NGGP), demonstrate that gas, as a fuel, is becoming more acceptable in the country.

Oil and Gas: Upstream

The upstream component of the oil and gas industry includes exploration operations, such as geological surveys, and production activities, such as onshore and offshore drilling. Geological surveys are carried out in a variety of ways, ranging from testing subsoil for onshore exploration to seismic imaging for offshore exploration.

Crude oil is an important source of energy for India. It is the country's second biggest source of total primary energy supply and its highest source of total final consumption. In recent decades, there has been a significant increase in oil consumption, with the demand for oil increasing by over 50 per cent. This surge can be attributed mostly to the rapid growth in the transportation sector, which is the largest consumer of oil, as well as the use of liquefied petroleum gas for cooking. With the significant increase in oil consumption and diminishing domestic production, India has become more reliant on oil imports, which accounted for almost 83 per cent of total imports in 2018. India has expanded its strategic alliances through international bilateral investment and foreign direct investment in India, with the goal of diversifying the country's import sources and suppliers. To build its strategic reserves, the government established the strategic petroleum reserves.[25]

Oil Reserves and Production

In April 2022, India's projected crude oil reserves were 651.77 million tonnes, up from 591.92 million tonnes in 2021. It represents a greater than 10 per cent increase over the previous year. According to the geographical distribution of crude oil reserves, the western offshore has the most reserves

(33 per cent), followed by Assam (23 per cent)[26] (Figure 4.4). The ONGC controls 71 per cent of crude oil reserves, with Oil India Limited (OIL) and the PSC regime controlling 13 per cent and 16 per cent, respectively.[27]

Figure 4.4: Crude Oil Reserves in India as of 2022

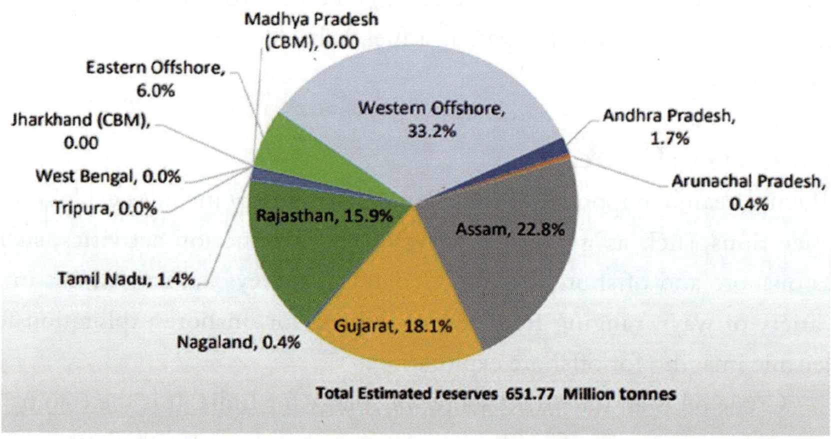

Source: Ministry of Statistics and Programme Implementation, Government of India, Energy Statistics, 2023.

While approximately half of India's crude oil production is sourced from offshore fields, this ratio has been decreasing. The ageing of key offshore fields, for example, Mumbai High, has contributed to this decline. ONGC's KG-D5 deepwater oil and natural gas development is the only project anticipated to come online in the next several years. This initiative has the potential to mitigate some of the reductions in mature fields. According to the Indian Petroleum and Natural Gas Statistics report, India's proven crude oil and condensate reserves were about 595 Mt (approximately 4.4 billion barrels), enough to continue production for around 14 years at current levels. The majority of oil production in India comes from three onshore states: Assam, Gujarat, and Rajasthan. These three states contribute to over 96 per cent of the onshore oil output. Additionally, there is also oil production from the ageing offshore Mumbai High Field. Recent findings in Rajasthan and the offshore Krishna-Godavari (KG) region demonstrate promising prospects.[28]

By easing contract conditions for private and international enterprises and encouraging national oil corporations to spend more on upstream development, the government is attempting to attract more investment and reduce India's oil imports. For instance, in 2021, India permitted 100 per cent foreign direct investment in upstream projects. In addition, the Ministry of Petroleum and Natural Gas announced in 2022 its intention to increase the oil and natural gas exploration area to around 310,000 square miles by 2025 and to 620,000 square miles by 2030 as a means of promoting further development.[29]

Figure 4.5: Production of Crude Oil in India (2013-2023)

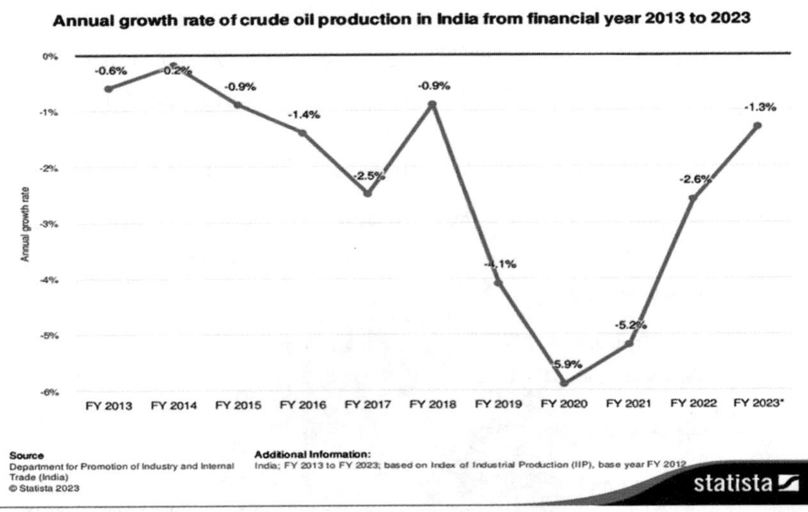

Source: Statista, 2023.

Figure 4.5 above demonstrates that India's domestic crude oil production has been negative during the past decade. The major cause of this reduction is the depletion of the country's oil reserves. Because of the fall in crude oil output, India has become more reliant on imports to satisfy its energy demands, as evidenced by India's import ratio of 85 per cent of its crude oil in 2022. Despite an anticipated future decline in domestic crude oil production, the government is taking proactive steps to increase output. These efforts include expanding exploration and production activities in new regions.

Gas Reserves and Production

India's consumption of natural gas is presently minimal. However, it is steadily rising. Most of the gas is utilised in industry and electricity generation. Although residential gas consumption is currently low, India is rapidly expanding its gas distribution networks, which is expected to result in a considerable increase in this area. India wants to boost natural gas' share of the energy mix to 15 per cent by 2030 from approximately 6.3 per cent in 2022.[30] Natural gas reserves were predicted to be 1,138.67 billion cubic metres as of April 2022. The western offshore has the most natural gas reserves (29.6 per cent), followed by the eastern offshore (23.6 per cent)[31] (Figure 4.6). Most of the natural gas exploration and production operations are performed by two PSUs, ONGC and OIL. Here, the Product Sharing Contracts (PSC) regime controls 50 per cent of natural gas reserves, followed by ONGC at 40 per cent and OIL at 10 per cent.[32]

Figure 4.6: Natural Gas Reserves in India as of 2022

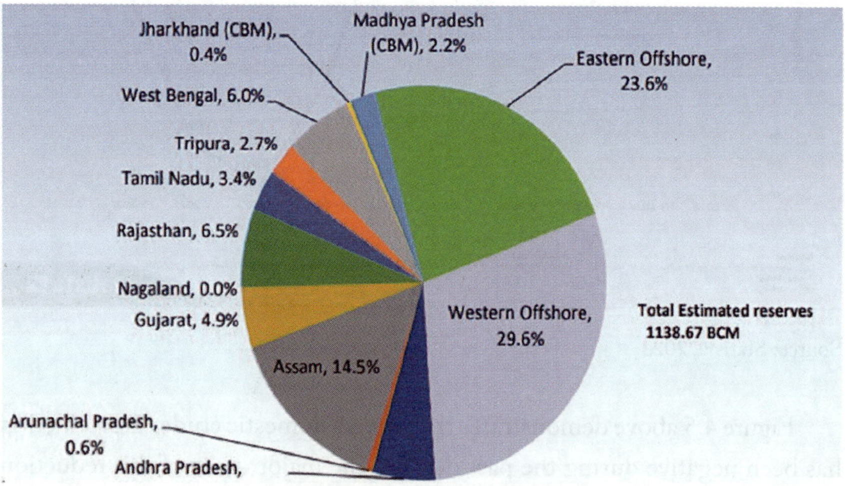

Source: Ministry of Statistics and Programme Implementation, Government of India, Energy Statistics, 2023.

The natural gas production from the offshore fields of the Mumbai Basin accounts for 33 per cent and 16 per cent of total production, respectively, from the ONGC-operated Bassein and Mumbai High fields.[33]

Following a significant decline from peak output in 2010, India's dry natural gas production stayed steady between 2015 and 2019, at around 31.4 billion cubic metres. Natural gas output fell to a little under 28.3 billion cubic metres in 2020 due to countrywide lockdowns imposed in response to the COVID-19 outbreak, before rebounding to 31.13 billion cubic metres in 2021. In a latest development, Reliance Industries and BP's MJ project in the KG-D6 block is a major project that started production in June 2023 and is expected to reach a peak of approximately 30 million standard cubic metres of gas a day, according to Reliance.[34] India's natural gas output has been falling over the previous decade (Figure 4.7). The major cause for this drop is the depletion of the country's gas reserves. Because of the fall in natural gas output, India has become more reliant on imports to satisfy its energy demands, as seen by the importation of 50 per cent of its gas requirements in 2022.

Figure 4.7: Production of Natural Gas in India, 2013-2023

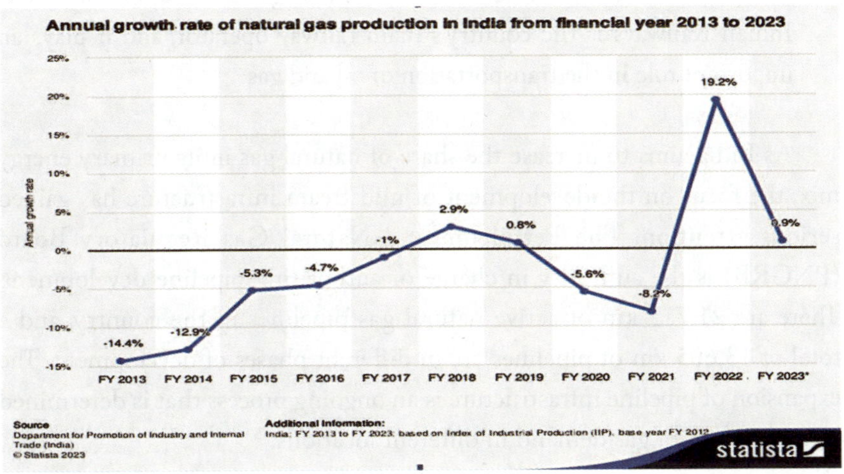

Source: Statista, 2023.

Oil and Gas: Midstream

The midstream sector includes transportation of oil and gas and storage infrastructure. The midstream transports energy from remote or distant locations to population hubs. Crude oil, in its unrefined form, is transported by tankers and pipelines. Similarly, natural gas is conveyed by pipelines or as liquefied natural gas (LNG) using specialised tankers. By utilising cost-effective underground storage options, the crude oil and natural gas storage system helps to balance out supply and demand fluctuations.

Oil and Gas Transportation

Oil and gas transportation in India is a complicated and multimodal system. In India, the primary ways of transportation for oil and gas are:

(a) Pipelines: They are the most efficient and cost-effective means of oil and gas transportation. India has a huge pipeline network that transports oil and gas from producing sites to refineries and consumption centres.

(b) Tankers: These vessels deliver oil and gas across large distances by water. There are several ports in India that handle the import and export of oil and gas. Mumbai, Chennai, and Cochin are the major oil import terminals in India.

(c) Railroads: These are utilised to carry oil and gas across great distances. Indian Railways is the country's main railway operator, and it plays an important role in the transportation of oil and gas.

As India aims to increase the share of natural gas in its primary energy mix, the focus on the development of midstream infrastructure has gained serious attention. The Petroleum and Natural Gas Regulatory Board (PNGRB) is the authority in charge of authorising pipeline development. There are 21,715 km of active natural gas pipelines in the country, and a total of 13,605 km of pipelines are in different phases of development. The expansion of pipeline infrastructure is an ongoing process that is determined by evaluations of gas demand in different locations.[35]

Oil and Gas Storage

The Strategic Petroleum Reserve (SPR) aims to defend against supply interruptions while also adding commercial storage to enable smooth refinery operations. As of March 2018, India's total crude oil and oil product storage capacity was roughly 38 million metric tonnes (281 million barrels), including 5.33 million metric tonnes (39 million barrels) of strategic reserve capacity under Phase I of the SPR Programme, which consists of facilities at three locations—Visakhapatnam, Mangaluru, and Padur. As per the consumption pattern in 2018-19, these strategic reserves are anticipated to contain around 9.2 days of India's crude demand. In 2018, the government provided permission for Phase II of the Strategic Petroleum Reserves initiative, which has a capacity of 6.5 Mt (almost 50 mb) at two locations, Chandikhol and Padur (Table 4.2).[36] Unlike oil, India does not have storage for natural gas. It is critical to note that the present contribution of natural gas in India's energy mix is 6.2 per cent, with a target of reaching 15 per cent by 2030. With India's energy consumption increasing, development in gas storage infrastructure is of utmost necessity.[37]

Table 4.2: SPR Location and Capacity (in Million Metric Tonnes)

Location	Capacity	Status
Visakhapatnam	1.33	Completed
Mangaluru	1.5	Completed
Padur	2.5	Completed
Chandikhol	4	In progress
Padur (Phase II)	2.5	In progress

Source: Ministry of Petroleum and Natural Gas Data. https://mopng.gov.in/en/pdc/investible-projects/oil-amp-gas-infrastructure/strategic-crude-oil-storage

Based on Global Data's prediction for India, there will be a total of 129 projects starting operations by 2027. Among these projects, trunk/transmission pipeline projects will be the largest, with 59 projects. Oil storage projects will be second with 42 projects, followed by LNG regasification projects with 25 projects. Transmission pipeline developments are expected to account for about 46 per cent of all midstream project launches in India between 2023 and 2027. The oil storage projects will account for about 33 per cent of all midstream project launches in India from 2023 to 2027. With a capacity of 30 million barrels, Chandikhol is a large oil storage project in the country and is scheduled to begin operations in 2025 (Figure 4.8).[38]

Figure 4.8: Upcoming Midstream Projects in India by Segment, 2023-27

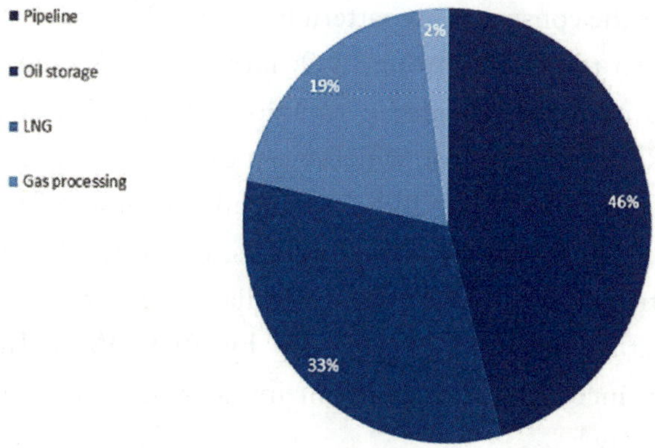

Source: Global Data, "India to lead midstream oil and gas project starts in Asia, with 129 projects planned during 2023-2027, forecasts Global Data", 2023.

Oil and Gas: Downstream

Downstream includes energy refineries and distribution companies. The process of refining is intricate, and its goal is to transform crude oil into petroleum products that are used for various purposes, including heating residences, powering vehicles, and producing petrochemical products. Marketing refers to the wholesale and retail distribution of refined petroleum products to businesses, industries, government, and the public.

According to the Ministry of Petroleum and Natural Gas, the Indian refining sector is emerging as a hub. India's refining capacity has increased from 62 million metric tonnes in 1998 to 251 million metric tonnes in 2023. The refining sector comprises 19 public sector refineries, 3 private sector refineries, and 1 joint venture refinery. Figure 4.9 illustrates the increasing capacity of refineries between 2014 and 2022. With 23 refineries, India's refining capacity is 251 million metric tonnes per annum as of October 2022 (Figure 4.9), and it aims to expand its refining capacity to 450 million metric tonnes per annum by 2030.[39] India has also planned to build a 'greenfield refinery'. In contrast to an existing refinery that is extended or modified, a greenfield refinery is a new refinery built in a wholly new location. Greenfield refineries are larger and more complicated than the current refineries, and they employ cutting-edge technology to create greener fuels. The HPCL Rajasthan Refinery Ltd. (HRRL) in India, founded in 2013, is an example of a greenfield refinery. Public sector marketing firms, such as Indian Oil Corporation Ltd, Hindustan Petroleum Corporation Ltd, and Bharat Petroleum Corporation Ltd, market petroleum products, as do private corporations, such as Reliance Industries, Essar, and Shell.[40]

Figure 4.9: Refining Capacity (2014-2022)

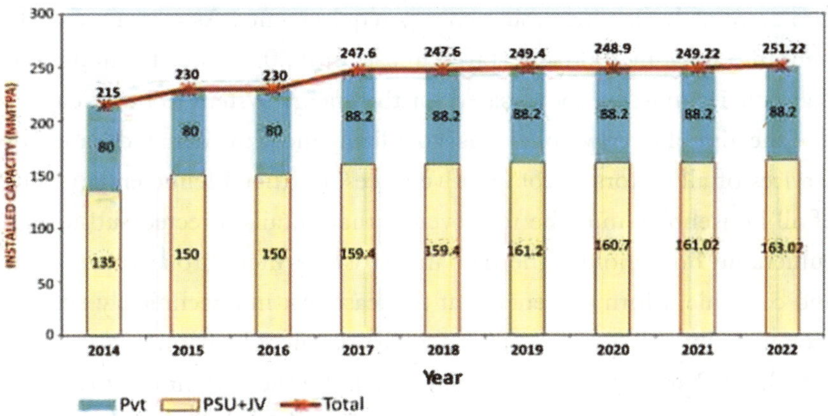

Source: Ministry of Petroleum and Natural Gas, Government of India, Annual Report 2022-23.

Government Policies and Regulations

India's energy policy aims to provide energy security for all. The country's rising energy concerns, along with a growing awareness of climate change and global warming, have prompted it to undertake a multipronged local and international strategy. The Indian government has implemented various measures to stimulate domestic oil and gas production. These measures include encouraging Indian companies to enhance their domestic operations and fostering closer collaboration with multinational corporations, as well as creating more avenues for their involvement in oil and gas exploration within India.

Integrated Energy Policy (IEP)

Over the last two decades, there has been a shift towards a more integrated approach to India's energy strategy. The initial initiative at the domestic level was observed in the Planning Commission's 12th Five-Year Plan, which delineated a comprehensive and inclusive policy strategy known as the Integrated Energy Policy (IEP). The origin of this study can be traced back to a committee of experts that was established in 2004 by the 10th Planning Commission. The group was formed at the behest of the Indian Prime Minister with the aim of creating a detailed energy policy that takes into account India's increasing energy requirements. As a result, the IEP went into force in 2006 and stayed in use until 2016. The IEP underlined that policies must be coordinated for the energy system to be efficient. It sees the aim of energy policies as "to reliably meet the demand for energy services of all sectors at competitive prices. Further, lifeline energy needs of all households must be met even if that entails directed subsidies to vulnerable households. The demand must be met through safe, clean, and convenient forms of energy at the least cost in a technically efficient, economically viable, and environmentally sustainable manner."[41]

The IEP presented various policy options for the government to consider in its pursuit of energy security. The choices primarily included the following strategies:

(a) The policy prioritised the goals of diversifying and improving the efficiency of energy sources. Considering the projected increase in energy usage, the IEP identified coal as a significant and primary energy source in India beyond the year 2030.

(b) The strategy proposed that energy demand should be met by conventional hydrocarbon sources like petroleum and liquid natural gas, as well as alternative energy sources like nuclear and renewable energy.

(c) The strategy advocated for the promotion of research and development in technical innovation through the sponsorship of educational institutions and the expansion of investment in research and development. Additionally, it aimed to establish a national energy fund to provide financial support for commercially feasible solutions that enhance energy efficiency and promote the use of renewable energy. It proposed directing energy research toward all viable renewable energy sources.[42]

In the context of oil and gas, the IEP acknowledged the importance of considering the supply and availability aspects of energy security within the framework of foreign policy. It highlighted the necessity for improved technology to make use of local resources; the susceptibility of energy supply, specifically oil and gas, due to unstable political situations in the countries from which India sources its energy; and the requirement for diplomatic efforts to ensure energy security within the framework of foreign policy and geopolitical risks.[43]

The policy suggested the following initiatives for the oil and gas sectors: "(a) pricing of petroleum products; (b) petroleum & natural gas regulation; (c) subsidy; (d) reserve enhancement and competition; (e) strategic reserves; (f) natural gas allocation and pricing; (g) gas pipeline network; and (h) using gas abroad."[44] The last initiative aimed to get access to inexpensive natural gas under long-term (25-30 year) agreements and consider setting up gas liquefaction plants in such countries, which would effectively increase India's energy availability.

Sharma[45] regarded the IEP as the Planning Commission's comprehensive assessment of India's energy security scenarios. The IEP acknowledged the various energy challenges that the Indian government had to address, including meeting energy demands, ensuring supply security, addressing environmental concerns, and transitioning to renewable and alternative energy sources. The IEP's strategy may be described as futuristic, with the goal of solving the issue of India's energy security while balancing economic growth and climate change issues.

National Energy Policy (NEP)

The NEP focused on "access at affordable prices, improved energy security and independence, greater sustainability, and economic growth."[46] The NEP advances upon the achievements of the previous energy strategy, the Integrated Energy Policy (IEP), and sets forward a fresh agenda that aligns with the revised role of emerging energy advancements.[47] To achieve objectives, the following seven areas of intervention were identified: "(a) energy consumption by businesses, households, transportation, and agriculture; (b) energy efficiency/decarbonisation measures on the demand side; (c) production and distribution of coal; (d) electricity generation, transmission, and distribution; (e) augmenting/increase in supply of oil and gas, both by domestic exploration and production (E&P) and through acquisition of overseas acreages; (f) refining and distribution of oil and gas; (g) installation, generation, and distribution of renewable energy."[48]

On oil and gas, the NEP's India Vision 2040 anticipated that by 2040, oil and gas would have almost maintained their 2015-16 proportions of 26 per cent and 6.5 per cent, respectively, to 25-27 per cent and 8-9 per cent. With renewables accounting for 7-10 per cent of India's energy mix by 2040, overall primary energy imports are predicted to climb significantly. Imports of oil and gas will account for the majority of the growth, with estimates of 81-88 per cent and 35-51 per cent increases, respectively. As a result, the country's reliance on foreign supplies is likely to grow.[49]

Experts on energy policy opined that the NEP proposes a possible solution to India's current and future energy difficulties, as well as a template for future policy. The NEP is primarily concerned with supply planning and objectives, but it fails to identify the variables influencing individual demand sectors. Despite covering a wide variety of concerns in the energy industry, the NEP fails to assess priorities, preparation, or uncertainty. Furthermore, it was said that guaranteeing energy security through clean, safe, and inclusive means is the key challenge, not a shortage of supply.[50]

New Exploration and Licensing Policy (NELP)

The introduction of the NELP in 1997 was the Government of India's first major step towards reforming the oil and gas upstream sector. It went into effect in 1999 and stayed in force for all government contracts signed between 1997 and 2016. Since the implementation of the NELP, hydrocarbon E&P licenses have been awarded exclusively through a competitive bidding mechanism. The NELP facilitated the entry of private and international investors into the oil and gas exploration industry by allowing 100 per cent foreign direct investment. It facilitated fair competition between domestic and foreign companies, both public and private, for licences to explore petroleum reserves.[51]

The NELP planned to attract capital from Indian and global corporations, as well as cutting-edge technology, novel geological ideas, and best management practices for the exploration of oil and gas resources in order to meet the country's expanding demand for oil and gas. The salient features of the NELP were: The policy allowed for 100 per cent foreign direct investment without any requirement for state participation or government carried interest. The allocation of blocks was done through an open international competitive bidding mechanism. The ONGC and the OIL were allowed to compete with each other to gain petroleum exploration licences. The contractors are granted freedom to market crude oil and gas in the domestic market. They are subject to a royalty rate of 12.5 per cent for land areas and 10 per cent for offshore areas. Production from blocks offered under the NELP is exempt from cess. Additionally, companies are exempt from import duty payments on goods imported for petroleum operations.[52]

The NELP was effective in attaining its primary goals, particularly in encouraging private and international corporations to participate in hydrocarbon E&P activities. It introduced cutting-edge technologies and streamlined processes to enhance the operation and management of India's hydrocarbon exploration and production. It also fostered healthy competition and encouraged public participation.

India Hydrocarbon Vision of 2025

In 1997, the Committee on Energy declared that "the most important problems in the energy sector are the lack of a long-term policy, which leads to inefficiencies in the supplying and use of energy." The 'Hydrocarbon Vision 2025' document released in 2000 was an endeavour to design long-term strategy. The Vision document outlines the key pillars of India's energy strategy:

(a) To assure energy security by achieving self-reliance through increased indigenous production and investment in equity oil abroad;

(b) To enhance quality of life by progressively improving product standards to ensure a cleaner and greener India;

(c) To develop the hydrocarbon sector as a globally competitive industry, which could be benchmarked against the best in the world through technology upgradation and capacity building in all facets of the industry;

(d) To have a free market and promote healthy competition among players and improve the customer service;

(e) To ensure oil security for the country, keeping in view strategic and defence considerations.[53]

As stated in the Vision document, the energy supply mix of the country until 2025 indicates that oil and gas will remain the dominant sources of energy to meet the country's needs, with the oil and gas industry meeting 45 per cent of overall energy demands. Table 4.3 shows the expected oil and gas shares in 2025 as per the document.

Table 4.3: Share of Future Energy Supply in India (in per cent)

Year	Coal	Oil	Gas	Hydel	Nuclear
1997-98	55	35	7	2	1
2001-02	50	32	15	2	1
2006-07	50	32	15	2	1
2010-11	53	30	14	2	1
2024-25	50	25	20	2	3

Source: Directorate General of Hydrocarbons Data, Government of India, 2014.

Although the Vision statement prioritises domestic exploration and production, it also recognises the importance of international cooperation and participation for oil and gas. The document highlights the need to acquire acreages abroad for exploration and production in the oil sector to diversify energy resources. By investing in exploration externally, the country aims to tap into potential reserves while reducing dependency on a single region for oil resources.

The emphasis on oil security is seen in the strategic approach to exploration and production initiatives. By concentrating efforts in countries like Russia, Iraq, Iran, and north African countries, recognised for their energy-rich landscapes, the strategy aims to establish strong relationships in regions with high potential for oil extraction. This not only secures access to vital resources but also fosters diplomatic ties that can enhance long-term energy security.

Ensuring adequate availability of gas, as highlighted in the strategy, involves a mix of domestic production, pipeline imports, and the import of liquefied natural gas. This diversified approach minimises risks associated with supply disruptions and market fluctuations. Additionally, the pursuit of diplomatic and political initiatives for gas imports, especially through transnational pipelines, underscores a commitment to regional cooperation and energy partnerships. By emphasising collaboration with neighbouring and other nations, the strategy seeks to create a network of reliable energy sources, further enhancing energy security.

In essence, this multifaceted strategy demonstrates a forward-thinking approach to securing energy resources. It encompasses exploration abroad, targeted E&P projects, a mix of domestic and international gas sources, and diplomatic efforts for collaborative energy ventures. Such a strategy not only ensures energy sufficiency but also promotes economic growth, diplomatic ties, and stability in the energy sector.

Hydrocarbon Exploration and Licensing Policy

The Hydrocarbon Exploration and Licensing Policy (HELP), implemented in 2016, was developed with the distinct goal of increasing oil and gas production in the Indian sedimentary basin, in keeping with the ambition of lowering hydrocarbon import reliance by 10 per cent by 2022. The HELP mechanism has established an Open Acreage Licensing Policy (OALP), which allows investors to carve out blocks of their choosing by reviewing E&P data accessible at National Data Repository and filing an Expression of Interest.[54] It aimed for a "uniform license for exploration and production of all forms of hydrocarbon, an open acreage policy, an easy-to-administer revenue-sharing model, and marketing and pricing freedom for the crude oil and natural gas produced."[55]

The contractor will have authorisation to explore both traditional and non-traditional oil and gas reserves, including coalbed methane (CBM), shale gas/oil, tight gas, and gas hydrates, under a unified licence. The OALP will enable upstream companies to choose specific blocks within the designated zone. The fiscal system of production, which relies on investment multiples and cost recovery/production-linked payments, will be substituted with a revenue-sharing model. In the past, contracts were based on the concept of profit sharing, where the government and the contractor divided the earnings after covering the costs. The implementation of the profit-sharing scheme necessitated the government to examine the cost particulars of private participants, leading to numerous instances of postponement and discord. Under the new system, the government's focus will shift from costs to obtaining a percentage of the overall revenue generated from the sale of oil, gas, and other commodities. This is consistent with the government's 'ease of doing business' programme.[56]

HELP represents a significant shift in India's energy policy, moving away from government control and towards government assistance for upstream exploration and production. The OALP eliminates limitations on exploration by providing enterprises with both the data and the autonomy to investigate areas of their preference. The upstream oil and gas exploration and production policy in India has faced criticism due to protectionist measures and excessive government bureaucracy, which have hindered the progress of oil and gas exploration and production. This policy, aimed at promoting upstream investment and enhancing productivity, has the potential to attract greater participation from private and international entities in the oil and gas industry.[57] Overall, the significance of HELP lies in boosting domestic oil and gas production, attracting investments, creating employment opportunities, enhancing transparency, and fostering a conducive environment for the oil and gas sector's growth. The Indian government has been on the path of increasing domestic exploration and production of oil and gas, as Union Minister Puri highlighted, "…objective of increased domestic production of oil and gas, target to increase the area under exploration and production to 0.5 million sq km by 2025 and achieve 1 million sq km by 2030."[58] Since 2016, seven rounds of OALP have been completed, with 134 E&P blocks totalling 207,691 square kilometres distributed across 19 sedimentary basins. The government has taken significant measures to reduce 'No-Go' regions in India offshore by 99 per cent.[59]

Assessment

The 4-plank strategy demonstrates India's maturity to accommodate different forms of energy in its energy basket in accordance with the prevailing domestic and international energy milieu. It is certain that oil and gas will continue to be a crucial component of India's energy blend due to the anticipated rise in demand for these resources. Additionally, the recent increase in the share of imported oil from Russia amidst the Ukraine crisis and the Indian government's approval to invest 5000 crore rupees to refill its Strategic Petroleum Reserves in 2023-24[60] demonstrate India's appetite for oil and gas despite growth in other forms of energy.

India's energy policies and regulations, as outlined through various initiatives such as the IEP, NEP, NELP, Hydrocarbon Vision 2025, and the more recent HELP, reflect a comprehensive and evolving strategy to address the country's energy needs.

The IEP, with its focus on diversification, efficiency, and security, laid the groundwork for a coordinated approach to energy policy. It recognised the significance of traditional hydrocarbon sources while also advocating for investments in alternative and renewable energy. Similarly, the NEP built upon these foundations, aiming for affordability, security, sustainability, and growth in the energy sector.

The NELP marked a significant shift by allowing private and international players into India's oil and gas exploration, promoting technological advancements and healthy competition. The India Hydrocarbon Vision of 2025 emphasised the importance of both domestic and international cooperation in securing oil and gas resources, with a strategic focus on specific regions known for their energy potential.

The more recent HELP, with its OALP, represents a move towards a more liberalised and efficient system. By shifting towards a revenue-sharing model and providing autonomy to exploration and production companies, HELP aims to boost domestic production, attract investments, and foster growth in the oil and gas sector. The government's commitment to increasing exploration zones and reducing bureaucratic hurdles is evident through the successful completion of multiple OALP rounds.

It is important to note that India's rising oil demand is unlikely to be supplied solely by new production initiatives, given the country's limited resource base. Along with the government's drive for domestic E&P, proven oil reserves remain limited in comparison to local requirements, thereby increasing India's reliance on imports dramatically in the upcoming decades. Imports are predicted to rise from 78.6 per cent in 2022-23 to more than 80 per cent in 2027-28.[61]

The growing significance of gas in the energy mix can be noticed in the government's decision to boost its share up to 15 per cent by 2030. Natural gas has been promoted as a transition fuel in India. To meet this share, India has made considerable investments in infrastructure projects, such as liquefied natural gas (LNG) import terminals, gas pipelines, and compressed natural gas (CNG) stations.

Despite the positive prognosis for renewables, the energy balance remains heavily reliant on fossil fuels. It is critical to recognise that not all energy sources are interchangeable with modern technologies. For instance, the aviation and shipping industries will continue to rely largely on fossil fuels. Regardless of continuing research and development, the energy sector is still not in a position where renewable forms of energy can completely replace oil and gas. As a result, oil and gas will continue to be an integral part of the energy mix. Finally, in India Energy Week 2023, Prime Minister Modi's recognition of embracing all types of energy, including fossil fuels and low-carbon fuels, to meet increasing demand shows the significance of oil and gas in the decades to come.

Notes

1. "India's Import of Russian Oil Scales New High in May", *The Hindu*, June 04, 2023, https://www.thehindu.com/news/national/indias-import-of-russian-oil-scales-new-high-in-may/article66930404.ece#:~:text=Russia%20now%20makes%20up%20for,individual%20country%20in%20recent%20years.&text=The%20rise%20in%20Russian%20share,suppliers%20in%20the%20Middle%20East. Accessed on June 10, 2023.

2. Press Information Bureau, "India has been ranked third largest primary energy consumer in the world", March 22, 2022, https://pib.gov.in/PressReleasePage.aspx?PRID=1809204. Accessed on June 10, 2023.
3. Ministry of Petroleum and Natural Gas, "Energising the Nation: Annual Report, 2021-22", https://mopng.gov.in/files/TableManagements/Final-Annual-Report-2021.pdf. Accessed on June 10, 2023.
4. United States Energy Information Administration, "India", November 17, 2022, https://www.eia.gov/international/analysis/country/IND. Accessed on June 10, 2023.
5. Anant Sudarshan and Ligia Noronha, "Contextualizing India's energy security", in Anant Sudarshan and Ligia Noronha, eds., *India's Energy Security,* (London and New York: Routledge, 2009).
6. G. Bothun, "Past and Future Global Energy Mix", in Walter Leal Filho et al., *Affordable and Clean Energy,* (Switzerland AG: Springer, 2021).
7. Shubhangi Mathur, "Oil to retain largest share of energy mix until 2045: OPEC", *Money Control News,* February 07, 2023, https://www.moneycontrol.com/news/business/oil-to-retain-largest-share-of-energy-mix-by-2045-opec-10023761.html. Accessed on June 30, 2023.
8. Ibid.
9. This paper employs both the U.S. Measuring System (e.g., barrels, million cubic feet) and the Indian Measuring System (e.g., metric tonnes, cubic metres) for oil and gas measurements. A conversion table between these units is provided in Appendix I.
10. International Energy Agency, "India 2020: Energy Policy Review", January 2020, https://iea.blob.core.windows.net/assets/2571ae38-c895-430e-8b62-bc19019c6807/India_2020_Energy_Policy_Review.pdf. Accessed on June 10, 2023.
11. Ministry of Statistics and Programme Implementation, "Energy Statistics India 2023", https://www.mospi.gov.in/sites/default/files/publication_reports/Energy_Statistics_2023/EnergyStatisticsIndia2023.pdf. Accessed on June 30, 2023.
12. This paper employs both the U.S. Measuring System (e.g., barrels, million cubic feet) and the Indian Measuring System (e.g., metric tonnes, cubic metres) for oil and gas measurements. A conversion table between these units is provided in Appendix I.
13. United States Energy Information Administration, n. 4.
14. Press Information Bureau, "India's 4-plank energy security strategy is based on diversifying supplies, increasing E&P, alternate energy sources and energy transition through a gas-based economy, Green Hydrogen etc." January 10, 2023, https://www.pib.gov.in/PressReleasePage.aspx?PRID=1889967#:~:text=India%20has%20been%20able%20to,sources%20and%20meeting%20energy%20transition. Accessed on June 30, 2023.
15. Ibid.
16. Ibid.
17. Nishant Ugal, "India's ONGC outlines $24.2 billion investment to meet net-zero emissions target", *Upstream,* August 31, 2023, https://www.upstreamonline.com/

energy-transition/india-s-ongc-outlines-24-2-billion-investment-to-meet-net-zero-emissions-target/2-1-1509322. Accessed on September 5, 2023.

18. Sanjeev Choudhary, "India's fossil fuel import bill could triple by 2040: IEA study", *The Economic Times,* February 09, 2021, https://economictimes.indiatimes.com/industry/energy/oil-gas/indias-fossil-fuel-import-bill-could-triple-by-2040-iea-study/articleshow/80763811.cms?from=mdr. Accessed on August 31, 2023.
19. Asia Pacific Energy Research Centre, Institute of Energy Economics, "A quest for energy security in the 21st Century: Resources and Constraints", https://aperc.or.jp/file/2010/9/26/APERC_2007_A_Quest_for_Energy_Security.pdf. Accessed on August 31, 2023.
20. Press Information Bureau, "Shri Pradhan says India is all for a reasonable and responsive pricing of crude", December 02, 2020, https://www.pib.gov.in/PressReleasePage.aspx?PRID=1677636. Accessed on August 31, 2023.
21. Sukalp Sharma, "The dramatic transformation of India's oil trade with Russia, in seven charts", *The Indian Express,* July 25, 2023, https://indianexpress.com/article/explained/explained-economics/india-russia-oil-trade-transformation-seven-charts-https-indianexpress-com-article-business-india-iraq-oil-trade-public-sector-refiners-crde-oil-russian-oil-8853397/#:~:text=During%20the%20April%202022%2DMay,watchers%2C%20appears%20to%20have%20peaked. Accessed on August 31, 2023.
22. Ibid.
23. Fatih Birol and Amitabh Kant, "India's clean energy transition is rapidly underway, benefiting the entire world", *International Energy Agency,* (January 2022), https://www.iea.org/commentaries/india-s-clean-energy-transition-is-rapidly-underway-benefiting-the-entire-world. Accessed on August 31, 2023.
24. Press release, "Oil and gas industry needs to step up climate efforts now", International Energy Agency, January 20, 2020, https://www.iea.org/news/oil-and-gas-industry-needs-to-step-up-climate-efforts-now. Accessed on August 31, 2023
25. International Energy Agency, n. 9.
26. Ministry of Statistics and Programme Implementation, "Energy Statistics India: 2023", https://static.investindia.gov.in/s3fs-public/2023-04/EnergyStatisticsIndia2023.pdf. Accessed on August 31, 2023.
27. Indian Bureau of Mines, "Indian Minerals Yearbook 2021: Mineral Reviews (60th edition)", March 2023, https://ibm.gov.in/writereaddata/files/16821575926443b01812260Petroleum_NaturalGas_2021.pdf. Accessed on August 31, 2023.
28. International Energy Agency, n. 9.
29. United States Energy Information Administration, n. 4.
30. Press Information Bureau, "The government has set a target to raise the share of natural gas in energy mix to 15% in 2030 from about 6.3% now", July 2022, https://pib.gov.in/PressReleasePage.aspx?PRID=1844630#:~:text=The%20Government%20has%20set%20a,2030%20from%20about%206.3%25%20now&text=i).,Km%20from%20current%2021%2C715%20Km. Accessed on August 31, 2023.

31. Ministry of Statistics and Programme Implementation, "Energy Statistics India-2023", https://static.investindia.gov.in/s3fs-public/2023-04/EnergyStatistics India2023.pdf. Accessed on August 31, 2023.
32. Indian Bureau of Mines, "Indian Minerals Yearbook 2021: Mineral Reviews (60th edition)", https://ibm.gov.in/writereaddata/files/16821575926443b01812260 Petroleum_NaturalGas_2021.pdf. Accessed on August 31, 2023.
33. International Energy Agency, n. 9.
34. British Petroleum, "Reliance and BP commence production from third deepwater field in India's KG D6 block", June 30, 2023, https://www.bp.com/en/global/corporate/news-and-insights/press-releases/reliance-and-bp-commence-production-from-third-deepwater-field-in-indias-kg-d6-block.html. Accessed on August 31, 2023.
35. Press Information Bureau, "One Nation One Gas Grid Project", July 2022, https://pib.gov.in/PressReleasePage.aspx?PRID=1843445. Accessed on August 31, 2023.
36. International Energy Agency, n.9.; see also, Ministry of Petroleum and Natural Gas, "Strategic Crude Oil Storage", https://mopng.gov.in/en/pdc/investible-projects/oil-amp-gas-infrastructure/strategic-crude-oil-storage, Accessed on August 31, 2023.
37. Manish Gupta, "Gas storage infra must for shift to cleaner fuel: Regulator", *Financial Express,* July 11, 2023, https://www.financialexpress.com/industry/gas-storage-infra-must-for-shift-to-cleaner-fuel-regulator/3163821/. Accessed on August 31, 2023.
38. Global Data, "India to lead midstream oil and gas project starts in Asia, with 129 projects planned during 2023-2027, forecasts Global Data", 27 April, 2023, https://www.globaldata.com/media/oil-gas/india-to-lead-midstream-oil-and-gas-project-starts-in-asia-with-129-projects-planned-during-2023-2027-forecasts-globaldata/#:~:text=Oil%20storage%20projects%20constitute%20around,to%20 start%20operations%20in%202025. Accessed on August 31, 2023.
39. Make In India, "Oil and Gas", https://www.makeinindia.com/sector/oil-and-gas. Accessed on August 10, 2023.
40. Ministry of Petroleum and Natural Gas, "Annual Report 2022-23: Marketing and Distribution", https://mopng.gov.in/files/TableManagements/annualreport2223.pdf. Accessed on August 10, 2023.
41. Planning Commission, "Integrated Energy Policy: Report of the Expert Committee", August 2006, https://lpr.adb.org/sites/default/files/resource/846/india-integrated-energy-policy.pdf.pdf. Accessed on August 10, 2023.
42. Ashok Sharma, *India's pursuit of energy security: Domestic measures, foreign policy and geopolitics,* (India: SAGE Publications, 2019).
43. Ibid.
44. Planning Commission, "Integrated Energy Policy: Report of the Expert Committee", August 2006, https://lpr.adb.org/sites/default/files/resource/846/india-integrated-energy-policy.pdf.pdf. Accessed on August 10, 2023.

45. Ashok Sharma, *India's Pursuit of Energy Security: Domestic Measures, Foreign Policy and Geopolitics,* (India: SAGE Publications, 2019).
46. Press Information Bureau, "Objectives of New Energy Policy", November 21, 2016, https://pib.gov.in/newsite/PrintRelease.aspx?relid=153952. Accessed on August 10, 2023.
47. Ibid.
48. International Energy Agency, "National Energy Policy", 2017, https://www.iea.org/policies/2461-draft-national-energy-policy. Accessed on August 16, 2023.
49. NITI Aayog, "National Energy Policy", 2017, https://policy.asiapacificenergy.org/sites/default/files/Draft%20National%20Energy%20Policy%20%28NEP%29.pdf. Accessed on August 8, 2023.
50. Rahul Tongia and Sahil Ali, "Is the draft national energy policy actionable?" *Mint News,* August 22, 2017, https://www.livemint.com/Opinion/5h2buHAGm6ZrVEEAg6CBCM/Is-the-draft-national-energy-policy-actionable.html. Accessed on July 20, 2023.
51. Ministry of Petroleum and Natural Gas, "New Exploration and Licensing Policy", https://mopng.gov.in/files/ExpAndProd/PSC/4.NELP.pdf. Accessed on August 16, 2023.
52. Ibid.
53. Directorate General of Hydrocarbons, "Policy for Geo-scientific Data Generation for Hydrocarbons in Indian Sedimentary Basins and the Agreement to Carry out Non-exclusive Multi-client Geo-scientific surveys/Activities relating to Hydrocarbons", 2014, https://www.dghindia.gov.in/assets/downloads/5e749d1a0448bNonExclusiveMultiClientPolicyForGeoScienceDataGenerationForHydrocarbonsInIndianSedimetaryBasins.pdf. Accessed on August 18, 2023.
54. Ministry of Petroleum and Natural Gas, "Hydrocarbon Exploration and Licensing Policy", https://mopng.gov.in/en/exp-and-prod/help. Accessed on August 16, 2023.
55. Press Information Bureau, "Hydrocarbon Exploration and Licensing Policy", March 10, 2016, https://pib.gov.in/newsite/printrelease.aspx?relid=137638. Accessed on August 16, 2023.
56. Ibid.
57. Sarah Ladlslaw and Sharmlla Bellur, "India's Hydrocarbon Exploration and Licensing Policy (HELP): Will it Help India's Upstream Oil", Centre for Strategic & International Studies, March 21, 2017, https://www.csis.org/analysis/indias-hydrocarbon-exploration-and-licensing-policy-help-will-it-help-indias-upstream-oil. Accessed on August 20, 2023.
58. "India to double down on oil. Gas exploration: Hardeep Singh Puri", *The Hindu News,* February 04, 2022, https://www.thehindu.com/business/Economy/india-to-double-down-on-oil-gas-exploration-hardeep-singh-puri/article38376594.ece. Accessed on August 20, 2023.

59. Press Information Bureau, "MoP&NG launches OALP Bid Round-VIII, accelerates exploration and production (E&P) activities", June 5, 2023, https://www.pib.gov.in/PressReleasePage.aspx?PRID=1929908. Accessed on August 20, 2023.
60. PRS Legislative Research, "Demand for Grants 2023-24 Analysis: Petroleum and Natural Gas", February 20, 2023, https://prsindia.org/files/budget/budget_parliament/2023/DfG_2023-24-Petroleum_and_Natural_Gas.pdf. Accessed on August 20, 2023.
61. "India's Dependency on Oil Imports Likely to Rise Above 80% By 2027, Informs Centre", *Business World News,* August 05, 2023, https://www.businessworld.in/article/India-s-Dependency-On-Oil-Imports-Likely-To-Rise-Above-80-By-2027-Informs-Centre-/05-08-2023-486716/. Accessed on August 20, 2023.

5

Fostering Energy Cooperation: India and the Caspian Sea States

An increase in the quantity of oil and gas imports from Russia was observed in India during the initial months of 2023. In January, India imported 1.3 million barrels per day (mbpd), with the private sector accounting for approximately 60 per cent of the imports.[1] This increase in imports from Russia is the result of India's appetite for profitable hydrocarbons, a point that was emphasised by Indian External Affairs Minister S. Jaishankar when he said, "... we buy oil from multiple sources, but it is sensible policy to go where we get the best deal...."[2] Presently, a major portion of oil comes from Russian fields located in Western Siberia and the Far East of Russia. Before Russia's military operation in February 2022, more than 60 per cent of India's need for crude oil was met by the West Asian region. North America accounted for approximately 14 per cent, West Africa around 12 per cent, Latin America almost 15 per cent, and Russia for about 2 per cent of India's crude oil imports.[3] Despite India's impeccable history of import diversification, it has hardly shown interest in the Caspian region. New Delhi's interest has been historically limited to Iran's Persian Gulf region, and its attitude towards the Turkmenistan-Afghanistan-Pakistan-India (TAPI) project has been unsteady because of various uncertainties associated with the project.

Amidst the ongoing conflict in Ukraine, Russia and Western powers have started to deepen their engagement with Caspian region states. For instance, the European Union (EU) signed a recent MoU on 'Strategic Partnership in the Field of Energy'. Under the agreement, Azerbaijan will double the capacity of the Southern Gas Corridor (SGC) to provide approximately 20 billion cubic meters[4] (bcm) to the EU yearly by 2027. Additionally, the success of the SGC has renewed interest in the Trans-Caspian Gas pipeline (TCP) project. The EU supports the TCP as it aims to diversify energy imports. In the past, the EU and the U.S. have aligned when it comes to introducing energy routes from the region. Likewise, at the 6th Caspian Summit, underlining the significance of the region, Russia emphasised the need to improve the region's transportation and logistics architecture and specifically pointed to the International North-South Transport Corridor (INSTC). It is no surprise that because of international sanctions, Moscow is searching for an alternative route to access markets in Asia. Moscow has strong incentives to prioritise the development of the Caspian region's infrastructure due to several key factors: the opportunity to tap into energy-deficient markets in South Asia and Southeast Asia, the desire to prevent Europe from accessing Caspian energy resources, and the intention to undermine Western nations in their attempts to isolate Russia. For instance, Russia's interest in participating in the development of the TAPI pipeline, which was expressed by Russian Foreign Minister Lavrov, suggests that Moscow will endeavour to enhance its influence in the Caspian region moving forward.

India heavily depends on crude oil imports, as domestic production is inadequate to meet the country's growing needs. In the past ten years, India's net imports of crude oil have increased by more than 90 per cent to reach 4.3 million barrels per day in 2017. The top three providers were Iraq, Saudi Arabia, and Iran, accounting for 21 per cent, 18 per cent, and 11 per cent, respectively. In 2017, Iraq overtook Saudi Arabia as the primary source of crude oil for India. Approximately 62 per cent of India's imported crude oil is obtained from West Asia via the Strait of Hormuz. Another 15 per cent is sourced from Africa, 10 per cent from South America, and the remaining amount is acquired from various other countries. The Indian Oil Corporation Limited (IOCL) has entered into a contract with the United States to acquire 3 million metric tonnes (approximately 61 thousand barrels per day) of U.S. crude oil in 2019.[5] During the period from 2020 to 2021, Iraq maintained its position as India's primary source of oil, representing 24 per cent of the nation's total crude oil imports.

In 2016, after the U.S. and European countries removed their restrictions on Iran's oil exports, India increased its purchases of crude oil, including condensates, from Iran. Following the re-imposition of sanctions by the U.S. on Iran's oil exports in 2020 and 2021, India's imports from Iran ceased completely. Between 2020 and 2021, the U.S. experienced a fourfold increase in the amount of crude oil it exported to India. This accounted for almost 5 per cent of India's total crude oil imports in 2020 and nearly 10 per cent in 2021. In 2021, India's total imports from Russia accounted for 2 per cent of its entire imports. In 2023, India saw a significant increase in its oil imports from Russia, with the latter supplying almost 42 per cent of all crude oil. This was due to Russia offering discounted prices on its oil to boost sales, following its military intervention in Ukraine.[6]

India's gas imports have steadily risen as India's liquefied natural gas (LNG) terminal capacity has expanded. In 2017, the entire volume of natural gas imports amounted to 27 billion cubic metres, with Qatar being responsible for 49 per cent of this amount. India has expanded its supply sources in recent years, purchasing from over 13 countries in 2017. Notably, Nigeria, Equatorial Guinea, and Australia made substantial contributions to India's imports.[7] In 2021, India ranked as the fourth largest importer of LNG worldwide, with around 1.2 trillion cubic feet,[8] or 7 per cent of the total global trade volume. Qatar accounted for 42 per cent of India's LNG imports, with the U.S. and the United Arab Emirates following at 16 per cent and 13 per cent, respectively. Despite currently representing only 6 per cent of the country's energy consumption, India aims to increase the market share of natural gas to 15 per cent by 2030. This is in line with the country's strategy to combat air pollution and promote the use of cleaner burning fuels.[9]

Over the past three decades, the Caspian region's capacity for energy production and its significance as a transportation route for Central Asian energy resources have attracted numerous international stakeholders. The chapter aims to examine the energy dynamics between India and the

Caspian Sea countries amid this development. This paper attempts to answer two main research questions: First, what is the present status of India's energy relations with Caspian Sea states? Second, how can energy cooperation (bilateral and multilateral) with Caspian Sea states facilitate India's energy security? In this regard, the focus will be on the Caspian connectivity initiatives, such as the INSTC and the TAPI project, and their potential to address India's energy concerns. The focus will be on exploring the energy dimension of these connectivity initiatives.

Understanding Regional Energy Cooperation

The post-World War II period witnessed a proliferation of regional organisations aimed at fostering regional cooperation. In the 1960s, regional groupings were formed in many developing countries. In the 1980s and 1990s, integration among developed and developing countries was witnessed through closer economic and trade connections as an alternative to globalisation, for instance, the EU, the Association of Southeast Asian Nations (ASEAN), the South Asian Association for Regional Cooperation (SAARC), the Central European Free Trade Agreement, etc. The drivers and justifications for regional cooperation vary depending on the geographic region as well. For instance, in Africa, attempts were made for economic integration, whereas in Asia, attempts were aimed at promoting cooperation in the fields of culture, politics, and economics rather than pursuing integration. In Europe, the interest in economic integration grew in response to the emergence of common markets. In Latin America and the Caribbean, regional groupings grew because of countries' need to overcome foreign exchange constraints.[10] In general, regional cooperation can be understood as "political and institutional mechanisms that countries in a general geographical region devise to find and strengthen common interests as well as promoting their national interests, through mutual cooperation and dialogue."[11] From an energy security standpoint, regional energy cooperation agreements can be understood as "the political and institutional mechanisms that neighbouring countries devise to interact with one another and pursue common objectives or economic interests that either directly or indirectly involve their energy sector or access to energy resources."[12] Regional energy cooperation offers various long-term advantages through the establishment of collaborative structures for the sharing of energy production, generation, import, transit, or distribution.

For this study, regional energy cooperation is identified in two categories: multilateral cooperation and bilateral cooperation. Multilateral cooperation involves more than two countries, whereas bilateral cooperation involves only two parties, and they are intraregional.[13] Regional cooperation involves setting common rules, regulations, and formal agreements that institutionalise the relationships among neighbouring countries,[14] and this study explores India's engagement with the Caspian Sea states specifically in the field of oil and gas. The goal is to understand and anticipate how regional energy cooperation can serve as a tool to secure India's energy security.

Bilateral Energy Cooperation: India's Energy Engagement with Caspian Sea Countries

The dissolution of the Soviet Union resulted in a significant transformation in regional geopolitics. The emergence of four new countries—Azerbaijan, Russia, Kazakhstan, and Turkmenistan—has significantly altered the balance of power in the region. Since 1991, they have attracted global attention due to their internal conflicts, varied foreign policy orientations, and abundant natural resources. Also, various international and regional entities are engaged in competition within the region, driven by their strategic, economic, and political objectives. Although the Caspian Sea region has a long history of being a significant supplier of oil and natural gas, it has not fully realised its maximal capacity. The region has been hindered from achieving its full potential due to disputes between coastal states regarding competing assertions to oil and gas reserves, uncertainty in regulations, and excessive expenses for extracting hydrocarbons, as it requires significant investment to cover the rising costs of production. The extreme weather conditions, particularly winter freezes, further add to the challenges. Finally, sanctions against Russia and Iran have made matters more difficult, given the Caspian region's strong interdependence among the littoral states.

For India, energy cooperation with the Caspian Sea region is vital for the following reasons: First, India is becoming a dominant consumer in the global energy industry amidst the Ukrainian crisis. Second, India consumes a significant portion of its domestically produced oil and gas. Third, India is urgently exploring external energy sources in response to its domestic hydrocarbon shortfall and rising energy demands. Fourth, India's geographical proximity to the closest external energy source is vital.

India and Russia Energy Cooperation: Current Scenario

Energy forms one of the main pillars of the bilateral relationship between India and Russia. Over 80 per cent of India's energy requirements are fulfilled by coal, oil, and biomass. Coal is supporting the expansion of electricity and industry and remains the largest fuel source in the country's energy basket. Oil imports and consumption are increasing because of the rising use of road transportation and vehicle ownership. Between 1990 and 2018, coal supplied 45 per cent of total energy consumption, followed by oil, which supplied around 26 per cent, and biomass around 20 per cent.[15] Between 2011 and 2015, there has been an increase in coal imports from 100.84 metric tonnes (mt) to 216.54 mt. But, in 2020-2021, imports declined by 14 per cent.[16] Between 2011 and 2020, oil imports rose from 171.73 mt to 226.95 mt,[17] and gas imports increased from 18 bcm to 33.89 bcm.[18]

As an oil and gas deficit country, India relies on imports. For instance, approximately 59 per cent of crude oil was imported from the West Asian region in 2019, mostly from Iraq and Saudi Arabia. Africa and the Americas also contributed 16 per cent and 17 per cent, respectively. In the natural gas sector, India was the 4th largest importing country in 2019, with approximately 1.2 tcf of global trade. Here, Qatar has been the main gas provider with an approximate share of 41 per cent, followed by the U.S., Oman, Australia, and African countries. In the coal sector, India became the 2nd largest importer of coal after China. Indonesia accounts for almost 49 per cent of coal imports, and Australia and South Africa account for 20 per cent and 16 per cent, respectively.[19]

It has been projected that India's demand for oil is expected to rise to 10 million barrels per day by 2040 from 4 million barrels per day. Likewise, natural gas consumption is also expected to increase to 175 billion cubic metres from 50 billion cubic metres.[20] So, it is no surprise that hydrocarbon imports will play an important role in mitigating increasing oil and gas demand in the years to come despite increasing endeavours toward new energy.

Indo-Russian energy collaboration has been majorly confined to nuclear energy and hydrocarbons. In the field of hydrocarbons, as per India's Ministry of Petroleum & Natural Gas, oil and gas account for a 35.7 per cent share of India's energy mix. India imports 83.7 per cent of its overall oil consumption and 45.7 per cent of its natural gas.[21] In its huge energy basket, "India imported approximately 1 percent of its overall imports from Russia in 2021, and it accounts for approximately 0.2 percent of Russia's gas exports."[22] But, at the same time, India has made gradual strides as a few Indian energy companies' investments in Russia are estimated to be worth around US$ 16 billion. Examples include Sakhalin-I, Imperial Energy, and Vankorneft, and the signing of a 'first-term contract' in 2020.[23] Russia's Rosneft has invested approximately US$ 13 billion in a private oil refiner, Essar Oil, renamed Nayara Energy.[24] Despite their close friendship, both Moscow and New Delhi need to make significant strides in the hydrocarbon sector. As India's industrialisation and urbanisation are generating huge energy demands, the country's main objective is to access energy at reasonable prices and in sufficient quantities.

Earlier, highlighting the significance of bilateral energy cooperation, Indian Prime Minister Modi, at the 6th Eastern Economic Forum in 2021, said, "… the India-Russia energy partnership can help bring stability to the global energy market."[25] The significance of India-Russia cooperation lies in the fact that India is an energy-deficit country, and Russia is an energy-surplus country.

Before Russia's special military operation in Ukraine, New Delhi imported approximately 1 per cent oil from Moscow in 2021 and 0.2 per cent of natural gas as a result of GAIL's deal with Gazprom to purchase 2.5 million tonnes of LNG.[26] However, the import volume suddenly shifted after international sanctions on Russia and Europe's decision to cut energy imports from Russia. India's crude oil imports increased and reached approximately 10 per cent by May 2022.[27] Gazprom has expanded its deliveries to GAIL in order to achieve the objective of 2.85 million metric tonnes by 2023.

In the context of asset acquisitions, Indian energy firms have made bids to purchase assets shunned by Western companies. The Oil and Natural Gas Corporation (ONGC) has submitted an offer to acquire Shell's 50 per cent stake in the Salym oilfield in Siberia, Shell's 27.5 per cent stake in Sakhalin-2, and ExxonMobil's 30 per cent stake in Sakhalin-1. GAIL has also expressed interest in acquiring oil and gas assets. In April, Indian companies, including Bharat Petroleum, ONGC, Indian Oil, and Oil India, were in discussions to evaluate the possibility of acquiring BP's 20 per cent stake in Rosneft.[28]

This sudden increase in India's oil imports from Russia cannot be attributed only to low prices. Previously, the imposition of Western sanctions on Iran, with whom India has established long-standing energy ties, had an adverse effect on its energy security. As an oil and gas deficit country, India should not devalue its ties with Russia, which could jeopardise or undermine India's energy interests.

India and Azerbaijan Energy Cooperation: Current Scenario

India recognised Azerbaijan as a sovereign nation shortly after it gained independence in December 1991 and formalised diplomatic relations with it in February 1992. In 1998, the two nations entered into an agreement on economic and technological cooperation. Subsequently, in April 2007, they inked a pact to establish the India-Azerbaijan Intergovernmental Commission on Trade, Economic, Scientific, and Technological Cooperation. As a result, India was able to forge a more robust and significant alliance with Azerbaijan, opening fresh avenues for collaboration and shared advantages. India's trade with Azerbaijan has shown significant growth over the years, rising from approximately US$ 50 million in 2005 to US$ 739 million in 2021. Bilateral trade between Azerbaijan and India reached US$ 1.882 billion in 2022, marking a significant rise of 154.6 per cent. As a result, India now ranks as Azerbaijan's fifth largest trading partner, following Italy, Turkey, Russia, and China. Azerbaijan's exports to India during the time amounted to US$ 1.663 billion, representing a significant rise of 179.7 per cent compared to the previous year. Similarly, imports from India to Azerbaijan reached US$ 219.5 million, showing a notable growth of 51.7 per cent.[29]

In Azerbaijan's oil and gas sector, ONGC Videsh Ltd. was able to acquire shares of 2.72 per cent in the Azeri-Chirag-Gunashli (ACG) oil field and 2.36 per cent in the Baku-Tbilisi-Ceyhan (BTC) pipeline from the U.S. energy firm, Hess Corporation. The ACG field was discovered in the 1970s during the Soviet period and is the largest oil and gas field in Azerbaijan, located in the southern part of the Caspian Sea.[30] With almost 80 per cent of Azerbaijan's crude oil being sent to Europe, European countries hold the highest priority for Baku in terms of its exports.[31]

India's position in the hydrocarbon sector is notable, but its market share is smaller than that of other foreign entities in the country. India accounts for less than 13 per cent of Azerbaijan's total exports. Considering the longer journey hydrocarbons must undertake to reach India from Azerbaijan via Georgia, it is advisable for Azerbaijan, India, and Russia to contemplate the implementation of the INSTC design to establish new energy channels.

India and Kazakhstan Energy Cooperation: Current Scenario

India was among the earliest countries to acknowledge the sovereignty of Kazakhstan after diplomatic relations were officially established in 1992. The first partnership between India's ONGC Videsh Ltd. (OVL) and Kazakhstan's KazMunaiGas (KMG) was established in 2005 to collaborate in the oil and gas industry. New Delhi has been trying to establish a strong presence in the hydrocarbon industry of Kazakhstan. However, the agreement between OVL and KMG was only inked in 2009. In June 2010, KazMunaiGas (KMG) and the Ministry of Oil and Gas of Kazakhstan signed a government contract for exploration and production in the Satpayev block. The Satpayev block is situated in the northwest section of the Kazakhstani sector of the Caspian Sea. In 2011, KazMunaiGas and OVL signed an agreement to facilitate the latter's purchase of a 25 per cent stake in the Satpayev oil block. This agreement was the result of the 5th session of the India-Kazakhstan Intergovernmental Commission on Trade, Economic, Scientific, Technological, Industrial, and Cultural Cooperation in 2005.

Energy has remained one of the primary areas of India's engagement with Kazakhstan. During his initial term as Prime Minister, Narendra Modi undertook visits to Central Asian countries, such as Kazakhstan, where multiple bilateral agreements were reached regarding the fields of energy and military. At the 12th meeting of the India-Kazakhstan Inter-Governmental Commission on Trade, Economic, Scientific, Technical, Industrial, and Cultural Cooperation in 2015, emphasis was placed on energy cooperation.[32]

The first exploratory drilling of the block was jointly inaugurated in Astana in July 2015 by Prime Minister Modi and Prime Minister Massimov. The Satpayev oil block is a hydrocarbon reservoir located in an offshore region, and the site is situated in the Atyrau region, positioned in the northern section of the Caspian Sea. The field is believed to contain around 1.8 billion barrels (250 million tonnes) of prospective crude oil and natural gas reserves. Extraction of the initial oil from the block was anticipated to occur by the year 2020. The Satpayev field was projected to achieve a peak production rate of 287,000 barrels per day.[33] However, this endeavour did not bear fruit, and India pulled out of the region in 2018.[34]

India is a relatively new partner in the country, and Satpayev was its first step on the Kazakhstan side of the Caspian region. At present, Kazakhstan depends on the Caspian Pipeline Consortium system, the Transneft pipeline system (through Russia), and the Kazakhstan-China pipeline to China for exports; hence, the main challenge for India would be to find common ground for cooperation.

India and Turkmenistan Energy Cooperation: Current Scenario

India swiftly recognised Turkmenistan's independence and formalised diplomatic relations in April 1992. India and Turkmenistan are both signatories of the Ashgabat Agreement, with India joining in February

2018. Additionally, Turkmenistan has shown interest in being a member of the INSTC by including its Turkmenbashi port located on the Caspian Sea. It has also shown interest in using the Chabahar Port in Iran, which was constructed with support from India, for the purpose of transshipping cargo.[35]

Turkmenistan sees a lack of infrastructure as limiting its exporting capabilities. Foreign governments or organisations are welcomed when they decide to tie up with either Turkmenneft or Turkmengaz (both are state-owned oil and gas companies). More than 70 per cent of gas goes to China, followed by Russia and Iran.[36] India's share in the country's energy sector is nil. In 2015, the construction of the TAPI pipeline showed a promising future for India's energy security. The pipeline was planned to transport 90 million cubic metres of gas from the Galkynysh field (Turkmenistan), which holds 16 trillion cubic feet of gas reserves. However, work on the pipeline has been halted several times due to security and political reasons. For Turkmenistan, the TAPI gas pipeline project is a route to diversify its exports to overcome its dependency on Russia and China. In mid-2020, after the Taliban established its de facto control over Afghanistan, the former agreed to resume the TAPI project, and Turkmenistan, too, announced to start working on the project.[37] The TAPI project clearly demonstrates Turkmenistan's unwavering commitment to alternative routes and the pursuit of new energy partnerships.

The latest state visit of Indian President Ram Nath Kovind to Turkmenistan in 2022 was an important stepping stone toward India's energy security. President Ram Nath Kovind held a meeting with his Turkmen counterpart, Serdar Berdimuhamedov, to discuss enhancing bilateral ties between the two countries. They deliberated on the Ashgabat Agreement on the International Transport and Transit Corridor and the TAPI gas pipeline project and reached a consensus to convene technical meetings to address the security and commercial aspects of the project.[38] Although the project has been progressing slowly in the past, it has provided India with an impetus for anticipating future cooperation in the development of the region's energy infrastructure.

India and Iran Energy Cooperation: Current Scenario

Traditionally, hydrocarbons dominated Indo-Iran relations. Tehran has always viewed New Delhi as a favourable market for its energy resources, and the latter also occupied an advantageous spot in the former's energy export. Before the sanctions on Iran, it used to be India's second largest oil supplier. In 2009-10, India's oil imports amounted to 21.2 million tonnes, which were later reduced to 11 million tonnes in 2013-14.[39] The lifting of sanctions in January 2016 made way for India to advance with new opportunities. In May 2016, India signed two key agreements with Iran and Afghanistan. In the first, India has inked a bilateral agreement with Iran that grants the former the rights to develop and manage terminals and berths at the Chabahar port for a duration of ten years. This agreement allows India to handle all types of cargo at the port. Second, a trilateral agreement among India, Iran, and Afghanistan was signed for the Trilateral Transport and Transit Corridor connecting Chabahar with Afghanistan's roads and railways.[40] With this development, India was looking forward to expanding its engagement in the region's energy sector.

India's endeavour or initiative in the development of the Farzad-B gas resources, as agreed upon with Iran, represents a notable accomplishment, with estimated reserves exceeding 212 million barrels of oil and 350 billion cubic metres of natural gas.[41] With these deals, India has not only cemented its role in the region's infrastructure development but also flagged its presence there. These deals also provide India an opportunity to connect with other Caspian region countries. In 2017-18, India was the second largest market next to China. It imported nearly 480 barrels of crude oil per day[42] and by 2019, New Delhi imported oil worth US$ 12.11 billion from Tehran. However, the U.S. sanctions shook India's position in Iran's energy share as a result of the Significant Reduction Exemption (SRE) termination.[43] The sanctions also halted India's years of accomplishments in the Farzad-B block in the Persian Gulf.

Of late, Iran has proposed to supply crude oil to India in light of the Ukrainian crisis. This initiative indicates that, despite previous setbacks,

India maintains a crucial role in Iran, as reflected in the Iranian ambassador's assertion: "Iran is ready to meet India's energy security needs by launching rupee-rial trade for exports of oil and gas."[44]

Multilateral Energy Cooperation: India's Approach Toward Connectivity

The Indian government, under the leadership of Prime Minister Modi, prioritised connectivity as a policy objective since the beginning of 2014. Addressing the significance of the Indo-Pacific region at the 2018 Shangri-La Dialogue, Prime Minister Modi stated:

> "Connectivity is vital. It does more than enhance trade and prosperity. It unites a region. India has been at the crossroads for centuries. We understand the benefits of connectivity. There are many connectivity initiatives in the region. If these have to succeed, we must not only build infrastructure, we must also build bridges of trust."[45]

In 2016, at the first Raisina Dialogue, Sushma Swaraj, then Indian Minister for External Affairs, emphasised the significance of connectivity for India in the following way:

> "Connectivity today is central to the globalisation process. It is, of course, particularly important for Asia's growth and development. Indeed, the past many decades have witnessed the restoration and modernisation of connectivity as an integral element of the continent's revival. Where India itself is concerned, whether it is domestic, external, or regional, connectivity will determine how we meet our promise of growth, employment, and prosperity"[46] … "connectivity is not just key to India's development ambitions but an important and integral aspect of its vision for international cooperation. It will drive our interests and relationships in Asia and beyond. We bring to bear a cooperative rather than unilateral approach and believe that creating an environment of trust and confidence is the prerequisite for a more inter-connected world. This is in our DNA;

> after all, we are the inheritors of two powerful connectivity legacies—the message of Buddha and the Spice Route."[47]

Further, India's approach towards the Caspian Sea region can be observed in her statement when she said,

> "...our efforts to work with Iran on the Chabahar Port are getting underway. Perhaps less well known are other initiatives under discussion to cooperate with Iran as a transit corridor to Central Asia and Russia."[48]

Her statement underscores the importance of connectivity in achieving India's developmental objectives and its wider ambition for global collaboration. In this context, connectivity pertains to the creation and enhancement of several forms of linkages, including infrastructural, economic, and cultural bonds, both domestically and internationally, with other countries. It implies that connectivity serves not just as a method to accomplish India's economic goals but also as a vital element of its approach to the region. The mention of a 'cooperative rather than unilateral approach' suggests that India advocates for collective efforts, promoting cooperation and reciprocal advantages with other countries. The objective is to provide a setting characterised by trust and assurance, highlighting the significance of constructive and cooperative connections for a more interconnected global community. The reference to 'the message of Buddha and the Spice Route' emphasises India's historical and cultural ties to the concept of connectivity. The essence of the Buddha's message pertains to the doctrines of peace, empathy, and interdependence that are closely linked with Buddhism. The Spice Route, in contrast, refers to the ancient trade routes that linked India with other regions, enabling the interchange of commodities and ideas. Connectivity is firmly embedded in India's cultural and historical legacy. India seeks to actively contribute to the formation of an interconnected and cooperative society by placing emphasis on a collaborative approach and leveraging its historical heritage.

In the 2nd Raisina Dialogue (2017), Prime Minister Modi emphasised that India's approach to international engagement is centred on "Rebuilding connectivity, restoring bridges, and rejoining India with our immediate and extended geographies."[49] He observed the need for regional connectivity in achieving peace, advancement, and economic well-being. In addition, he underscored the need for preserving the sovereignty of the countries involved to fully realise the potential of regional connectivity and avoid the creation of tensions and disputes.[50]

In his recent visit to Iran on January 14-15, 2024, concerning the Chabahar Port, External Affairs Minister Dr Jaishankar said, "...we discussed India's involvement in the development and operation of the Chabahar port, a joint project with a joint vision of connectivity...discussed how we can establish a firm, sustainable, and long-term roadmap for India's continued involvement over the coming years."[51] Further, on the INSTC, he continued, "Regional connectivity has been a critical pillar of India-Iran relations, ... I reiterated India's interest in benefiting from Iran's unique geographical position to access markets in Central Asia, Afghanistan, and Eurasia. We discussed the prospects of energising the INSTC."[52] The statement underscores the importance of connectivity in achieving India's developmental objectives and its wider ambition for energy cooperation.

Connectivity, in theory, can help ensure energy security in the following ways: First, it can broaden the range of oil and gas supply sources and routes. Countries can access a broader selection of suppliers and lessen their dependency on any one supplier by connecting with multiple oil and gas markets. This can help to reduce the likelihood of supply disruptions and price shocks. Second, new oil and gas resources or fields can be developed. Connectivity can help isolated places develop new oil and gas resources by providing access to infrastructure and markets. This can help to improve oil and gas supply and lessen the likelihood of supply shortages. Third, the efficiency and dependability of oil and gas infrastructure can be enhanced. Countries may build a more connected and robust oil and gas system that can survive interruptions by connecting diverse pipelines and storage facilities. This can facilitate an increase in supply reliability and reduce the danger of price shocks.

The Indian leadership's position on connectivity highlights the need for upholding sovereignty, adhering to the rule of law, and promoting openness, transparency, and equality. Ensuring the preservation of regional peace and stability takes precedence over engaging in geopolitical rivalry. New Delhi acknowledges the need for expanding roads and railways and enhancing digital connections to foster regional cooperation. India's connectivity policy prioritises a rules-based approach that is economically feasible and environmentally sustainable while also respecting sovereignty.[53]

Exploring Energy Potential of the International North-South Transport Corridor

To assess the energy dimension or potential of the International North-South Transport Corridor, it is first important to examine the distribution of oil and gas reserves alongside the corridor route (Map 5.1 and Map 5.2). The INSTC consists of three routes: (a) The *Trans-Caspian section* is a maritime transportation route that connects northern Russia to southern Iran, crossing the Caspian Sea. From there, goods may be sent via the Strait of Hormuz to reach the Arabian Sea. This section comprises the Russian seaports of Astrakhan, Olya, and Makhachkala, as well as the Iranian ports of Bandar-e-Anzali, Nowshahr, and Amirabad. (b) The *Western section* is a land route that combines rail and road transportation. It starts from northern Russia and goes south through Azerbaijan, reaching northern Iran. From there, it continues to a southern port on the Persian Gulf, where the goods are sent by sea. The transportation route consists of a rail connection that passes directly through the Samur and Yalama crossing points, connecting Russia and Azerbaijan. It further extends into Iran by means of the transborder segment between Astara in Azerbaijan and Astara in Iran. (c) The most recent rail and road route, known as the *Eastern section*, extends from northern Russia in a south-eastern direction through Kazakhstan and Turkmenistan, ultimately reaching Iran. The transportation route consists of a railway connection that passes through Kazakhstan and Turkmenistan, ultimately connecting to Iran's railway network at two border-crossing points: Serakhs (Turkmenistan)-Sarakhs (Iran) and Ak-Yayla (Turkmenistan)-Incheboron (Iran).

Map 5.1 Oil and Gas Fields in the Caspian Sea Region

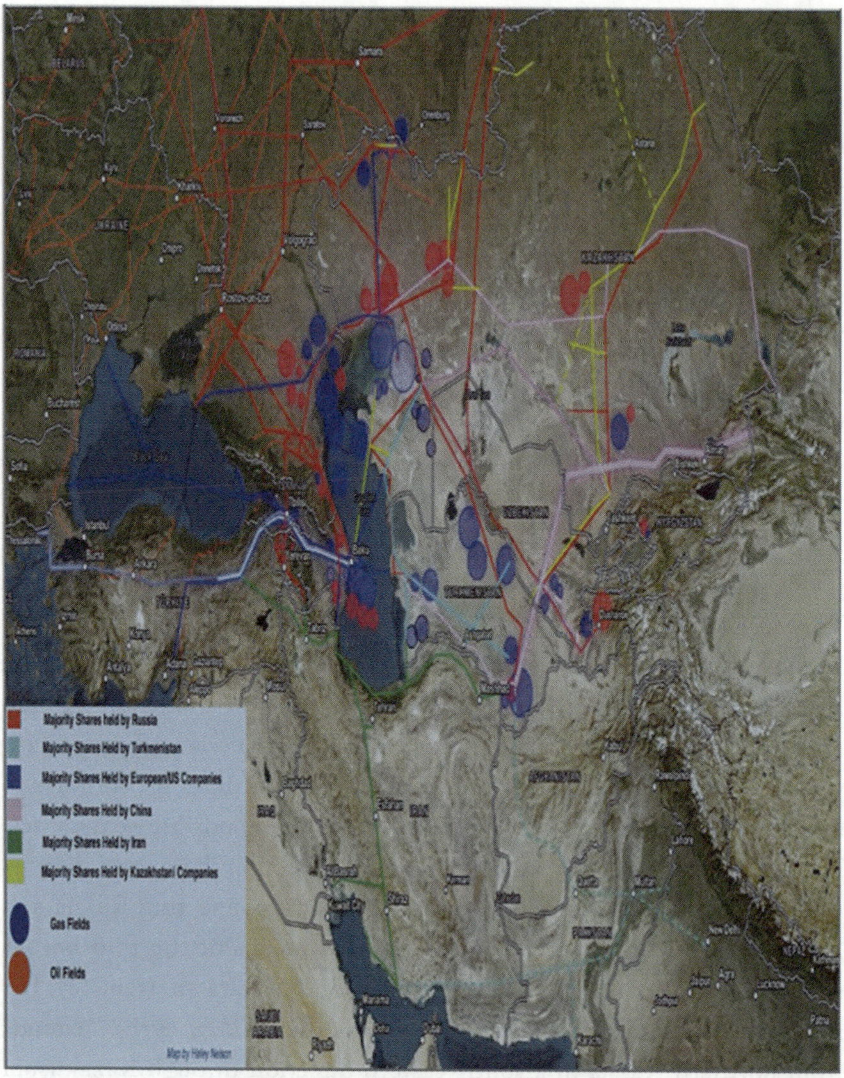

Source: Heley Nelson and Richard E. Hoagland, *The wealth of the Caspian Region: A modern history of oil and natural gas export routes,* Caspian Policy Center, 2023.

Map 5.2 INSTC Transport Routes and Seaports

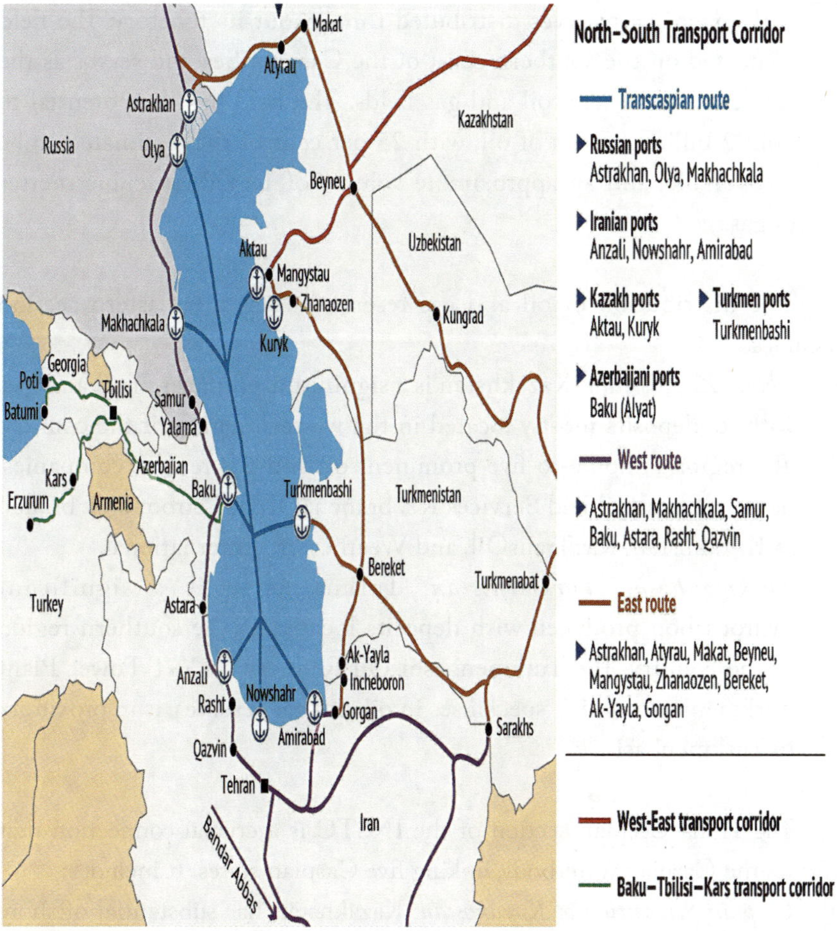

Source: Valdai Club.

The distribution of oil and gas reserves along the Western section includes:

- *Astrakhan, Russia*: The Astrakhan Oblast has oil and gas reserves located in areas such as the Astrakhan gas condensate field and the Kasatskoye field. As of 2022, 11 hydrocarbon deposits were listed on the state balance sheet at the beginning of 2022, with another 11 deposits on the Russian side of the Caspian Sea's seabed.

- *Sardar-e Jangal gas and oil field, Iran*: Iran is a major global oil producer, with extensive reserves distributed throughout its territory. The field is located on the southern coast of the Caspian Sea and serves as the residence for several oil and gas fields. The field has the potential to hold 2 billion barrels of oil, with 25 per cent of that estimated to be recoverable, and an approximate volume of 12 trillion cubic metres of gas.

The distribution of oil and gas reserves along the Eastern section includes:

- *Aktau, Kazakhstan*: Kazakhstan is a significant producer of oil and gas, with its deposits mostly located in the western region of the country. The region is home to five prominent oil and gas reserve companies, namely, Safar Oilfield Services KZ branch, OMV Petrom S.A. branch in Kazakhstan, KazTransOil, and Weatherford International.
- *Turkmenbashi, Turkmenistan*: Turkmenistan is a significant hydrocarbon producer, with deposits located in the southern region of the country. The Turkmenbashi Oil Refinery OCGT Power Plant Turkmenistan, which specialises in oil and gas reserves, is in proximity to Turkmenbashi.

The Trans-Caspian section of the INSTC is a crucial connection that crosses the Caspian waterbody, linking five Caspian states. It includes:

- *Caspian Sea section of Kazakhstan*: Kazakhstan has substantial offshore reserves in the northern part of the Caspian Sea, which include parts of the Kashagan field and other deposits, such as Karachaganak and Tengiz.
- *Absheron Peninsula, Azerbaijan*: The Azeri-Chirag-Guneshli (ACG) oil field, which is one of the biggest in the Caspian Sea, is located on this peninsula.
- *Gunashli and Shah Deniz fields, Azerbaijan*: The presence of these supplementary significant offshore deposits makes a substantial contribution to Azerbaijan's oil and gas production.

The Trans-Caspian section of the INSTC, while not having the highest number of reserves, is crucial in linking Caspian Sea producers to global markets. To fully maximise its potential in the future, it is essential to address logistical obstacles and prioritise environmental sustainability.

The Caspian littoral countries have recently placed increased importance on the INSTC, and the project has acquired significant momentum. However, the INSTC route had difficulties in garnering support; for instance, there was a lack of a minor rail segment on the train connection, little knowledge among prominent commercial organisations, irregular shipping services between India and Iran, and insufficient insurance coverage.[54] Therefore, amidst these challenges, India must develop a new strategy for moving oil and gas from the region. As a non-pipeline option, the INSTC's potential for oil and gas transportation needs to be explored.

Engaging in Hydrocarbon Initiatives through Regional Cooperation Frameworks

In recent times, the Iranian oil and gas sector has experienced new developments. In the upstream segment, Iran now permits international oil companies to participate in all phases of upstream projects under Iran Petroleum Contracts. The international oil companies can engage in the production phases in addition to the exploration and development phases, with an option of extending to the Enhanced Oil Recovery (EOR) phases. In the downstream segment, the Law on the Protection of the Downstream Oil and Natural Gas Sector with Private Investment (2019) was ratified to implement privatisation in Iran's energy industry. These recent developments provide an avenue for India to engage with Iran's oil and gas companies under the BRICS and Shanghai Cooperation Organisation (SCO) frameworks. The prospects for Indian energy companies include modernising Iran's oil and gas technologies, EOR projects, and the construction of LNG export facilities.

The significance of the SCO and BRICS stems from the fact that they bring together three Eurasian powers: India, Russia, and China. With the onboarding of new members, which include oil and gas-rich countries, the global heft of these groupings is projected to grow. In terms of energy cooperation, India and Iran must take a firm stance and present a united front. One of these instances was when India refused to join the 'price cap coalition' against Russia. Iran's importance to India stems from its dual nature as an energy-producing and energy-transit country. In sum, cooperation within the regional cooperative mechanisms—the SCO and the BRICS—holds significant potential for enhancing India's energy partnerships with Iran and catalysing a favourable impact on the geopolitical dynamics of the Caspian region.

Collaboration in Trans-Caspian Maritime Infrastructural Connectivity Initiatives

The maritime domain is one of the areas that has drawn the interest of many global players to the Caspian Sea region. It has played a pivotal role in the development of the oil and gas sector, particularly in terms of providing access to offshore oil and gas fields and allowing the exportation of oil and gas resources. In the last few years, new ports—Amirbad port in Iran (2017), Turkmenbashi port in Turkmenistan (2018), and Kuryk port in Kazakhstan (2018)—have emerged because of the littoral states' desire to become the region's key transportation hub and to promote a competitive climate in the Caspian Sea. Iran and Russia have maritime access, while Kazakhstan, Turkmenistan, and Azerbaijan are landlocked. Presently, Kazakhstan and Azerbaijan depend on two primary pipelines, namely the Caspian Pipeline Consortium (CPC) and the Baku-Tbilisi-Ceyhan (BTC) pipeline, for the purpose of exporting their oil. Over the past 20 years, tankers have emerged as a new method of exporting goods. At present, each of the five Caspian governments operates small fleets of tankers that navigate the world's biggest confined inland waterbody as regional trade continues to grow. Although Russia and Iran have tankers stationed in the Caspian Sea, their fleets are not very big. This is because they mostly rely on pipelines to transmit the majority of their energy exports to the Black Sea and Persian Gulf. From there, they are then transferred onto tankers for further transportation. The most notable advancement is the consistent growth in shipping activities in the affluent petroleum-rich nations of Azerbaijan and Kazakhstan. Turkmenistan, too, has decided to lease and construct ships for the transportation of Caspian hydrocarbons.

In Azerbaijan, the Azerbaijan Caspian Shipping Company (ACSC), the largest and oldest shipping company in the country, traces its origins back to the establishment of the Caspian Shipping Company in 1858. The ACSC fleet comprises a total of 97 vessels, which include 33 tankers and 13 ferries. Azerbaijan has built a new port on the Caspian Sea in Alat, which is located southwest of Baku. It is located at a transportation crossroads where rail and road networks intersect, enabling convenient and efficient transportation in both north-south and east-west directions. Additionally, Alat has the capacity to handle rail ferries.[55] Kazakhstan, too, initiated the transportation of a portion of its oil exports via tankers. In 2008, a company named Cross Caspian Oil and Gas Logistics LLC commenced the shipping of crude oil extracted from Kazakhstan's Tengiz field onshore, across the Caspian Sea, to Azerbaijan. Kuryk Port on the Caspian Sea shoreline, south of Aktau, benefits from direct railway connectivity, as it may be readily utilised for the transshipment of oil and gas. Turkmenistan, formerly using ACSC ships on a charter basis, has initiated the transportation of its oil via maritime routes. In 2001, Burren Energy Shipping and Transportation, the company responsible for managing the Nebit Dag Production Sharing Agreements in Turkmenistan, entered into agreements to construct 10 tankers for its subsidiary, Samara. These tankers would be used in Turkmenistan. Since 2006, Turkmenistan has been actively building its own fleet of tankers by acquiring vessels from Russia and the Baltic republics. These tankers are used to transport products along the Caspian coast and crude oil from Turkmen terminals, Aladzha and Ekerem, to Kenar. Turkmenistan has further declared its intentions in January 2013 to construct a shipyard along the Caspian coastline.

Another related development in the region was Turkmenistan's joining the INSTC project in 2023. Russia, Kazakhstan, and Turkmenistan have undertaken the task of establishing a joint venture to facilitate the advancement of the corridor, and the objective of this venture is to enhance transportation services, reduce cargo delivery times, and expedite customs procedures by implementing standardised information systems, referred to as the 'unified window'.[56] This development coincides with Turkmenistan's ongoing exploration and development of oil and gas reserves located on the Caspian Sea shelf. Eni, Dragon Oil, PETRONAS, and other businesses are involved in the extraction of oil and gas in designated regions of the Caspian Sea. The development of offshore fields in the Turkmen section of the Caspian Sea is another opportunity for attracting investment in the energy industry of Turkmenistan.[57]

Iran is projected to initiate operations at 27 midstream oil and gas projects between 2021 and 2025. In the context of investment in the midstream industry, "…the investments focus on building greater transport and storage to meet the growing demand for oil and gas, as well as for exports."[58] However, the present condition of the Iranian oil industry remains unstable. There is a pressing need for more investment and improved access to equipment and technology. Sanctions have discouraged foreign countries from participating in the Iranian oil and gas sector. The increasing maturity of Iran's gas fields poses a risk to the security of domestic gas supply. There is a need for liquefaction and compressor technology. Although Iran has the capability to produce some compressor components domestically, it lacks the necessary infrastructure and expertise to undertake large-scale design and construction. This scenario synchronises with Iran's endorsement of expediting the advancement of the Chabahar port initiative and its request to India to resume the purchase of crude oil from Iran while attempting to connect the INSTC with Chabahar port. As the port of Bandar-e-Anzali, through which Iran established links with other Caspian Sea ports to facilitate its economic integration in the region, is now being used for the transshipment of containers from the shores of Kazakhstan and Turkmenistan, it provides impetus for the INSTC's prospects for oil and gas transportation.

India should intensify its efforts in maritime infrastructure development. It is critical for India to take advantage of current and proposed maritime projects initiated by the Caspian countries. For example, it is important for New Delhi to give serious consideration to Astana's proposal for the construction of ports in the Caspian Sea to foster energy cooperation. Apart from its gradual increase in investments and the development of ports in the region, India should strive to undertake more measures. The recent manifestation of bilateral agreements between India and Russia, pertaining to shipbuilding activity in Astrakhan port, demonstrates the possibility for such initiatives with other Caspian littoral governments. Moscow intends to invest at least US$ 250 million (potentially up to US$ 1 billion) in the region by 2026, with the goal of increasing the port's capacity from 10 million to 25 million tonnes per annum. The project includes the construction of new piers, berths, terminals, and cargo handling equipment. Likewise, in January 2024, India and Iran engaged in a comprehensive dialogue regarding the establishment of a durable collaboration framework for the strategically significant Chabahar Port. The prioritisation of seaports as facilitators of energy cooperation is essential for India's energy security, as they have the potential to enhance maritime energy transit. Seaports facilitate the accessibility of offshore oil and gas reserves, hence allowing the streamlined transfer of people, equipment, and supplies to and from offshore platforms. They have the potential to facilitate the development of new offshore fields and enhance production capacity. Considering the geographical distance of India, it would be prudent for it to give priority to the development and progress of midstream projects. As ports would help improve marine energy transportation, the Indian shipping industry must prioritise them as essential components of energy security.

Collaboration in Rail Infrastructural Connectivity Initiatives

The railways have historically played a crucial role in transporting energy from the Caspian shores. Azerbaijan, as a littoral state, has a documented history of transporting oil and gas through railways. In the last three decades, with the introduction of pipelines such as the Baku-Novorossiysk pipeline in late 1997, the Baku-Batumi pipeline in early 1999, and the Baku-Tbilisi-Ceyhan pipeline in mid-2005, there was a decline in the transportation of oil, gas, and oil products by railways in the country. Nevertheless, rail transport has maintained its profitability.

Since the beginning of Russia's special military operation in 2022, the Caspian littoral governments have engaged in many bilateral and trilateral agreements for railway connections. For example, Iran and Turkmenistan inked a transit agreement on November 17, 2023, pertaining to the building of road infrastructure. The agreement also emphasised Turkmenistan's connection with Chabahar Port in Iran via a railway, providing it direct access to international waters. Turkmenistan and Kazakhstan have signed a contract regarding a transportation connection. On November 3, 2023, the companies, Russian Railways Logistics (RZD Logistics), Kazakhstan Railways (KTZ Express), and the Transport and Logistics Centre of Turkmenistan (TULM), signed a memorandum of cooperation for international and transit freight transportation. The parties have agreed to establish a collaborative railway service along the international 'North-South' route. These recent initiatives demonstrate that attempts are being made to strengthen railway connectivity infrastructure on the eastern side of the Caspian Sea.

On the other hand, railway networks in Russia and Azerbaijan in the South Caucasus region do not have a direct physical link with Iran on the western side of the Caspian Sea.[59] As Russia and Iran have agreed to complete the Rasht-Astara railway, which is part of the INSTC, the route has the potential to boost the number of products transited via Iran. The Rasht-Caspian railroad, spanning 35 km, is one of two railroads that complement the Rasht-Astara train line in Iran's Gilan Province. It connects the province to the Caspian port of Astara, which is situated in the Anzali Trade-Industrial Free Zone. Due to its sea access, the prospects of this line to facilitate the transportation of oil and gas require serious consideration by the INSTC members.

Further, railway infrastructure complements maritime (seaport) connectivity when it comes to transportation. Therefore, along with the development of the intra-regional railway network, the member countries need to work on the development of port transportation nodes in the region. Port transportation nodes are port complexes, which include a seaport with its facilities and infrastructure; a port rail hub, which includes stations, yards, freight areas, intra-node lines, and other facilities for waggon and locomotive maintenance; and industrial, automobile, pipeline, and urban transport. It enables the transportation of goods from the sea to land and vice versa. In the middle of the ongoing geopolitical unrest, as the Caspian littoral countries are revising their overseas trade strategies and building new logistical routes, India has a unique opportunity to shape its prospects for oil and gas transportation. To realise this, New Delhi must carefully coordinate its relations with the Caspian states to serve common interests.

Prospects of the Turkmenistan-Afghanistan-Pakistan-India Gas Pipeline

The TAPI project is one of the most significant projects in the Caspian-Central Asian region. In recent years, efforts have been made towards the implementation of the long-delayed TAPI project. It has been delayed due to various factors, such as regional security issues, tensions between the participating countries, insufficient funding and indifference approaches of financial institutions and energy companies, and the bankability of the project.

The recently held Turkmen Energy Investment Forum (TEIF) 2024, an international event aimed at attracting foreign investments in Turkmenistan's energy sector, has revived the TAPI project and its potential for ensuring India's energy security. It clearly demonstrates that finance is as pivotal as security. Mukhammetmyrat Amanov, Chairman of the Board of Directors of TAPI Pipeline Company Ltd., announced the completion of the Turkmen segment of the TAPI pipeline and invited international companies to invest in the construction of the pipeline. He emphasised Turkmenistan's effort to expeditiously execute the TAPI project and highlighted the negotiations with the present leadership of Afghanistan on crucial project agreements, including the host country agreement, gas transportation agreement, security arrangements, and land purchase agreement.[60]

Along with Turkmenistan's active efforts towards the TAPI project, its partner countries—Afghanistan and Pakistan—have also expressed their willingness to start the construction of the pipeline project. Afghanistan, under the Taliban de facto administration, has announced its decision to start construction on the TAPI gas pipeline project. Both Turkmenistan and Afghanistan considered it "a large and strategically important project."[61] Further, Turkmenistan and Pakistan, in 2023, signed the Joint Implementation Plan (JIP) on the project. Pakistan has emphasised its potential to act as a convenient entry point for accessing Turkmenistan's abundant energy resources.[62] It is evident from these initiatives that the operationalisation of the TAPI pipeline is quite likely, as it has received acceptance from both Afghanistan and Pakistan. To add further, in 2023, Russia also showed its readiness to join the gas project."[63]

Despite various agreements, many studies highlighted several challenges. Concerning India, Bibhu Routray observed the following challenges: First, India is deeply concerned about the insecurity in Afghanistan. The security situation in both Afghanistan and Pakistan is precarious, and involvement in the project may include direct engagement with, recognition of, and indirect financial support to the Taliban's Islamic Emirate. This could result in the Taliban becoming a stakeholder and beneficiary of the project. Second, India's concerns are also based on its susceptibility to potential gas supply disruptions, which could occur, depending on the condition of relations between India and Pakistan. The participation of China and the actuality of the Sino-Pakistan connection may exacerbate this vulnerability.[64] These issues serve as deterrents for India.

In his earlier visit to Ashgabat on the TAPI project, President Kovind emphasised the importance of resolving the security concerns regarding the pipeline and fundamental business principles during the technical and expert-level discussions.[65] In the context of the concerns highlighted, India may look into the following areas while making assessments on the project. The objective here is to propose some ideas to address India's prospects with the TAPI project:

(a) *Agreement on enhancing pipeline security cooperation:* An accord or pact is necessary to guarantee the protection and safety of pipeline infrastructure during transit. It is possible to explore joint agreements or legal instruments among TAPI member states that pertain to the security of infrastructure and the uninterrupted flow of natural gas. India has already emphasised its security concerns over the pipeline infrastructure. An agreement on this issue can establish a comprehensive framework to handle India's specific concerns about the project.

(b) *Expanding the project's stakeholder base:* By involving other regional countries and international institutions, there is potential for fostering a variety of viewpoints, enhancing the responsibility of its members, and establishing mechanisms for oversight and accountability. India can utilise regional organisations, such as the SCO and the BRICS, to further its energy cooperation. If the member states of the SCO choose to engage in the TAPI project through their Energy Club, the pipeline could potentially be realised. As countries like Russia and Iran, which are members of the SCO, are currently subject to sanctions, they would disregard penalties imposed on the Taliban. For instance, during the 27th St. Petersburg International Economic Forum held from June 5-8, 2024, Russian President Putin advocated for the strengthening of Moscow's relations with the Taliban de facto administration. In addition, Russian Foreign Minister Sergei Lavrov announced Moscow's plans to remove the Taliban from its list of proscribed terrorist groups.[66] Similarly, China, as another member of the SCO, will also disregard any sanctions imposed on the Taliban. China enjoys convenient access to Turkmenistan and Pakistan due to its existing strong diplomatic ties with both countries. It already possesses significant influence in Turkmenistan and Pakistan. Recently, China has begun to establish connections with the Taliban. For example, in 2024, China officially acknowledged Bilal Karimi, a former spokesperson for the Taliban, as a representative to Beijing. This makes the Chinese government the first in the world to recognise the Taliban as the ruling power in Afghanistan after their takeover in 2021.[67] These regional developments and changing dynamics within the SCO and the BRICS could enable China to play a role in facilitating the TAPI pipeline project. India's continued membership in the project will allow future studies to assess its viability, despite the limitations identified by experts. The recent statement by the Indian ambassador to Ashgabat reasserted India's active interest.

Assessment

This chapter underscores the significance of regional energy cooperation, both bilateral and multilateral, in ensuring India's energy security in the years to come. While domestic hydrocarbon exploration and production are crucial, India's dependence on energy imports necessitates strategic partnerships with resource-rich countries. The Caspian Sea states emerge as a significant source of energy for India due to their abundant oil and gas reserves and geographical proximity. At the same time, the Caspian region faces challenges that hinder its full potential. These include unresolved territorial disputes, regulatory uncertainties, and high transportation costs. Therefore, the complex geopolitical landscape, with the involvement of various global actors, necessitates a nuanced approach from India.

This chapter explores the dynamics of India's present energy cooperation with the five Caspian states: Russia, Azerbaijan, Kazakhstan, Turkmenistan, and Iran. Each country presents unique opportunities and challenges. While India has existing partnerships with some, its relations with others require further development. India needs to pursue a two-pronged approach: bilateral cooperation with individual Caspian states and participation in multilateral initiatives. By forging closer ties with these countries, India can ensure a stable and reliable supply of energy to meet its growing demands and support its economic development.

Indian leadership considers connectivity to be a fundamental aspect of its development plan and its ambition for global collaboration. Connectivity involves the construction of physical infrastructure, the promotion of commercial relationships, and the reinforcement of cultural connections. India promotes a cooperative strategy towards connectivity, highlighting the importance of trust, mutual benefit, and respect for each country's sovereignty. This method capitalises on India's rich historical legacy as a centre of trade and cultural interaction.

The INSTC and TAPI projects provide India with the opportunity to tap the energy resources of the Caspian region. However, there are various obstacles, such as inadequate infrastructure, security, and environmental issues, that need to be addressed. The resurgence of interest in the INSTC and the TAPI project underscores the necessity for a solid strategic approach from India. To solidify India's entry in the region, strengthening engagement with Iran (a new member of both the SCO and the BRICS) is crucial. As the Caspian states strengthen their transportation networks, creating new prospects, India can capitalise on this opportunity to shape regional connectivity in relation to the transportation of oil and gas by collaborating with the Caspian states.

Disclaimer: A part of this chapter appeared as the author's article in Air Power Journal at the Centre for Air Power Studies, Vol. 19, No. 2, (April-June), 2024.

Notes

1. Rishi Ranjan Kala, "India top buyer of Russian crude, private refiners lead", *The Hindu Business line*, January 19, 2023, https://www.thehindubusinessline.com/markets/commodities/india-largest-importer-of-seaborne-russian-crude-in-jan-as-private-refiners-get-aggressive/article66409575.ece. Accessed on March 20, 2023.
2. "India's Russian oil imports highest ever, makes up for 25% of all oil import", *Hindustan Times,* January 15, 2023, https://www.hindustantimes.com/business/indias-russian-oil-imports-highest-ever-makes-up-for-25-of-oil-import-101673776679684.html#:~:text=The%20previous%20record%20for%20most,all%20oil%20imported%20by%20India. Accessed on March 20, 2023.
3. "India's Russian oil imports top 1 million barrels a day in December", *Live Mint,* January 15, 2023, https://www.livemint.com/industry/energy/indias-russian-oil-imports-top-1-million-barrels-a-day-in-december-11673762196458.html. Accessed on March 23, 2023.
4. This paper employs both the U.S. Measuring System (e.g., barrels, million cubic feet) and the Indian Measuring System (e.g., metric tonnes, cubic metres) for oil and gas measurements. A conversion table between these units is provided in Appendix I.
5. International Energy Agency, "India 2020: Energy Policy Review", January 2020, https://iea.blob.core.windows.net/assets/2571ae38-c895-430e-8b62-bc19019c6807/India_2020_Energy_Policy_Review.pdf. Accessed on March 20, 2023.
6. Ibid.
7. Ibid.
8. This paper employs both the U.S. Measuring System (e.g., barrels, million cubic feet) and the Indian Measuring System (e.g., metric tonnes, cubic metres) for oil and gas measurements. A conversion table between these units is provided in Appendix I.
9. United States Energy Information Administration, "India", November 17, 2022, https://www.eia.gov/international/analysis/country/IND. Accessed on March 20, 2023.
10. A.S. Bhalla and P. Bhalla, *Regional Blocs: Building Blocks or Stumbling Blocks?* (Great Britain: Macmillan Press, 1997).
11. Babalola Abegunde, "Regional Cooperation and State Sovereignty", *Athens Journal of Law,* Vol. 7, No. 2, 2021, pp. 169-188.

12. Elai Rettig, "When regional energy cooperation fails: learning from the struggles of Northeast Asia's joint oil import mechanism", *Cambridge Review of International Affairs,* 2024, Vol. 37, No. 5, pp. 637–664.
13. Charles K. Ebinger, *Energy and Security in South Asia: Cooperation or Conflict?* (Washington DC: Brookings Institution Press, 2011), p. 142.
14. Aletheia Kerygma B. Valenciano and Aries A. Arugay, "Regional Security Organizations", in Scott N. Romaniuk and Peter Marton, eds., *The Palgrave Encyclopaedia of Global Security Studies,* (Switzerland: Palgrave Macmillan, 2023).
15. United States Energy Information Administration, n. 7.
16 Ministry of Statistics and Programme Implementation, "Energy Statistics India-2022", https://mospi.gov.in/documents/213904/1606151//Energy%20Statistics%20India%202022%1644825594802.pdf/aed59aac-4d5a-995b-1232-bb68397cd873. Accessed on July 26, 2022.
17. Ibid.
18. Ibid.
19. International Energy Agency, n. 4.
20. Vasily Shikin and Amit Bhandari, "Russia—India Energy Cooperation: Trade, Joint Projects, and New Areas", *Policy Brief,* Russian International Affairs Council, October 2017.
21. Ministry of Petroleum and Natural Gas, "Annual Report: 2019-20", https://mopng.gov.in/files/TableManagements/2020-12-08-115045-xyd7b-AR_2019-20E.pdf. Accessed on July 25, 2022.
22. "How dependent is India on Russia for oil, gas, and coal?" *The Economic Times,* February 17, 2022, https://economictimes.indiatimes.com/industry/energy/oil-gas/how-dependant-is-india-on-russia-for-oil-gas-and-coal/articleshow/89634954.cms. Accessed on July 26, 2022.
23. Suhail Nathani and Ambarish Sathianathan, "Russia Sanctions: An Overview of the Impact on India", *Mondaq,* March 2, 2022, https://www.mondaq.com/india/export-controls-trade-investment-sanctions/1167214/russia-sanctions-an-overview-of-the-impact-on-india. Accessed on July 26, 2022.
24. United States Energy Information Administration, "Energy Security", www.iea.org/topics/energysecurity/. Accessed on March 23, 2023.
25. Ibid.
26. "How much oil, gas, and coal India imports from Russia", *The Times of India,* February, 17, 2022, https://timesofindia.indiatimes.com/business/india-business/explainer-how-much-oil-gas-and-coal-india-imports-from-russia/articleshow/89631248.cms. Accessed on July 27, 2022.
27. Rakesh Kumar, "India's crude imports from Russia up 7.2 times April-May 2022", *The New Indian Express,* July 14, 2022 https://www.newindianexpress.com/business/2022/jul/14/indias-crude-imports-from-russia-up-72-timesin-april-may-2022-2476374.html#:~:text=NEW%20DELHI%3A%20India's%20crude%20oil,million%20for%20the%20same%20period. Accessed on July 27, 2022.

28. Ibid.
29. Embassy of India in Azerbaijan, "Brief on India-Azerbaijan Bilateral Relations", May, 2023, https://www.indianembassybaku.gov.in/page/bilateral-brief/. Accessed on March 31, 2023.
30. "Vankorneft", at http://www.rosneft.com/Upstream/ProductionAndDevelopment/eastern_siberia/vankorneft/. Accessed on March 31, 2023.
31 International Energy Agency, "Azerbaijan 2021: Energy Review Policy", https://www.euneighbours.eu/sites/default/files/publications/2021-07/Azerbaijan2021EnergyPolicyReview.pdf. Accessed on March 31, 2023.
32. Embassy of India in Kazakhstan, "12th meeting of the India-Kazakhstan Inter-Governmental Commission on Trade, Economic, Scientific, Technical, Industrial and Cultural Cooperation", https://www.indembastana.gov.in/news_detail/?newsid=94. Accessed on April 1, 2022.
33. Oil and Natural Gas Corporation, "Hon'ble PM launches drilling at Satpayev in Kazakhstan", July 15, 2015, https://www.ongcindia.com/wps/wcm/connect/en/media/press-release/honblepm-launches-drilling-kazakhstan. Accessed on April 1, 2022.
34. "OVL to exit Kazakhstan's Satpayev oil block", *Times of India,* September 18, 2018, https://timesofindia.indiatimes.com/business/india-business/ovl-to-exit-kazakhstans-satpayev-oil-block/articleshow/65855093.cms. Accessed on April 1, 2022.
35. Embassy of India in Turkmenistan, "India-Turkmenistan Bilateral Brief", https://www.mea.gov.in/Portal/ForeignRelation/Bilateral-brief23.pdf. Accessed on April 1, 2022.
36. United States Energy Information Administration, "Turkmenistan", https://www.eia.gov/international/analysis/country/TKM?pa=12&u=0&f=A&v=none&y=01%2F01%2F2019. Accessed on April 1, 2022.
37. "The long and troubled history of TAPI Pipeline: What you need to know about ambitious gas pipeline project", *Firstpost,* January 28, 2022, https://www.firstpost.com/world/the-long-and-troubled-history-of-tapi-pipeline-what-you-need-to-know-about-ambitious-gas-pipeline-project-10328721.html. Accessed on April 1, 2022.
38. "India, Turkmenistan sign 4 MoUs for cooperation, agree to expand bilateral trade", *The Indian Express,* April 02, 2022, https://indianexpress.com/article/world/india-turkmenistan-mou-cooperation-bilateral-trade-7849665/. Accessed on April 3, 2023.
39. "India Looks to Raise Oil Imports from Iran as Sanctions Lifted", *DNA India,* January 18, 2016, at http://www.dnaindia.com/money/report-india-looks-to-raise-oilimports-from-iran-as-sanctions-lifted-2167324. Accessed on April 3, 2023.
40. "India to Develop Iran's Chabahar Port", *The Hindu*, May 24, 2016, at http://www.thehindu.com/news/national/india-to-develop-irans-chahbahar-port/article8637558.ece. Accessed on April 3, 2023.

41. "Iran Reaches Basic Agreements with India on Farzad B", *Iran Daily*, April 12, 2016, http://www.iran-daily.com/News/139416.html?catid=3&title=Iran-reaches-basicagreements- with-India-on-Farzad-B. Accessed on April 3, 2023.
42. "US tells allies to halt Iran oil imports by Nov", *BBC News,* June 06, 2018, https://www.bbc.com/news/business-44621127. Accessed on March 22, 2022.
43. Ministry of External Affairs, "India-Iran Bilateral Relations", https://mea.gov.in/Portal/ForeignRelation/India-Iran__Aug_2020_.pdf. Accessed on March 21, 2022.
44. "After Russia, Iran offers oil to India, proposes revival of rupee-rial barter", *ET Now,* March 19, 2022, https://www.timesnownews.com/business-economy/economy/after-russia-iran-offers-oil-to-india-proposes-revival-of-rupee-rial-barter-article-90324533. Accessed on March 24, 2022.
45. Ministry of External Affairs, "Prime Minister's Keynote Address at Shangri La Dialogue", June 1, 2018, https://www.mea.gov.in/Speeches-Statements.htm?dtl/29943/Prime+Ministers+Keynote+Address+at+Shangri+La+Dialogue+June+01+2018. Accessed on 20 February, 2024.
46. Observer Research Foundation, "Raisina Dialogue: Conference Report-2016", 2016, https://www.orfonline.org/wp-content/uploads/2016/10/Raisina2016_Report.pdf. Accessed on February 22, 2024.
47. Ibid.
48. Ibid.
49. Observer Research Foundation, "Raisina Dialogue: Conference Report-2017", 2017, https://www.orfonline.org/wp-content/uploads/2017/09/Raisina_Report_2017-WEB.pdf. Accessed on February 22, 2024.
50. Ibid.
51. Ministry of External Affairs, "Joint Press Statement by EAM, Dr. S. Jaishankar with Minister of Foreign Affairs of Iran", January 15, 2024, https://www.mea.gov.in/Speeches-Statements.htm?dtl/37513/Joint+Press+Statement+by+EAM+Dr+S+Jaishankar+with+Minister+of+Foreign+Affairs+of+Iran. Accessed on February 22, 2024.
52. Ibid.
53. Manasi Singh, "India, Europe and Connectivity: From Shared Views on BRI to Mutual Cooperation?" in Rajendra K. Jain, eds, *India, Europe and Asia Convergence and Divergence,* (Singapore: Palgrave Macmillan, 2021).
54. Athar Zafar, "India and Russia in Central Asia: Growing convergence of interests?" *MGIMO Review of International Relations,* 2023, 16 (2), pp. 251-262.
55. United States Department of Commerce, "Azerbaijan: Country Commercial Guide", International Trade Administration, November 21, 2023, https://www.trade.gov/country-commercial-guides/azerbaijan-transportation-and-logistics. Accessed on February 22, 2024.
56. Dennis van der Laan, "Russia, Kazakhstan and Turkmenistan create INSTC joint venture", *Rail Freight,* February 28, 2024, https://www.railfreight.com/railfreight/2024/02/28/russia-kazakhstan-and-turkmenistan-create-instc-joint-venture/?gdpr=accept. Accessed on May 11, 2024.

57. "Turkmenistan Wants to Attract Foreign Investors to the Exploration and Development of the Caspian Shelf", *ROGTEC Magazine,* March 21, 2024, https://www.rogtecmagazine.com/turkmenistan-wants-to-attract-foreign-investors-to-the-exploration-and-development-of-the-caspian-shelf/. Accessed on May 11, 2024.
58. "Iran leads midstream project starts in the Middle East by 2025", *Natural Gas World,* January 6, 2022, https://www.naturalgasworld.com/iran-leads-midstream-project-starts-in-the-middle-east-by-2025-95269. Accessed on February 22, 2024.
59. Vali Kaleji, "Will Russia Complete Iran's Rasht–Astara Railway?" The Jamestown Foundation, May 16, 2022, https://jamestown.org/program/will-russia-complete-irans-rasht-astara-railway/. Accessed on February 22, 2024.
60. "Turkmenistan ready to accelerate TAPI project through closer cooperation with partners", *Interfax*, April 25, 2024, https://interfax.com/newsroom/top-stories/101802/. Accessed on May 10, 2024.
61. Daniel Onyango, "Taliban Announces Readiness to Begin Work on Afghan Portion of TAPI Gas Pipeline Project", *Pipeline Technology Journal News,* February 29, 2024, https://www.pipeline-journal.net/news/taliban-announces-readiness-begin-work-afghan-portion-tapi-gas-pipeline-project. Accessed on May 10, 2024.
62. "Pakistan, Turkmenistan ink Joint Implementation Plan for TAPI gas pipeline", *Business Standard,* June 9, 2023, https://www.business-standard.com/world-news/pakistan-turkmenistan-ink-joint-implementation-plan-for-tapi-gas-pipeline-123060900063_1.html. Accessed on May 11, 2024.
63. Habib Rahman Qooyash, "Russia Ready to Join TAPI Project: Envoy", *Tolo News,* January 25, 2023, https://tolonews.com/business-181698. Accessed on May 11, 2024.
64. Bibhu Prasad Routray, "Re-Reviving TAPI: Hardened Obstacles & Challenges for New Delhi", Mantraya Policy Brief No. 38, April 8, 2022, https://mantraya.org/policy-brief-re-reviving-tapi-hardened-obstacles-challenges-for-new-delhi/. Accessed on May 11, 2024.
65. "India, Turkmenistan sign 4 MoUs for cooperation, agree to expand bilateral trade", *The Indian Express,* April 2, 2022, https://indianexpress.com/article/world/india-turkmenistan-mou-cooperation-bilateral-trade-7849665/. Accessed on May 11, 2024.
66. "Putin Calls For Russia To "Build Up" Ties With Taliban Government", *NDTV News,* 06 June, 2024, https://www.ndtv.com/world-news/vladimir-putin-calls-for-russia-to-build-up-ties-with-taliban-government-5827416. Accessed on May 11, 2024.
67. Ruchi Kumar, "Why has China recognised Taliban's envoy to Beijing?" *Aljazeera News,* February 14, 2024, https://www.aljazeera.com/news/2024/2/14/is-chinas-recognition-of-afghanistan-envoy-a-diplomatic-win-for-taliban. Accessed on May 11, 2024.

6

Conclusion: Exploring the Potential for Future Cooperation

Since the beginning of Russia's special military operation in Ukraine, there have been significant changes in the global energy landscape. As the conflict in Ukraine has stretched into 2024-25, it is uncertain how the events on the ground will unfold. The conflict has compelled countries in Europe and Asia to revaluate their energy strategies in order to secure energy supplies. For instance, European countries such as Germany have cancelled their approval of a newly planned Russian gas pipeline and are now preparing to purchase liquefied natural gas from the United States (U.S.) and Qatar. Belgium is rethinking its departure from nuclear power. Italy, the Netherlands, and the United Kingdom are all stepping up their efforts to deploy wind power. Meanwhile, two Asian powerhouses—China and India—have increased their energy imports from Russia. Undeniably, Russia's special military operation in Ukraine has elevated the importance and concerns of energy security at a global level.

With Russia halting the supply of natural gas to Europe in response to Western sanctions on imports from it, Europe has turned its attention to the Caspian Sea states. In their quest for an alternative source of gas in the short term amidst the ongoing conflict, the European Union (EU) members have turned to Azerbaijan.[1] While Brussels seeks to improve its position, Russia also wants to secure its position in the Caspian region. The idea of a 'Trilateral Gas Union' among the three littoral states, proposed by Russian

President Putin, indicated Russia's haste in tying the littoral countries into some form of an energy consortium led by Moscow.

On the energy front, amidst the Ukrainian conflict, the littoral states are also increasing intra-regional cooperation amongst themselves and endeavouring to access alternative markets for their oil and gas. For instance, in June 2022, Iran and Azerbaijan signed an agreement to increase the volume of gas swaps between Azerbaijan and Turkmenistan. As per an earlier gas swap agreement signed amongst three littoral states in November 2021, Iran annually delivers 1.5 to 2.0 billion cubic metres[2] of Turkmen gas to Azerbaijan. From January 2022 onwards, the supply volume rose to 5-6 million cubic metres of gas per day. Iran receives Turkmen gas and then delivers an equal amount to Azerbaijan.[3] Iran also signed a US$ 40 billion energy cooperation deal with Russia in July 2022. This increasing energy cooperation was endorsed by Kazem Jalali, Iranian Ambassador to Russia, when he said, "Iran welcomes foreign investors, especially from friendly countries such as Russia, to implement relevant projects."[4] In the second Caspian Economic Forum held on October 5-6, 2022, the key focus was on increasing energy ties. The Caspian riparian countries emphasised increasing oil and gas swaps on the shores of the Caspian Sea, settlements based on national currencies, and cooperation in the energy field to counter sanctions.[5]

In recent times, Iran has emerged as an important factor in the geopolitics of the Caspian Sea region. The Brazil, Russia, India, China, and South Africa (BRICS) group held its 15th summit in August 2023, when members agreed to add new countries on January 01, 2024, Iran being one of them. Likewise, the 23rd Shanghai Cooperation Organisation (SCO) Summit in July 2023 welcomed Iran as a new member. Both the BRICS and the SCO have gained immense importance in Eurasian politics. The BRICS is known for its economic prowess and diversity, whereas the SCO is primarily concerned with security and regional cooperation in Eurasia. With the admission of Iran to the SCO and the BRICS, the geopolitics of the Caspian region is set to change. The Caspian region will witness an escalation in geopolitical tug-of-war amongst regional and non-regional actors. For Iran, membership in these organisations is linked to its 'Look East' policy. On the other hand, for Russia and China, Iran's admission in these organisations strengthens the notion of multipolarity. These organisations will provide Iran with regional platforms to strengthen engagements with Eastern economies. In sum, it is safe to conclude that Russia is looking toward east and south Asian markets; Azerbaijan, Kazakhstan, and Turkmenistan are looking toward European markets; and Iran is hoping to become a regional hub for energy.

The Caspian region offers India a promising source of energy, but based on the lessons learnt in the previous chapters, lack of and limited infrastructure and difficulty in reaching an agreement on the legal status of the Caspian Sea are factors that pose challenges. These challenges are intertwined and cannot be examined in isolation. The first challenge is the geographical distance between India and the Caspian Sea region. To establish transit connections, India needs to depend on land and sea routes. However, the land routes include the territories of Pakistan and Afghanistan, which poses challenges of security and instability. The land transit through Iranian territory also comes with its predicament of the ongoing Western sanctions. Second, lack of and limited transportation infrastructure is another challenge. Despite conceptualisation, there is no strong energy midstream infrastructure. Though work on the Turkmenistan–Afghanistan–Pakistan–India (TAPI) project has started, the Af-Pak factor can bring hurdles. Third, the difficulty in reaching an agreement on the legal status of the Caspian Sea hampers the development of energy projects, creates uncertainty about ownership, and reduces foreign investments.

Challenges in the Caspian's Hydrocarbon Sector

Challenges in Iran's Oil and Gas Industry

Sanctions and foreign investment: The depth of the Iranian sector in the Caspian Sea imposes technical difficulties. The condition necessitates the construction and installation of specific deep-water drilling rigs. This type of equipment necessitates substantial finances and advanced technologies; however, the Western sanctions have created significant challenges for

Iran.[6] Iran's capacity to export oil, acquire cutting-edge technologies, and allure international investment has been significantly curtailed due to the economic sanctions imposed by the U.S. and its allied countries. As a result, Iran's oil production capacity has been restricted, and its efforts to modernise its infrastructure have been hindered. Iran's oil sector has been unable to attract necessary foreign investment to revitalise its established oil reserves and explore new discoveries. Iran will continue to encounter challenges domestically in attracting new investment needed to increase output, as put forward by Hamid Hosseini, Board Member, Iran's Oil, Gas, and Petrochemical Products Exporters' Union in Tehran, when he said, "As long as there is no opening in our foreign relations, providing major foreign investment to this end is definitely impossible."[7]

Shortage of natural gas for reinjection: Iran relies on the method of reinjecting natural gas into oil fields to sustain its pressure and maintain production. The inadequacy of gas reserves for reinjection is hampering this process and accelerating the drop in oil production. For example, Erfan Afazeli, Chairman of the Iranian Federation of Petroleum Industry, highlighted Iran's need to introduce gas into its oil reservoirs in order to sustain the production flow. He cautioned that failure to do so will lead to substantial damage and further added that the progress of Iran's enhanced oil recovery initiatives is impeded by a lack of technical proficiency and insufficient financial means.[8]

Maturing energy infrastructure: Over the years, the sanctions and financial constraints have resulted in a lack of investment in Iran, causing oil and gas fields and refineries to become old and outdated. This leads to a decrease in efficiency and an increase in manufacturing costs. The research conducted by the International Energy Agency (IEA) in February 2024 concluded that Iran's reduction in oil output may speed up because of insufficient investment in new technologies and maintenance, exacerbated by ageing infrastructure. According to reports from Iran's Ministry of Oil and the US Energy Information Administration, around 80 per cent of Iran's oil production is derived from old oil fields that are experiencing decreasing pressure. As a result, Iran's annual oil production is declining by 8 to 10 per cent.[9] As per the Khazar Exploration and Production Company

(KEPCO), approximately US$ 12 billion is required to drill over 12 oil wells in the Caspian Sea, which would enable Iran to extract a minimum of 125,000 barrels[10] of oil per day over a 25-year span (Keleji quoted KEPCO). However, the challenging economic circumstances resulting from international sanctions have prevented Iran from investing in energy infrastructure in the deep seas of the southern Caspian.[11]

Challenges in Russia's Oil and Gas Industry

Stagnant demand: The shift towards renewable energy sources and an emphasis on energy efficiency in Europe, which is a long-standing consumer of Russian oil and gas, may result in a decrease in demand for these commodities. The EU's REPowerEU strategy, announced in 2022, aims to phase out Russian fossil fuel imports and increase the use of renewable energy sources.[12]

International sanctions: The Western sanctions implemented following the Russia's military operation in Ukraine restricted the availability of sophisticated technologies required for exploring and extracting resources in challenging regions. This can impede both effectiveness and security. For instance, in July 2023, the oilfield services company, SLB, declared ceasing transportation of products and technology to Russia from all SLB locations across the globe as a direct response to international sanctions. It imposed an embargo on shipments from the U.S., Britain, the EU, and Canada to Russia in the past.[13]

Challenges in Azerbaijan's Oil and Gas Sector

Declining oil production: The Azeri-Chirag-Guneshli (ACG) oil field in the Caspian Sea is presently experiencing a gradual decline in oil output as a result of natural factors. British Petroleum's regional president, Gary Jones, asserts the possibility to mitigate the rate of decline by increasing investment and embracing innovative technologies. Despite a decline, Azerbaijan's commitment to its oil industry can be observed, with the Baku-Tbilisi-Ceyhan (BTC) pipeline playing a vital role in transporting crude oil and condensate. The current negotiations aim to increase the oil supply from Kazakhstan by using Azerbaijan while considering the differences in quality between Azerbaijani and Kazakhstani oil.[14]

Challenges in Kazakhstan's Oil and Gas Sector

Mature fields and depletion: The decrease in production presents a substantial risk to the entire country, as it will negatively affect nearly all areas of the economy and might lead to a scarcity of oil and petroleum products. President Tokayev has stressed restoring the mineral resource base, which entails promptly identifying new resources and reserves. To enhance the recovery rate and extend the lifetime of depleted fields, it is imperative to utilise contemporary production techniques.[15] The present oil reserves in Kazakhstan have reached a state of maturity and require modern techniques for extraction. The exploration of new fields and more challenging areas, such as deepwater deposits, necessitate significant investments and expertise.

Export route vulnerability: Kazakhstan's existing oil export system is constrained, necessitating a renewed focus on identifying alternate transportation options for its energy. This challenge is more pertinent given the geopolitical tensions surrounding Russia. As Lidiya Parkhomchik (an expert at the Institute of World Economics and Politics) said, "Given the increased geopolitical turbulence around Russia, finding alternative options for Kazakhstan's oil exports continues to be relevant."[16]

Challenges in Turkmenistan's Oil and Gas Sector

Concerns over foreign investment: Over the years, Turkmenistan's cautious strategy towards foreign investment has limited the availability of vital technology and knowledge necessary for infrastructure development and diversification. Recently, the state corporations, Türkmengaz (Turkmen Gas) and Türkmennebit (Turkmen Oil), in partnership with Turkmen Forum and the British company, Gaffney Cline, arranged a forum with the objective of showcasing Turkmenistan's resource potential and investment prospects in the global energy transition. The primary objective of the Turkmenistan Energy Investment Forum (2024) was to attract foreign investments in the resources located in the Caspian Sea.

Limited options for export: At present, Turkmenistan's pipeline infrastructure is mainly dependent on Russia and China, which limits its capacity to access new buyers. This was apparent during the recent decline in energy prices when Turkmenistan faced difficulties in locating other purchasers. For example, Turkmenistan has experienced a decline in its natural gas exports to Western countries, which has necessitated the search for new partners. Turkmenistan exports significant amounts of gas to Russia, China, and Iran. Due to the prevailing uncertainty and instability in the region and economic difficulties in Russia and Iran, Turkmenistan has shifted its efforts towards increasing gas exports to China.[17]

Cooperation over Competition

Opportunities in the Upstream Sector

To guarantee energy cooperation, India has a strategic opportunity to form a partnership with the Caspian littoral states in the upstream oil and gas sector, which includes activities such as exploration, development, and production. India possesses notable advantages. State-owned firms, like the Oil and Natural Gas Corporation (ONGC), possess substantial expertise in exploration and production. Moreover, Indian private enterprises, such as Reliance Industries, have actively allocated funds to international oil and gas ventures, showcasing their substantial financial resources. India could cooperate with regional businesses in Azerbaijan, Kazakhstan, and Turkmenistan in the following domains:

(a) Exploit untapped oil and gas reserves: The Caspian Sea region harbours vast hydrocarbon resources, including multiple fields that remain mostly unexplored. India's proficiency in the upstream sector can be pivotal in uncovering and extracting these resources, resulting in mutual benefits for both.

(b) Obtain ownership shares in established oil and gas fields: The Caspian Sea is home to multiple operational oil and gas fields. India has the option to invest by purchasing shares in the companies operating them, which would provide it with instant access to production and revenue streams. For example, the ONGC has already obtained ownership interests in ongoing ventures in Kazakhstan. Similar endeavours might be undertaken in other littoral countries that require financial assistance in the upstream development.

(c) Provide technical know-how: India's strong oil and gas service industry can provide valuable technical knowledge. This may encompass aspects, such as storage management, drilling techniques, and higher oil recovery, ultimately resulting in heightened output for the region.

Collaboration in the early stages of a project provides a situation where the parties involved can benefit. As the Caspian states require crucial financial resources and advanced technological expertise, India's technological expertise and growing energy demands position it as a serious player in driving the progress of the oil and gas sector in the Caspian Sea region.

Opportunities in the Midstream and Downstream Sectors

Although ensuring a consistent and reliable supply of oil and gas is of the utmost significance, India has the potential to expand its influence beyond its current role as a simple consumer. India can strengthen its economic partnerships and position itself as a significant participant in the energy infrastructure of the Caspian Sea region by making strategically important investments in the midstream and downstream sectors. India possesses the means for cooperation with regional Caspian companies to establish and enhance this vital infrastructure. This cooperation could encompass various facets:

(a) Building new pipelines and focusing on the energy transit potential of the International North–South Transport Corridor (INSTC): Currently, there is no direct pipeline connecting the Caspian Sea's vast reserves to India. Investing in infrastructure projects like the SAGE pipeline will negate the security-related fears related to the TAPI and would ensure a stable and cost-effective flow of energy resources. Further, until now, experts have only concentrated on the commercial and trade aspects of the INSTC. Moving forward, the INSTC members should focus on exploring and utilising the multimodal transportation network in the region to transfer oil and gas to India.

(b) Providing technical expertise: India has a well-established oil and gas midstream base with significant expertise. By offering technical assistance and services to the Caspian littoral states, India can foster knowledge sharing and strengthen partnerships. This could involve training local personnel, sharing best practices in refinery operations, or cooperating on pipeline maintenance projects.

(c) Support and active participation in various regional storage projects: In recent times, Turkmenistan has shown intentions to execute large gas projects to enhance its export capacity, including the setting up of an underground gas storage facility, the Karakum and Shatlyk compressor stations at gas condensate fields, and the construction of Zyakli-Derveze gas cleaning units.[18] As these initiatives will be undertaken with the involvement of foreign contractors, India should assess and seriously consider the prospects for cooperation.

India's entry into the midstream and downstream segment of the Caspian Sea offers a win-win scenario, as India secures a reliable source of energy, while the Caspian states benefit from the development of infrastructure and possible new markets. India can strengthen its position as a significant participant in the energy sector of the Caspian Sea by developing robust partnerships and making strategic investments in these essential industries.

Energy Cooperation through Regional Framework

India should use multilateral organisations such as the SCO, the Eurasian Economic Union, and the BRICS to develop an energy strategy. Through regional energy cooperation, India can propose the bifurcation of existing energy export routes or new routes from the Caspian region. Iran's geographical proximity to South Caucasus and Central Asia and its existing domestic midstream network can be used for transporting energy resources. A proposal can be put forward for using the Iranian energy network for exports. The realisation of a trans-Iranian transit corridor will open access gates for India, as it would connect the Caspian Sea to international waters. The South Caucasus Gas Pipeline (from Azerbaijan to Turkey) and the Baku-Tbilisi-Ceyhan Oil Pipeline (from Azerbaijan to Turkey via Georgia) are such instances. Similar initiatives would require strong political will and investments from the participating countries to be put into effect. Recently, Iran has encouraged neighbouring Caspian countries to make use of its transit connections. Hojatollah Abdolmaleki, Advisor to the President and Secretary General of the Supreme Council of Free Economic Zones of the Islamic Republic, has encouraged neighbouring countries to take advantage of affordable and unobstructed transit routes that run through Iran.

Russia's 2023 foreign policy described the Russia-India relationship as a 'privileged strategic partnership'. It emphasised the need to enhance and broaden cooperation in all areas, with a focus on increasing bilateral trade, strengthening investment and technological connections, and safeguarding against harmful actions by hostile countries and their alliances. Given that Russia and India are both members of the SCO and the BRICS and are currently in the process of negotiating a free trade agreement with the Eurasian Economic Union, it is important for New Delhi to secure Moscow's participation and collaboration in energy-related opportunities in the region. It is necessary for India to engage in strategic collaboration with Russia for it to make significant advancements in the region.

Iran is another important partner in the region. In recent times, Moscow and Tehran have intensified bilateral cooperation in the oil and gas sector. As Tehran has joined the SCO and the BRICS, New Delhi needs to speed up new avenues of partnership with the former. Tehran, like Moscow, has been subjected to harsh Western sanctions, which are expected to remain in place. Given Moscow's penchant for New Delhi, the latter should think about initiating similar endeavours. Further, on its part, India can propose an energy consortium with Iran and Russia, like President Putin's 'tripartite gas union' proposal in 2022. This consortium will bring together not only the largest producers but also the largest consumers in the world. As Moscow backed Iran's admission to the SCO as a full member, as well as its application to join the BRICS, creating a regional energy consortium would not be a difficult assignment.

The Last Word

India's energy strategy is characterised by the diversity of energy supplies, with a strong emphasis on expanding its alternate energy capacity. The government has set goals for the adoption of renewable energy, and it has made significant progress in this regard. However, given the present ratio of massive energy consumption, the predicted increase in consumption patterns in the coming years, and the inconsistent availability of renewable energy sources, the significance of hydrocarbons will continue. Additionally, though essential and inevitable, the energy transition to renewables is a gradual process that requires financial capital, the latest technology, and considerable time. In this regard, the importance of oil and gas cannot be negated, considering their value as intermediate fuels during the energy transition, giving ample time to facilitate this transition.

Although India has made significant progress in obtaining oil and gas from different regions, more attention and efforts are required to explore the potential advantages of the Caspian region. The limited attention given to the Caspian region is because of the complex relationships among the littoral countries, uncertainty on territorial issues, lack of connectivity, and tug-of-war among major powers in the region. These factors may create challenges for India to establish stable and long-term energy partnerships. Nonetheless, these challenges are not insurmountable. India's proficiency in the energy industry and regional cooperation mechanisms can facilitate forging energy partnerships in various oil and gas segments and leveraging diplomacy to secure access to the region's energy resources. Given the significant opportunities in the Caspian region, this book has endeavoured to understand energy dynamics from India's perspective, highlighting the importance of focusing on the Caspian region to secure India's energy future.

Notes

1. Nigar Bayramli, "President Aliyev inaugurates Greece-Bulgaria Interconnector to launch direct gas supplies to Bulgaria", *Caspian News,* October 02, 2022, https://caspiannews.com/news-detail/president-aliyev-inaugurates-greece-bulgaria-interconnector-to-launch-direct-gas-supplies-to-bulgaria-2022-10-2-0/. Accessed on December 18, 2023.

2. This paper employs both the U.S. Measuring System (e.g., barrels, million cubic feet) and the Indian Measuring System (e.g., metric tonnes, cubic metres) for oil and gas measurements. A conversion table between these units is provided in Appendix I.
3. Aygul Ospanova, "Azerbaijan president, Turkmen official discuss energy, transport ties", *The Caspian News,* November 29, 2022, at https://caspiannews.com/news-detail/azerbaijani-president-turkmen-official-discuss-energy-transport-ties-2022-11-29-53/. Accessed on December 23, 2023.
4. Nigar Bayramli, "Iran, Russia sign $40 billion energy cooperation deal", *The Caspian News,* July 19, 2022, at https://caspiannews.com/news-detail/iran-russia-sign-40-billion-energy-cooperation-deal-2022-7-19-0/. Accessed on December 23, 2023.
5. SHANA Petro Energy Information Network, "Increased energy ties key topic in Caspian talks", October 11, 2022, https://en.shana.ir/news/462904/Increased-Energy-Ties-Key-Topic-in-Caspian-Talks. Accessed on December 23, 2023.
6. Vali Kaleji, "Four Obstacles to Iranian Oil and Gas Production in the Caspian Sea", November 17, 2021, *Eurasia Daily Monitor*, Vol.18, No. 175, https://jamestown.org/program/four-obstacles-to-iranian-oil-and-gas-production-in-the-caspian-sea/. Accessed on March 27, 2024.
7. Rosemary Griffin and Aresu Eqbali, "Iran's crude production upside faces risk of further Western sanctions", *S&P Global Commodity Insights*, https://www.spglobal.com/commodityinsights/en/market-insights/latest-news/oil/032624-irans-crude-production-upside-faces-risk-of-further-western-sanctions,. Accessed on March 27, 2024.
8. "Iran's Booming Oil Exports Threatened by Looming Gas Shortages", *Iran International,* 11 November, 2023, at https://www.iranintl.com/en/202311133462. Accessed on March 27, 2024.
9. Ibid.
10. This paper employs both the U.S. Measuring System (e.g., barrels, million cubic feet) and the Indian Measuring System (e.g., metric tonnes, cubic metres) for oil and gas measurements. A conversion table between these units is provided in Appendix I.
11. Vali Kaleji, n. 5.
12. European Commission, "REPowerEU: A plan to rapidly reduce dependence on Russian fossil fuels and fast forward the green transition", May 18, 2022, https://ec.europa.eu/commission/presscorner/detail/en/IP_22_3131. Accessed on March 27, 2024.
13. "Top Oil Field Service Company Halts Shipments of Technology to Russia", *RadioFreeEurope/RadioLiberty,* July 15, 2023, https://www.rferl.org/a/32504699.html. Accessed on March 27, 2024.
14. "Azerbaijan's energy landscape: Navigating oil decline and gas expansion", *AZE Media,* January 24, 2024, https://aze.media/azerbaijans-energy-landscape-navigating-oil-decline-and-gas-expansion/. Accessed on March 27, 2024.
15. Farkhat Abytov, "Kazakhstan's Oil and Gas Industry: Prospects, Trends, Look into Future", *The Astana Times*, October 10, 2023, at https://astanatimes.com/2023/10/

kazakhstans-oil-and-gas-industry-prospects-trends-look-into-future/. Accessed on March 28, 2024.

16. "Kazakhstan on its Way to Oil Supply Diversification", *The Astana Times,* March 25, 2023, https://astanatimes.com/2023/03/kazakhstan-on-its-way-to-oil-supply-diversification/. Accessed on March 28, 2024.
17. Xu Changzhi et al., "Turkmenistan exploring more devt. opportunities with China", *Global Times,* January 18, 2024, https://www.globaltimes.cn/page/202401/1305675.shtml. Accessed on March 28, 2024.
18. NEBIT-GAZ, "OGT - 2024: Turkmengas invites foreign companies to participate in the implementation of large gas projects", October 26, 2024, https://www.oilgas.gov.tm/en/posts/habarlar/12223/ogt-2024-turkmengas-invites-foreign-companies-to-participate-in-the-implementation-of-large-gas-projects. Accessed on November 10, 2024.

Appendix I

Main Conversions used in the Petroleum Industry

Item	Conversation factor	
Crude oil	1 tonne	- 7.33 barrels
		- 1.165 m^3 (kilolitres)
	1 barrel	- 0.136 tonnes
		- 1.159 m^3 (kilolitres)
	1 m^3	- 0.858 tonnes
		- 6.289 barrels
	1 MT	- 1.111 BCM natural gas
		- 39.2 BCF natural gas
		- 0.805 MT (LNG)
		- 40.4 trillion Btu
Natural gas	1 MCM	- 35.3 BCF natural gas
		- 0.90 MT crude oil
		- 0.73 MT LNG
		- 36 trillion Btu
		- 6.29 million barrels of oil equivalent
LNG	1 MT	- 1.38 BCM natural gas
		- 48.7 BCF natural gas
		- 1.23 MT crude oil
		- 52 trillion Btu
		- 8.68 million barrels of oil equivalent
CNG	1 Kg	- 1.244 standard cubic metres natural gas
		- 1.391 litres of petrol
		- 1.399 litres of HSD oil

Btu - British thermal units; BCF - billion cubic feet; BCM - billion cubic metre; CNG - compressed natural gas; HSD - high-speed diesel; LNG - liquefied natural gas; MT - million tonnes.

Source: TERI Energy & Environment Data Directory and Yearbook, 2013/14.

Index